THE

ENGLISH

HERITAGE

VOLUME I: TO 1714

THE ENGLISH HERITAGE

VOLUME I: TO 1714

Third Edition

FREDERIC A. YOUNGS, JR.
ROGER B. MANNING
HENRY L. SNYDER
E. A. REITAN

HARLAN DAVIDSON, INC.
WHEELING, ILLINOIS 60090-6000

Libary of Congress Cataloging-in-Publication Data

Youngs, Frederic A., 1936–
        The English heritage / Frederic A. Youngs, Jr. . . . [et al.].—3rd ed.
            p.   cm.
        Includes bibliographical references and index.
        ISBN 0-88295-980-8 Volume I (alk. paper)
        ISBN0-88295-981-6 Volume II (alk. paper)
        Contents: v. 1. To 1714—v. 2. Since 1689
        1. Great Britain—History. 2. England—Civilization. I. Title.
        DA30.Y68   1999
        941—dc21   99-18849
                                                                        CIP

Cover photo: Ruins of Whitby Abbey by Earl A. Reitan
Cover design: DePinto Graphic Design

Manufactured in the United States of America
01 00 99 1 2 3 VP

CONTENTS

Volume I: To 1714
Volume II: Since 1689

PREFACE

 Like its popular predecessors, this third edition of *The English Heritage* is intended to introduce students (and all readers) to a remarkable national heritage stemming from the four main nations of the United Kingdom: England, Wales, Scotland, and Northern Ireland. Many Americans and Canadians are descended from British stock; many others received the English heritage as immigrants or as the descendants of immigrants. The fruits of that English heritage have extended throughout the world, bringing the English language and English concepts of government, law, literature, and religion to former colonies and beyond. No longer the exclusive property of any nation, race, religion, or culture, the English heritage today is global in scope and influence.

This book reflects the authors' belief that a concise, introductory text best serves both the student and the instructor. It quickly grounds the student in the main aspects of British history and presents the themes that will be further developed in class. A dependable reference to which the student can return for clarification, this book also features an excellent collection of illustrations, photographs, and maps that provide visual supplements to the text. Also, a brief text such as this allows the instructor to incorporate a variety of supplementary readings and other resources to enrich the course. To this end, suggestions for further reading (which also may serve as good sources for student papers) conclude each chapter.

The English Heritage, third edition, includes the work of several authors, though it has been carefully developed as an integrated text. Some of England's great contributions to the world have been in the form of government, political ideas, and law, and a chronological consideration of these provides the main narrative thread. However, considerable attention is also given to economic development, social relationships, and religion. Furthermore, this book includes character sketches, not only of political leaders but of important people in many walks of life. Among the special features in this third edition are periodic overviews of London—including Chaucer's London, Shakespeare's London, the eighteenth-century London of Samuel Johnson, Victorian London, and modern London—one of the great metropolitan centers of the world.

Because the story of the English heritage spans more than a thousand years, the narrative pauses at crucial points to help the reader assess where England stood in its development: at the close of the Middle Ages; in 1783, when King George III presided over a nation of expanding power and high civilization but was badly shaken by defeat in the American Revolution; and in the mid-nineteenth century, the height of the Victorian Age. Finally, the last chapter assesses Britain's position in the world today and its prospects for the future.

For this third edition of *The English Heritage*, the original authors have been joined by Dr. Roger B. Manning of Cleveland State University, who contributed Chapters 5, 6, and 7. Dr. Earl A. Reitan of Illinois State University revised all chapters beginning with Chapter 11 and brought the final chapter through December 1998. Many of the illustrations were provided from a private collection. Special thanks are due to the capable and helpful staff of Harlan Davidson, Inc., for producing a handsome and highly usable book.

Earl A. Reitan, General Editor

The Earliest Britons
to 1066

When the glaciers of the ice ages receded, Britain was part of the European landmass, but about 8000 B.C. glacial melting raised the level of the sea to form the North Sea and the English Channel and to leave Britain as an island. The sea was no real protection—wave after wave of invaders came from continental Europe. The story of the creation of the English heritage is at first an appreciation of what the different invading peoples—Celts, Romans, Anglo-Saxons, and Vikings—successively contributed to an emerging British culture.

EARLY INVADERS AND THE CELTS

Stone-Age Settlers

The earliest large migration of Europeans across the Channel came around 2750 to 2500 B.C. These settlers are called Windmill Hill people after the name of the archaeological site where the remains of their camps were found. Because the weapons and utensils of their Stone Age culture were not very versatile, they settled on the open unforested plains of the south and east where hunting, the grazing of animals, and some light plowing were possible. For protection they dug circular ditches around the camps and used the dirt to form stockades.

The Celtic Tribes

From about 2000 B.C. onward, the invaders of Britain were the Celts, the people of an ancient civilization probably originating in the lower area of the Danube

River in eastern Europe. Although they were not a distinct ethnic group, they were a linguistic group with a shared culture. Their military prowess was such that they spread across the European continent. Among the earliest documented Celts in Britain were the Beaker people, so called by archaeologists of modern time because of the characteristic shape of their drinking vessels. This wave of Celtic invaders became so economically successful from grazing and breeding animals that they were able to undertake trade with lands thousands of miles distant, selling not only agricultural products but also beautifully fashioned bronze ornaments and jewelry, which symbolized the transition from the Stone Age to a more sophisticated one.

Celtic tribal life was characterized by holding the area they occupied in common. Although some lands were set aside for the chieftain and his associates in rule and some for the poor and ill, most land was held without individual ownership. There were six classes in society, ranking upward from the unfree who had broken tribal law to the chieftain. Some were distinguished by the right freely to till the soil, others by profession, as for example the poets or bards, or the priestly druids. Women had equality of status with men. The idea of common ownership and the ease of moving from one class to another prompted a cooperative activity in which advanced techniques such as making better plows, manuring, and harvesting implements were developed.

Celtic Culture

The cultural activities of the Celts were many and varied. They fashioned ornamental jewelry of exquisite beauty and made musical instruments such as harps and trumpets on which accomplished artists developed a musical heritage that still lives today in Scottish and Irish tunes. The Celts believed in immortality. Death merely marked the passage of a soul from this world to the other world, a process which came full circle in due time when the soul migrated from there to another person in this world. The druids or priests were a caste of great prestige, an international order whose influence spread far beyond religious ritual to education and natural science. Among the four great religious festivals was one on the last day of October. Spiritual contacts with the other world, with all attendant fear and mystery, were celebrated by a feast transformed in a later Christian era into a feast of All Hallows (All Saints). The evening before the feast gained the name of Hallowe'en.

Some idea of the Celtic people's level of development can be gained from their impressive monuments. At Avebury the largest of the concentric circles of massive stones had a diameter of 1,400 feet and included nearly thirty acres. At Stonehenge the inner ring consisted of vertical stones thirty feet high, which weighed five tons apiece, joined by equally large stones laid horizontally across them. The whole site included outer concentric rings and was probably a temple

Stonehenge. Private collection.

for sun worship, but from recent computer-assisted calculations an astrono-
mer has argued that Stonehenge was also an astronomical calendar and clock
of great sophistication. The farreaching implications of such a theory suggest
that the monument's builders had the economic means and religious commitment needed to dedicate labor and material to a construction project that took
many years, the mathematical competence to make alignments and take measure-
ments of celestial movements with amazing accuracy, the engineering skill to move
huge stones hundreds of miles from the quarry, and perhaps the political unity
that guaranteed the peaceful conditions needed to erect the monument.

From the eighth to the first centuries B.C. there were successive waves of
Celtic invaders who used iron in their weapons, tools, and implements. Iron
plows could turn the soil and make agriculture more productive, and the Celts
worked skillfully with iron and other metals to fashion swords, daggers, shields,
and luxury goods such as brooches. As regions began to specialize in different
products, trade between them was facilitated by the use of minted coins. The
new Britons exported to continental Celts many products such as grain, leather,
animals, and highly prized tin, which was mined in the western regions.

The increase in populations from newer migrations caused a severe competition for land. The Celts grew more warlike and aggressive, erecting hill-
side forts and venerating the warriors as an aristocracy. As a result of continued fighting several more stable kingdoms were formed from the smaller tribal

groups. About 75 B.C. a particularly fierce group of Celts called the Belgae occupied Britain, and they continued to assist their relations who had remained behind in northern Gaul. When nearly twenty years later the Roman general Julius Caesar conquered Gaul, he became convinced that Gaul could be held only if he also subdued Britain.

ROMAN BRITAIN

The Military Conquest

The forty-seven-year-old Julius Caesar was a man of boundless energy, ability, and ambition, a statesman who had earlier shared rule in Rome with two other outstanding politicians and who had then embarked on military campaigns as a way to gain the glory and prestige necessary to catapult him into single rule back in Rome. His conquest of Gaul, modern-day France, in the years just before 55 B.C. opened up the possibility of continuing conquest in the British Isles.

The attack that Caesar and his two Roman legions mounted in 55 B.C. nearly cost him his reputation: the Celts resisted fiercely, gaining a technological edge by using chariots against which the Romans had not previously fought and a psychological edge as many Celts, their naked bodies painted blue to instill terror, temporarily restrained the invading Romans to the beachhead. A few subsequent Roman victories not far from the point of invasion did demonstrate enough Roman might and discipline so that Caesar could salvage his reputation, then withdraw until a better-prepared force could make a better-prepared invasion the following year.

When the Romans brought five legions in 54 B.C., their disciplined troops carried the fight to the home area of the most powerful Celtic chief, and the decisive victories established the reality of Roman domination so well that when Caesar's forces left, the Celts acknowledged the Roman lordship and continued to pay tribute for 100 years in the absence of any sustained Roman presence in Britain. During those years the Celts took advantage of the great opportunities for trading within the Roman Empire and gained a breathing space for political consolidation, but chafed at their dependent status. In A.D. 43 the Romans decided to invade and to occupy Britain in order to end the military and political dangers which the Celts posed.

This time the Roman invaders skillfully separated the Celtic forces and won decisive victories at the onset. In the next thirty years the Romans moved their control westward and northward into the mountainous regions. They suffered occasional defeats as when Queen Boudicca led her people in rebellion in A.D. 60 and destroyed nearly an entire Roman legion in battle. When in A.D. 70 a previously friendly buffer state in the north turned hostile, the Ro-

Hadrian's Wall. Private collection.

mans mounted a massive military effort and then erected the town of Eboracum (later called York) to consolidate the hard-won successes.

The Roman Military Frontiers

The Romans succeeded because their army was such a formidable fighting force. Each legion was a self-sufficient and mobile town which carried the equipment needed to overcome man-made fortresses and to deal with natural barriers by erecting bridges and roads. The soldiers were extensively trained in marching and fighting, and the state offered them special privileges after twenty-one years of well-paid and respected service if they would settle in areas near the frontier to be available if their military talents were ever needed again.

Such a settlement of retired soldiers and their families was called a *colonia*. The colonia usually retained marked military characteristics: as at Roman York, for instance, where the headquarters of the legion defending the northeastern frontier occupied half the town's area, all the settlement on the north side of the river. Although there were probably three other coloniae—at Colchester guarding the eastern shore on the English Channel, at Gloucester guarding the western frontiers, and at Lincoln—the Romans built other fortified towns. These were called *castra*. The survival of names in variant English forms—as, for example, Chester, Chichester, and Exeter—shows how extensively the

Romans organized the conquered country. Three legions, about a tenth of the Roman Empire's entire fighting force, were normally stationed in Britain, but the Romans were still unable to conquer all the island. The northern frontier was set soon after the troops in the north suffered a severe defeat in A.D. 122; the Emperor Hadrian then had a wall built across an eighty-mile narrow stretch to keep out the Picts who occupied what later would become Scotland.

Life in Roman Britain

Secure behind the military shield, the civilian areas of Roman Britain enjoyed the most advanced civilization in the western world in common with the rest of the Empire. "Civilization" refers generally to the social heritage of ideas, attitudes, and style of living which one people passes on to its descendants. For the Romans civilization meant life in cities, and thus Roman Britain was a network of cities linked together by well-engineered, straight roads.

The cities had wide streets laid out at right angles and enclosed within protective walls. The center was the forum, an open square onto which faced the basilica, the hall for public meetings. There were temples, baths, shops for the highly developed economic life of the town, and homes whose exteriors were often shops but in which the domestic area centered interiorly on open courtyards. The floors of the richer homes were made of tiled mosaics, the walls were plastered and colorfully painted, the windows were made of glass, and the whole was heated by central heating which used a system of pipes and water. Underground sewers kept the cities clean, and outside the walls there was sometimes an arena for pageants and sports.

Life within the cities was varied and cultured. Young men and women were tutored in Greek and Roman literature and philosophy and practiced oratory. There were theaters for plays and baths for relaxation and gambling. The emperor was worshipped officially for the sake of political unity, but other gods were venerated as well. Christianity came to Britain at first as one of many religions, then in later years finally became the religion of the Empire.

Roman London

In his second campaign Julius Caesar had sought a place at which his armies could successfully ford the broad river Thames, a natural barrier along his invasion route from extreme southeastern England to the homelands of the major Celtic chiefs. Just to the east of the fordable site he located was a rudimentary settlement destined to be a major part of subsequent British history. The area came to be called London, a site geographically distinguished by the commanding presence of two major hills, by two rivers flowing from north and west through the site into the Thames, and by being the meeting point of several adjoining Celtic tribal lands.

Within five years after the successful invasion of A.D. 43, which established permanently a Roman presence, the conquerors turned London into the provincial capital. Within the first hundred years the Romans erected a fifteen-foot-high wall to encircle all but the river frontage of the nearly square mile area, heavily protected the five gates that opened through the massive walls onto the Roman roads which acted as spokes of communication into the hinterlands, and built a bridge across the river Thames. In addition to the full range of typical Roman buildings—a forum of unusually large size and the temples, basilicas, baths, and other monuments to the Roman presence—there was a palace for the governor of the province. At the height of the Roman period, the population of London perhaps reached 50,000.

The upper ranks of British society were greatly influenced by Roman culture, but the vast majority of Britons were completely unaffected. Their lives were focused in the rural settlements on farming and raising animals. The only important Roman presence in the countryside was on estates known as villas. They differed considerably in size but in general were large-scale farming operations with many workers under a well-to-do and highly romanized owner. Because the villas were self-sufficient they had little impact on the native Britons nearby.

Roman Baths, Bath.
Private collection.

The first decay in Roman life in Britain came when many city dwellers started to move to the countryside to escape the high taxes and public demands of city life. The decline in urban living sapped the cultural vitality of Roman Britain and contributed to a loss of political unity. In the third and fourth centuries many soldiers stationed in Britain were recalled to the continent because of political difficulties in the crumbling Roman Empire.

Faced with the prospect of being left defenseless, the British appealed to Rome for assistance—only to be told by the Emperor Honorius in 409 to look after their own safety. The Britons were ill-prepared for fighting because the Roman soldiers had guaranteed the peace for centuries. Thus the British sought the services of German mercenaries to protect their island. Ironically, in time the Germans would be responsible for totally eradicating Roman culture from Britain. Roman ways would indeed have a role in shaping later Britain, but that came only when in later centuries the Christian church reintroduced many Roman practices.

ANGLO-SAXON BRITAIN, 450 TO 870

The Anglo-Saxons

The Angles and Saxons of northern Germany were closely related in language, customs, culture, and especially in their reputation as fierce fighters. Their territories had never been part of the Roman Empire so that they were untouched by Roman civilization and Christianity. Loyalty to the tribe was paramount and military skill was highly praised, but because they were illiterate the details of their gradual conquering of Britain from about 450 to 600 are sparse. Some evidence of their settlements can be gained from archaeological remains and from such place names as *ingas*, which survives in the names Reading and Hastings, and *tun*, as in Southampton.

Legend has it that when the Romans left and the Saxons were hired, the mercenaries liked what they saw and began to conquer Britain, coming up the rivers to penetrate deep into the interior. At first the British were able to resist the small bands of invaders, and under the leadership of Arthur they stopped the Germans temporarily at Mount Baldon. Although Arthur's existence and military skill cannot be doubted, the legends about him and his Round Table are many, and the site of the battle and of his kingdom of Camelot, if indeed he was a king, are actually unknown.

By about 600 when the conquest was complete there were nearly a dozen independent Anglo-Saxon kingdoms. In time many of the names of the settlers had become the names of the kingdoms so that the lands of the East Saxons, West Saxons, and South Saxons had become, respectively, Essex, Wessex, and Sussex, and the East Angles had given their name to East Anglia.

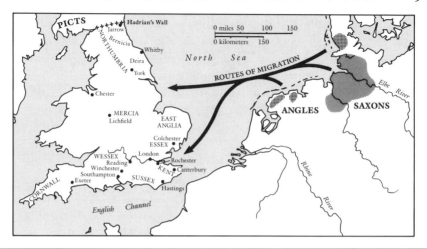

Anglo-Saxon Migrations

A slower advance northward produced several kingdoms, notably Bernicia and Deira, which were later unified as Northumbria ("north of the river Humber") and Mercia ("the borderers' area") in the midlands. The old cities were naturally inhabited, but the urban Roman style of life was totally foreign to the invaders. Many of the Romano-Britons had fled northward and westward into the mountainous areas to avoid the waves of pagan invaders. By the end of the seventh century the native British people had been forced into three geographically separate kingdoms. In the far southwest was Cornwall, which would later be conquered by the Anglo-Saxons. The kingdom of Wales in the west would flourish until well into the Middle Ages. The Scots, who were originally from Ireland, and the Picts created the northern Celtic kingdom known from about 850 as Scotland.

The Conversion of the Anglo-Saxons

There were two distinct missionary efforts to bring Christianity back to Britain, one from the Celts in the north and west and the other sent from Rome. About the year 575 a monk in Rome had seen several youths from Anglo-Saxon Britain and had been deeply moved by their ignorance of Christ. When he became pope soon after, the monk (known to history as Pope Gregory the Great) commissioned another monk named Augustine to lead a band of missionaries to Britain, and in 597 they arrived in the extreme southeast corner of the island. Augustine and his companions preached to various kings in the hope that a converted king would allow the evangelization of his kingdom. The first to be won was Ethelbert of Kent, a well-disposed ruler whose wife had been raised a Christian in her native Frankland. As the faith was spread the gains were consolidated by the erection of dioceses, geographic areas under the supervision of a bishop, such as Canterbury where Augustine himself settled.

The Celtic missionaries, the second missionary group, had a distinctly different character. The Roman traditions had been learned by the Celts during Roman rule, and St. Patrick (ca. 389–461) had established the church in Ireland by erecting dioceses which were coterminous with the tribes. But soon after his death the diocesan organization was abandoned, and the tribal chiefs established monasteries whose influence was unlimited by geographic borders. When Oswald became king of Northumbria in 633 he opened his realm to the Celtic monks who had been responsible for his earlier conversion.

The Roman and Celtic missionaries also differed in religious customs. A particular problem arose over the different ways of calculating the date of Easter, the central feast of the Christian year. The clergy in Rome had accepted newer and improved mathematical techniques for measuring cycles upon which the church's liturgical calendar was based, but the Celts who had been isolated from Rome when the Anglo-Saxons invaded had retained the older ways of calculation.

The issue over the date of Easter was merely one of many which arose from the fundamental question of whether British Christianity would develop in union with the universal church based on Rome or would maintain its by now unique features. At a Council in Whitby in Northumbria in 664, which both groups attended, they agreed to follow the Roman ways and to develop monasticism in the diocesan framework. The ecclesiastical unity that resulted made the missionaries' work easier and provided an example for and a stimulus to political leaders to bring about themselves the ideal of political unity instead of the multiplicity of the Anglo-Saxon kingdoms.

The Legacy of the Law

One of the most precious gifts of the invading Germanic tribes was their tradition of an unwritten but binding customary law. As they settled in different parts of Britain their tribal law became the law of the territory they occupied. The laws of the kingdoms were generally similar but there were differences, just as there were differences between the East Saxons and the West Saxons. All the laws sought to provide protection and to ensure a fair way to handle disputes.

The Germanic law had been intended as an alternative to the endless feuds and bloodshed between families seeking revenge for what outsiders had done to their kin. Each person had his own "peace," and it was far more serious to attack someone and break his peace within the privacy of his home than elsewhere. If a crime was committed the law sought to prevent revenge by

Saxon church. Private collection.

ordering the guilty to pay money as damages. If the accused had not been caught in the act or if there was no other presumption of guilt, he was allowed to swear an oath asserting his innocence. The value of his oath was based on his rank so that a nobleman's was many times more valuable than any other person's. If his oath was not deemed sufficient to free him from the accusation, he could bring in oath-helpers who swore to his trustworthiness, and the latter were unlikely to support a guilty person because of the penalties for perjury. When guilt had been determined then damages were assessed depending on the extent of the injury and the victim's rank. Thus the damage for the loss of a nose was twice that for a thumb or ear and nearly seven times as much as for a finger. The damage for causing a death, called the *wergeld,* was of course the highest amount that could be assessed.

If the procedures of oath-taking had not determined guilt or innocence, and after elaborate safeguards for the rights of all parties, the decision was left to God through one of several types of ordeal. In the ordeal by water, for example, the defendant first prepared himself by prayer, fasting, and the sacraments. Then a priest blessed a body of water such as a small pond. The defendant was thrown into the water and a struggle on his part was taken as a sign of guilt because the purified water would not receive a defiled criminal. If the water received him unstruggling, he was in time brought up and declared innocent.

Toward Political Unity: The Bretwaldas

Not until the tenth century was there political unity in Britain. From about 600 the different Anglo-Saxon kingdoms struggled for political dominance, with warfare the tactic and overlordship the result. The victorious kings who dominated others were called *Bretwaldas*. The crucial question was the quality of that overlordship: was it to be a recognition as the first among many essentially independent kings, or was it to be so effective politically that the lesser kingdoms under a Bretwalda's control would lose their independence and become absorbed within his own kingdom? To a striking extent the answer depended on the leader's strength of character. A series of able rulers could consolidate their predecessors' gains, but a weak successor could lose in a single battle the advances made over many years.

Kent was the first of the dominant kingdoms, but when Ethelbert died in 616 Kent's overlordship ended. Northumbria dominated during the remainder of the seventh century. Of necessity it was militarily oriented because as the northernmost Anglo-Saxon kingdom it was exposed on its frontiers to the hostile Celts, Welsh, Picts, and Scots. King Edwin (616–632)* won Northumbria's independence from the Celts, and his successor Oswald reunified the kingdom; a third Bretwalda maintained Northumbria's dominance until late in the century when weak kings gained the throne.

Mercia dominated during the eighth century, principally because of the ability of two kings who ruled for a total of eighty years. Ethelbald (716–757) combined military power with a ruthless personality, if a letter by the saintly missionary Boniface, which condemned the king's morality, accurately reflects the situation. Offa (757–796) enjoyed the greatest esteem of any Anglo-Saxon king up to that time. His wisdom in government was profound, his reputation on the continent so renowned that the great king of the Franks, Charlemagne, considered marrying one of his sons to Offa's daughter, and his importance to the church sufficient to move the pope to send a legate to him and even found (temporarily, as it turned out) a third archbishopric at Lichfield in Mercia. Under Mercia's control there was a striking acceleration of the movement toward political unity. The kingdoms of East Anglia, Essex, and neighboring areas were wholly incorporated in Mercia and lost their independence so that the number of competitors for power was significantly reduced. Thus London became a Mercian city and lent its prestige to the kingdom.

The dominant power in the ninth century and later was Wessex. Mercia had attempted to divert the crown in Wessex from Egbert, the proper successor, and placed one of its own claimants on the throne. Egbert fled to Charlemagne's court where in time he absorbed a thorough schooling in statecraft at that most important of European kingdoms while awaiting a promis-

*Dates given are the dates of the reign.

ing time to return from exile. In 825 he came back to win a crushing victory over Mercia and in the next several years he became overlord of all southern Britain as well. But the logical advance toward political unity which he represented was interrupted by an external force of great power, the Vikings.

The Vikings

Out of the north swept the fierce Vikings, attacking not only Britain but most of Europe as well. These Scandinavians were well schooled on the seas: the mountain ridges that dominated their homelands had rendered internal travel difficult and forced them to rely on the sea, and the extreme climate turned them away from the land to seek a living by trade or by fishing, or by the much more lucrative profession of piracy. The long, sleek Viking boats, propelled either by sails or by oars, had such an extended range that they even reached North America.

The Viking raids on Europe began in the eighth century. Their vessels were so swift that they could strike quickly and surprise victims both along the seacoast and even many miles inland along rivers which emptied into the sea. They terrorized the inhabitants of towns, looted extensively in nearby areas, and then withdrew before any help for the hapless victims could arrive. The undefended wealthy monasteries of Britain's eastern seacoast were particularly ripe targets.

Although the name Viking is used generically of all Scandinavians, the Danes concentrated their attacks against Britain and the Norse struck at Ireland. The Danish efforts against Britain continued intermittently for many years, but from 865 onward they abandoned the tactic of strike and withdrawal and began to make permanent settlements in Britain. As the Norse had begun their settlements on Ireland's eastern coast at Dublin, so the Danes settled Britain's eastern shore first. Their roving army quickly reduced the east and then subdued major parts of Mercia. Within a few years the only English kingdom totally free of Danish occupation was Wessex.

ALFRED THE GREAT
AND THE CREATION OF ENGLAND

Alfred the Great

The only English king ever to be called "Great" succeeded to Wessex's throne, determined to overcome the Vikings. Alfred (871–899) began to build his military strength, rallying the men of Wessex and forming an alliance with the unoccupied part of Mercia. The combined forces stopped the Danes' second campaign in 875, and in 878 Alfred led his forces to defeat them decisively when they mounted a third attempt. An agreement left eastern Britain to be governed by Danish custom (the area came to be known as the Danelaw) and the west to the Saxons. Alfred then used the twenty remaining years of his life to lead and inspire the kingdom, developing its military and naval strength. He organized the navy to protect the coastline and cut off the Viking lines of communications, and on land he consolidated his victories by erecting forti-fied strongholds to protect the countryside and people. Although the time to begin a sustained campaign to recapture the Danelaw was not yet ripe, he had prepared the military base which his descendants would need.

Alfred was an inspiration to his people culturally as well. If it had not been for his zeal, few writings in English (as the Anglo-Saxon language came to be called) would have survived. In addition to the *Anglo-Saxon Chronicle*, in which Alfred had a role, and legal documents from his government, Alfred translated Pope Gregory's *Pastoral Care* from Latin so that his bishops might be guided in properly shepherding their flocks. To give his people a sense of their heritage he translated the *Ecclesiastical History of the English People*, writ-ten by the Northumbrian monk Bede. To encourage learning he rendered Boethius' *Consolation of Philosophy* into English, and to stimulate his subjects' piety he had lives of the saints translated. There can be few more appealing pictures than that of this king who lamented his own lack of an early educa-tion, but who painstakingly worked to learn to read and write, first English and then Latin, and who later gathered around him educated men to instruct others. His encouragement of learning led other Englishmen to study Latin, the international language of scholarship and of the church. Thus horizons to European culture were expanded.

The Creation of England

At Alfred's death there were five major and a number of smaller kingdoms in Britain. The two Saxon kingdoms of Wessex and Mercia controlled the south-west and had been united politically by marriages between their royal families. The east was controlled by the Danes, primarily in the Danelaw but also in a few lesser kingdoms in the northeast. There were two Celtic kingdoms, Wales in the far west and Scotland in the north, the latter dating from a union of the Scots and Picts about 850. The most important steps toward political unifica-tion were the successive military victories of Alfred's son Edward (899–924) and grandson Athelstan (924–939) which resulted in the conquest of the Danelaw and the minor Danish kingdoms in the north and in the stopping of any Celtic movements southward. By the middle of the tenth century an agree-ment had been made with Scotland as to territories, the entire area south of the river Tweed to be the one unified kingdom of England.

Thenceforth England was a political unit never to be subdivided. When outside kingdoms threatened to invade, the whole of England was to be the prize. The kings were now the kings of England, solemnly bound to the realm as was demonstrated by the coronation oath of Edgar in 973. The ceremonies of coronation were traditional and included crowning, anointing, and investing with the royal insignia; the oath was new—the king's sworn promise to govern England well and lawfully, to give justice to his people and protection to the church.

The Powers of Kingship

An Anglo-Saxon king's immediate claim to power had rested on his military ability; thus he was the greater as he conquered or subdued more territory. But once England had been unified, kingship had to be expanded to include non-military tasks as well, and the king's prestige grew accordingly. Because the Germanic kingdoms had been communities which stressed the law, the pre-eminence of the king developed first in that area.

   The king grew to paramount importance in the law in three ways. First, the wergeld on his life was set so high that no one could pay it, and thus an offender would be executed. The king, therefore, had a unique form of protection. The crime of taking his life came to be considered a separate legal offense, treason. Second, the king became the normal person to make the decisions about the unclear or undeveloped areas in the customary law. His decisions, called "dooms," were in fact accepted as declarations of law—indeed, the first written law while remaining, however, of much less importance than the main body of unwritten law. Third, the kings began to develop a system of separate royal law administered exclusively by royal agents. The kings took the notion of "peace" which was so important in Germanic law and expanded the "king's peace" greatly. It was made to apply to persons other than the king (such as his family and royal officers), to places other than his royal court (churches, fairs, highways), and to times other than the king's ceremonial wearing of his crown (Sundays, feast days of the church). A small number of offenses were defined as breaking the peace on those occasions, and the case was to be heard before a royal officer. The guilty party upon conviction had to pay a fine to the king as well as damages to the injured.

   The king was advised by a council, a group of his closest advisors called the *witan*. He was not bound to take their advice, but it was to his advantage to consult them since he thereby associated the leading men of the realm with royal policies. The witan had the right to designate the successor to the throne; usually it chose the king's son although this was not always done since a hereditary right to the crown was not yet an unquestioned legal right. In practice the witan chose the obvious candidate, often passing over a very young son of a deceased king to choose an older relative or someone else who could actively exercise the office.

As nonmilitary administration became more important with an expanded kingdom, two offices within the royal court grew to greater importance. The chamberlain, who was at first the keeper of the king's bedding and personal effects, began to keep the king's treasure as well and thus received and disbursed royal funds on command. The clergy, who cared for the king's spiritual needs, were often the only literate men in the court and also served by writing the king's orders (the writs) and his grants of privileges and rights (the charters). These documents were cut so that a tongue of parchment hung down from the main writing, to which wax shaped with a mold (the royal seal) was affixed as an authentication.

Local Administration

As Wessex led the unification of the realm the kings needed to assert and assure their control over an increasing number of localities. A system of shires was developed, shire meaning "a share" or part of the whole. When former kingdoms such as Essex or Sussex were deemed small enough for administrative efficiency they became shires in themselves, but larger kingdoms such as Wessex were subdivided into several artificial shires as was done also for the land won back from the Vikings. Eventually over thirty shires were formed.

The king's representative in the shire was at first an *ealdorman*, but so many new shires were eventually created that it became unwieldy for the king to have to deal with so many of them. Alfred's successors began to group three or four shires under one ealdorman, but this increased responsibility made the ealdorman so important that he could even pose a threat to the king's exclusive power, and thus in time the ealdormen were relieved of any administrative responsibility. From the tenth century onward the principal royal officer in the shire was the sheriff (*shire reeve*). He collected the revenues of the king (rentals of land and profits of justice primarily), transmitted royal writs, oversaw the militia of the shire, and assisted in keeping the peace, especially by presiding over the shire court. The shire in turn was subdivided into hundreds or *wapentakes*, the latter a name which prevailed where the Vikings had had influence. It is not clear whether "hundred" referred to men, to units of land, or to units capable of producing a certain revenue. The constable was in charge of the hundred, below which were *tithings* ("tenths") which were charged with keeping the peace.

Standing outside this system were the boroughs. The word *burh*, which was the root of "borough," implied a fortified place, often strategically located at the junction of rivers or on hilltops which commanded an area. It was natural that these centers would come to have economic and governmental importance as well and so the boroughs acquired grants of privileges through royal charters, one of the most important of which was exemption from supervision by the sheriffs and constables. The population of boroughs remained generally small, a reflection of the new emphasis on rural life which differed so markedly from when the Romans had dominated Britain.

EARLY ENGLISH SOCIETY

The People of Saxon England

To understand the people who made up early English society first requires putting aside more modern terms such as upper, middle, or lower class because those terms are based primarily on differences in wealth and occupation. Anglo-Saxon society was almost totally agricultural, and distinctions were based on degrees of legal and economic freedom. There were three basic grades: slaves who had no freedom at all, *ceorls* who enjoyed legal but not economic freedom, and a nobility who enjoyed both legal and economic freedom. Persons became slaves when they were captured in battle by men of another kingdom, when they were punished for very serious crimes, or when they voluntarily exchanged their freedom for protection or for food during times of acute strife or famine.

The ceorls were husbandmen, tillers of the soil who headed agricultural households and worked in part on their own behalf and in part for their lord. The lowest ranking ceorls spent most of their time in unpaid labor for the lord—in sowing, tending, and harvesting his crops, in minding his animals, and in performing many other menial tasks. They were able to work on their own lands only after completing their legal obligations. The ceorls with the greatest freedom were those who merely paid the lord some rent and did not have to perform personal services. Because their energies could be spent on developing their own lands they could prosper and settle their obligations that much easier. Many ceorls owed a combination of personal and money services. The state of legal freedom but economic unfreedom which English ceorls and men of similar standing on continental Europe had is generally called serfdom.

The nobility of early English society gained their special privileges in the period of the Saxon conquests by their military services to the king. In later centuries they were rewarded also with land and were called *thegns.* Many thegns served the kings as administrators, most notably the ealdormen. As the latter were relieved of administrative duties and replaced by sheriffs in the shires, the Danish title of *eorl* (later earl) was adopted, and to its holders it became a more important rank of nobility with preeminence over the others.

Mobility between grades of society was possible. It was to the lord's advantage to make enterprising slaves ceorls, not only because the church encouraged this Christian act but also because the ceorl then became responsible for maintaining himself and yet still owed the lord service. A ceorl might accumulate enough wealth to buy exemptions from the economic services he owed and thus become economically and legally free even though not of noble status. It was also possible to move downward—many were unable to protect themselves from the constant dangers of the Viking invasions or were wiped out by a series of bad harvests and so voluntarily gave up some freedom to a lord in return for protection and the necessities of life. This practice was called commendation and became common in later years so that many people were less free than in the early part of the Middle Ages.

The Countryside

Early English settlements consisted not of single dwellings scattered around the countryside but of villages which were surrounded by the fields that people worked. Some villages were clusters of houses around an open space and others had a single road lined with dwellings through the village. Rarely would there have been any buildings of stone, although some more important churches and the homes of some nobles used stone in construction. The rest of the buildings varied as much as the social standing of the village's families. Prosperous ceorls might live in timbered structures with walls made of mud and wattle, but the poorer ones often lived in hovels, sunken huts covered with straw. The villages usually had a common pasture on which all could graze their animals.

The fields which surrounded the villages were divided, half to be sown while the other half lay fallow to regain its fertility. By the tenth century a system of strip farming had become quite common, perhaps introduced by the Danes. A ceorl would have several strips of land just over twenty yards wide in various parts of the fields, none adjacent but rather separated by the strips of other ceorls. Because oxen were used to pull the plow the strips would be as long as possible so that the team did not have to turn often. When the harvesting was completed in one field the other was immediately sown with wheat and rye, to lie dormant over the winter until germination in the spring, at which time barley and oats were also sown.

Barley was the most important crop and was ground in mills for making bread and also made into malt for brewing beer, the staple drink. Pigs and sheep were raised, but because it was so hard to keep animals alive in the winter due to the lack of fodder, most animals were slaughtered in the autumn; the rest often occupied the houses along with the people. Many areas of Britain were simply not suited for farming, and thus animals were grazed in the steep pastures.

Christian Life

The pattern for early Christianity had been set by its rapid spread in earlier periods, and by 700 it had been accepted in all of Britain. Dioceses were created, sometimes coinciding with smaller kingdoms as London did for Essex, sometimes consisting only of part so that Canterbury and Rochester served eastern and western Kent, respectively. The archbishop of Canterbury supervised the southern dioceses and the archbishop of York the northern. The real importance of Christianity lay in the impact it made on the lives of each person, substituting Christian ideals of love, respect, and unselfishness for pagan values. These new virtues were exemplified in the person of Theodore of Tarsus, a Greek who in his service of the universal church came to be archbishop of Canterbury from 669 to 690. He actively formed new dioceses and set a personal example of tireless devotion to his flock through teaching, preaching, confirming, and ordaining. He convened the clergy to draft codes for morals and penance in order to insure the sound formation of the people in Christian life, and his personal supervision of the higher clergy kept them zealous and dedicated.

The life in monasteries was devoted to Christian living. Men and women who wished to dedicate themselves to God in lives of worship and contemplation came to monasteries to withdraw from the world's distractions, binding themselves by vows of poverty to be rid of concern for worldly goods, chastity so that family responsibilities did not occupy their time, and obedience so that by losing their own will they might better do God's. In time the monasteries became centers of learning, especially when founders and benefactors presented them with handwritten manuscripts which were so rare in England. Some of the most beautiful examples of copied Bibles were made in northern monasteries such as Jarrow, and a particularly beautiful one of the early eighth century from Lindisfarne is an outstanding work of early English art. It was at Jarrow that the monk Bede prepared his *Ecclesiastical History of the English People,* an invaluable source for the history of Anglo-Saxon society which Alfred had translated. The manuscript has a rich and vivid style with unusually advanced descriptions of complex historical events.

The conversion of Britain did not exhaust the missionary vigor of the church. Northumbrians such as Wilfrid and Willibrord brought Christianity to Saxony and neighboring areas which were the original home of the Germanic invaders of Britain. The West Saxon Boniface evangelized down the Rhine in Germany to found Christianity there and to assist in reforming it in nearby Frankland. So famous was the monastery school at York under Alcuin that in 782 he was called by Charlemagne to head the school at his own court at Aachen.

The first Vikings had been pagans whose attacks on monasteries and churches dealt a crippling blow to Christianity. Gradually their conversion, both in England and in Scandinavia, led to a good deal of restoration, but the state of religion in the early eleventh century had not yet recovered to its earlier situation.

ENGLAND IN THE EARLY ELEVENTH CENTURY

Political Decline

For several generations the brilliance and wisdom of Alfred had continued in his descendants, but in the late tenth century there had been a considerable decline in the standards of English society which was personified in great part in King Ethelred the Unready (978–1016). He seemed to reflect the weakness, treachery, and selfishness of the time and his character was blemished by his contemporaries' suspicion that his mother had been implicated in the murder of Ethelred's older brother. When the second wave of Viking invasions began in the early years of his reign he sought to stop the invaders by paying them huge sums of money. England was greatly burdened in raising the thousands and thousands of pounds of precious metals which came to be known as the *danegeld.* The new invaders were a professional fighting force whose training and discipline made them a more effective army than western Europe had ever known before. Although this explains in part why Ethelred gave in, his flight in 1013 before another band of raiders, led this time by the Danish king, made many of his subjects esteem him as a coward.

Canute's Viking Empire

The successful invading Danish king died soon afterward and power passed to his son Canute. Most of the English recognized Canute as their king and when he defeated Ethelred's son Edmund Ironside in battle, and at Edmund's death soon afterward, Canute's acceptance was complete. Ethelred the Unready had been married to a Norman woman, Emma, whom Canute now married to further solidify his status in England. He thus became stepfather to the children of Ethelred and Emma.

Canute actively ruled a Scandinavian empire made up of the English, Danes, Norwegians, and Swedes. He was a remarkable man who combined the severity and cruelty of the military conqueror with the wisdom which realized that England's government was far superior to the Scandinavian institutions. Unlike earlier invaders he adopted England's government and law and by his military strength he guaranteed the opportunity for its economic growth. He safeguarded the church and appreciated English culture.

After Canute's death in 1035 his two sons who had little ability squandered his legacy. The last of them invited back from Normandy his half brother Edward, the son of Emma and her first husband, Ethelred the Unready, and thus made the transition of the crown easier. When Edward began to reign (1042–1066) he theoretically blended the three traditions which at Edward's death in 1066 would compete for the throne of England—the Saxons, the Vikings, and the Normans.

Edward the Confessor

Edward's religious devotion was inspiring to his contemporaries, and as "Edward the Confessor" he was recognized as a saint by the church soon after his death. Scholars today debate whether his saintly reputation was exaggerated, but they agree that the realm was certainly not peaceful. He had spent the first twenty-five years of his life in Normandy and had little appreciation of Englishmen or their values, so that when vacancies arose in the English government or church he filled them with trusted Normans. A resentful native opposition arose which was led by Godwin, Earl of Wessex, by his sons whose earldoms included most of southern England, and by his daughter Edith who was Edward's wife. The quarrels between these mighty English subjects and the king were complicated because Edward had no children, probably as a result of a vow of celibacy which he took just before his marriage.

It seems certain that in either 1051 or 1052 Edward had promised England's crown to his second cousin, William, Duke of Normandy. In later years when Edward withdrew from public life to devote more time to religion and to the building of his beloved Westminster Abbey, he allowed his cousin and brother-in-law Harold (a son of Godwin, who had died in 1053) to assume the practical direction of English affairs. Harold was a good fighter whose victories over the Welsh won much admiration. It seemed natural that when Edward died early in 1066 this capable English noble would be chosen king by the witan. His title was compromised, however, by Edward's promise to William and by an oath which Harold himself made to William, although the terms of the latter are still uncertainly known.

Harold's reign as king lasted but nine months. In September 1066 Harold Hardrada, the king of Norway, assisted by the English king's brother, landed on the northeastern coast of England to reassert the Scandinavian claim to the crown. King Harold of England marched his forces northward, and on September 25 at Stamford Bridge repelled the invasion, killing his brother and the Norwegian king in battle. But on September 27, William of Normandy set sail to demand the fulfillment of the promise of Edward the Confessor, so that King Harold of England had to turn his troops and march 250 miles southward to face yet another contender.

SUGGESTIONS FOR FURTHER READING

The Celtic and earlier cultures of pre-Roman Britain are described in V. Gordon Childe, *Prehistoric Communities of the British Isles* (1971); Lloyd and Jennifer Laing, *The Origins of Britain* (1980); and Lloyd Laing, *Celtic Britain* (1979). Rodney Castleden, *The Making of Stonehenge* (1993) is a thorough study of the archaeological and historical evidence which places Stonehenge in its cultural context.

Surveys of Roman Britain include: Peter Salway, *A History of Roman Britain* (1997); Malcolm Todd, *Roman Britain* (1981); and Sheppard S. Frere, *Britannia: A History of Roman Britain* (rev. ed., 1978). The arrival of the Romans in Britain is described by Graham Webster, *The Roman Invasion of Britain* (1981); and a contemporary account has become a historical classic: Cornelius Tacitus, *The Agricola and the Germania,* transl. H. Mattingly (1971). The reaction of the Britons is examined in *Boudica: The British Revolt against Rome, A.D. 160* (1978). For the social history of Roman Britain, consult Anthony Birley, *The People of Roman Britain* (1980). Urban settlements are studied in John Wacher, *The Towns of Roman Britain* (1974).

The Anglo-Saxon period is surveyed in H. R. Loyn, *Anglo-Saxon England and the Norman Conquest* (2nd ed., 1991); F. M. Stenton, *Anglo-Saxon England* (3rd ed., 1971); and Peter Hunter Blair, *Introduction to Anglo-Saxon England* (2nd ed., 1977). Leslie Alcock presents an argument for the historical existence of King Arthur in *Arthur's Britain* (1977). The notorious marauders of the British Isles are studied by H. R. Loyn, *The Vikings in Britain* (1977). The life of the defender of the Anglo-Saxons and the only monarch in English history ever to be called "the great" is examined in Eleanor Shipley Duckett's classic *Alfred the Great* (1958). Another royal biography is Frank Barlow's *Edward the Confessor* (1970). Contemporary accounts, chronicles and lives of various individuals are accessible in modern translations from the Latin and Old English. They include: St. Bede, *A History of the English Church and People* (1956) and *Alfred the Great: Asser's Life of King Alfred,* transl. Simon Keynes and Michael Lapidge (1983). This edition also includes *The Anglo-Saxon Chronicles.* A superb survey of the economic and social history of Anglo-Saxon England is provided by H. P. R. Finberg, *The Formation of England, 550–1042* (1974). For the artistic achievements of the Anglo-Saxons, consult C. R. Dodwell, *Anglo-Saxon Art* (1982). The best and most recent survey of women of all ranks and vocations in medieval society can be found in Henrietta Leyser, *Medieval Women: A Social History of Women in England, 450–1500* (1995).

CHAPTER TWO

Anglo-Norman England
1066–1189

When Edward died early in 1066 Harold was the logical successor to the crown, and in fact the witan proclaimed him king. Harold's title was at least in part compromised, however, by the promise Edward had made to William and by an oath which Harold himself made to William, although the terms of the latter are still uncertain. As has been discussed, Harold's reign as king lasted but nine months: after defeating his brother and the king of Norway in the northeast of England in September, King Harold of England had to march southward to meet a new threat. On September 27, William of Normandy set sail to demand the fulfillment of the promise of Edward the Confessor.

The achievements of William the Conqueror and his successors—the Anglo-Norman kings—shaped England into a much more powerful realm than it had been. The Anglo-Norman kings and the first of the Plantagenets, Henry II, fused Norman ideas and experiences with the best of the earlier Anglo-Saxon and Viking elements. By 1189 England had the most sophisticated governmental institutions in western Europe.

THE NORMAN CONQUEST

William the Conqueror

The Vikings had attacked and permanently conquered Normandy in the ninth and tenth centuries and had gradually fused their culture with the French, but early in the eleventh century Normandy was still a weak and divided duchy where great nobles were often competitors with the duke for power. William's resolute leadership dramatically changed that. He was a unique blend of statesman and soldier—a determined, courageous, and often brutal fighter who won control within the duchy and secured its borders against neighboring powers. He elaborated on feudal principles to subordinate and to harness the abilities of the Norman nobles. So that the Norman church served both God and the duke faithfully, William reformed the church vigorously according to the principles of the religious revival of the eleventh century. The promise of Edward the Confessor to Duke William gave him the opportunity to expand greatly his area of control.

Chivalry

The battle that Duke William fought against King Harold nine miles inland from Hastings on October 14, 1066, was a dramatic clash between two men who each claimed to be England's rightful ruler. Harold's army was drawn up in close order on a hilltop which could only be approached from the south. William sent charge after charge against the English, but neither the Norman soldiers nor their rain of arrows could break the English lines. The attackers soon discovered that a feigned retreat could cause some of the impulsive English soldiers to break ranks in pursuit, and then the Normans could ambush them piecemeal. This tactic was used repeatedly, and then a stray arrow struck and killed King Harold. Leaderless and with dwindling forces, the English retreated, and the first stage of the Conquest was complete.

William's political success depended on capturing London, but he advanced on it slowly to let the tales of his brutality toward townspeople who resisted him reach the Londoners. When his initial demands were rejected, he marched his army in a large arc through the areas neighboring London, burning as he went, until the Londoners capitulated to avoid the same fate. On Christmas Day, 1066, William was crowned king of England in Westminster Abbey.

In the next four years he gained effective control over northern England, at first confirming the titles and privileges of many English nobles in power if they would support him. William appreciated the more sophisticated practices of English government and wished to emphasize his claim to be heir to the crown by preserving the English nobility. In 1075 a rebellion of most English nobles brought this to an end, and, after William rewarded the Norman lords who helped him repress the rebellion with the rebels' lands, only a few English nobles remained.

The Feudal System

Although William retained English governmental institutions he did begin gradually to feudalize England. He acted as a lord in granting land called fiefs (from the Latin *foedum*, the root of the word feudalism) to vassals for which

Knight and his lady, monumental brass rubbing. Private collection.

they did homage by kneeling before him to swear their fealty, an oath of honor, loyalty, and service. The exact details of the manner and the pace with which William imposed feudalism are not known. It seems that as more and more lands were forfeited to him as the native English lords rebelled, the lands were regranted according to the new system. He also imposed the Norman custom of primogeniture, according to which the eldest son alone inherited his father's lands. William avoided the common continental European practice of granting all land within large areas or provinces to a single nobleman; by granting nobles many scattered fiefs he avoided making them all-powerful in their locality and denied them the means of mounting a concentrated opposition to royal policies.

Under the feudal system a lord kept part of his lands for his own use (as his *demesne*) and granted the remainder to a vassal in return for certain specified services. The obligations that the vassal owed to the lord were called the *servita debita* and varied considerably. The most common was knight service, in which a vassal had to furnish a certain number of men armed and ready for military duty at a set time. Churchmen usually owed prayer and religious services, officers in the king's administration owed their time and talents under the tenure of serjeanty, and occasionally a vassal merely paid a money rent.

Among the vassal's other responsibilities were attending the lord's court, offering him counsel, and paying "aids" and "incidents." Aids were paid when a lord's eldest son was knighted, when his eldest daughter was married, and as a ransom if the lord was captured in battle. The most important incident was the "relief," a money payment from a vassal's heir so that the lord would regrant the fief to him. Since a vassal often left minor heirs who were incapable of military or any other service, the lord managed the fief until the heirs came of age under a system known as wardship, and he could arrange the marriages of minor heiresses in order to protect his interests. If a vassal broke the feudal

A student making a brass rubbing,
Great St. Helen's Church, London.
Private Collection.

agreement he forfeited the fief to the lord, but if the lord was unfaithful then the vassal was entitled to rise in rebellion.

These elements were common to any lord–vassal relationship, but as the system was implemented the layers of subordination multiplied. A man who was a king's vassal could retain part of his grant as his own demesne and re-grant the remainder to other men who became his own vassals. This regranting was called subinfeudation and was quite common in England, doubtless because the possessions of individual lords had been purposely scattered by William. The result was a hierarchical structure of landholding, often sche-matically described as a pyramid, with the king at the apex and a number of tenants-in-chief holding land directly from him. There were many layers be-low as further subinfeudation took place. Because it was possible for one vassal to hold fiefs from different lords, the figure of a web can also be used for illus-tration to stress the tangle of interrelated loyalties implicit in feudalism. Be-cause a vassal's loyalties were most immediately dedicated to his own lord, feudalism tended to make minor vassals less concerned with tenants-in-chief or even the king who was far removed above in the pyramid. This diffusion of power and loyalties away from the king who stood at the center of the feudal kingdom can be likened to the centrifugal motion of ripples away from the center of a pond where a stone has been cast. William I attempted to mitigate this diffusion of loyalties by requiring all important men of the kingdom to take an oath of loyalty to him directly.

By means of the feudal system the Norman kings of England were able to weave the aristocracy into the fabric of the English state and to bind them to loyal service; approximately 200 tenants-in-chief were direct vassals of the king. The common people of England were little touched by the new develop-ments. The fief was the smallest legal unit of feudalism but, since it often coincided with the village which was the social and economic unit, the rights and duties which had long characterized the obligations of agricultural soci-ety were merely restated in newer legal terms.

The Normans and the Church

The monasteries had a well-established and traditional place in English life before the conquest, and at first only the leadership changed as Norman abbots were appointed. The Normans gradually began to appreciate the fervor of the English monks. As the new abbots introduced the continental reforms which had brought a revitalized spirit to monastic life, the abbeys fused the best of the old and the new. New orders of monks came to England, among them the Cistercians (often popularly called Trappists) who were a particularly austere and fervent order with a preference for settling in remote parts of the country.

The greatest ecclesiastical effect of the conquest was the Norman elabo-ration of the territorial structure of the church. England had long been divided into geographic dioceses under the direction of bishops, but the Normans rearranged the dioceses for greater efficiency. Later, smaller churches were built throughout the dioceses to serve people in geographic areas known as parishes. This expansion made it imperative to develop further the administrative machinery of the dioceses. Archdeacons were appointed in every diocese to handle administration and legal matters such as cases on marriages and morals; where a diocese included several shires, an archdeacon was usually appointed for each.

There was a special organization for the cathedral church of the diocese, a corporate body called the chapter, which was made up of important churchmen called canons. The canons elected one of their number to head the chapter as its dean. In addition to their responsibilities for maintaining the cathedral, the dean and chapter elected a new bishop when one died or was moved to a new diocese. This was only a theoretical right because the Norman kings told the deans and chapters whom to elect. The bishops were skilled administrators who had often begun their careers as chaplains in the royal court. Piety and spiritual dedication were important but, in many cases, were neglected in favor of managerial skills so that the zeal encouraged by the reforms and the effectiveness of this well-organized system was at times compromised by the character of some of its leaders. The archdeacons developed a reputation for pressing legal claims down to the last penny. In later centuries waggish university students were known to debate, half-seriously and half-mockingly, whether it was possible for an archdeacon to save his soul.

THE NORMAN STATE

The Norman Kingdom Divided

William the Conqueror and his nobles were forced to divide their time between England and Normandy, at times crushing rebellions of resentful English lords and at other times fighting less successfully to defend the Norman possessions from hostile neighboring French rulers. As William I neared death he adhered to tradition by willing Normandy to his eldest son, Robert, and England to his second son, William. The hard-won unity between the two possessions would be destroyed. The nobility who held lands in Normandy and England feared that if conflicts arose between the brothers they might be forced to choose one and thereby face the loss of possessions in the other's domains.

William Rufus

William II (1087–1100, called "Rufus" by his contemporaries because of his ruddy coloring) was an unappealing ruler who combined all the vices of a soldier with a blasphemy and immorality that scandalized a believing age. Only the code of the camp captured his respect; thus, he valued England merely as a source of revenue for battle. When some of his nobles sup-ported rebellions to supplant him with Robert and to reunite England and Normandy under one ruler, he responded with a military skill as effective as his father's and with a personal brutality which led him to blind, cas-trate, and hang the rebels. The governmental officials whom he left in charge in England were ruthlessly efficient and therefore very unpopular. William also took advantage of his brother Robert, an affable and coura-geous man who was irresolute in governing Normandy. When Robert wished to go on a crusade in 1095 he pawned part of his duchy to William to gain the funds. William in turn used Robert's absence to gain control of Normandy and to advance its frontiers militarily.

William often refused to fill vacant bishoprics so that he could appropri-ate their revenue, but, in 1093 when he believed that he was dying, he decided to make his peace. He accepted his councillors' advice to name Anselm arch-bishop of Canterbury—a man renowned for his holiness and as the most out-standing philosopher of the time. When William unexpectedly recovered his health he began to regret the choice. Anselm's behavior was a reproach to the king, and the archbishop combined a lack of administrative experience with a stubborn streak that further strained his relations with the king. These differ-ences were worsened by the investiture controversy. English feudal custom required a bishop to swear an oath of fealty to the king, as did other feudal lords, after which he was invested with his fiefs and the symbols of ecclesiasti-cal office. The pope objected to the king as a layman presuming to confer a spiritual office. Anselm insisted on the papal position, and William resisted lest his control over a feudal lord be reduced. At William's death matters were strained, and Anselm was in exile; only in the following reign was a compro-mise reached which was acceptable to all parties.

Henry I

William's successor was the Conqueror's third son who had been left a large treasure and no kingdom. Henry had played both sides in the struggle between his older brothers and had earned the distrust of both so that Robert and Wil-liam each made the other his heir to exclude Henry. When Rufus was on a hunting trip in 1100 he was "accidentally" struck in the neck with an arrow and killed. Henry just happened to be nearby and rode at once to Winchester to seize the English treasury and to proclaim himself king of England. William's body lay unclaimed for hours. Several years after he had been buried at Win-chester Cathedral the roof fell in over his tomb, and it was taken as a certain sign of divine disfavor.

Henry (1100–1135) was a capable statesman who immediately bid for the support of important leaders in order to gain their acquiescence in his usurpa-tion. He issued a Charter of Liberties which promised to repudiate William

II's abuses in the church and government, and he kept most of the promises by ruling fairly. He was called the "lion of justice." His governmental skill consolidated the achievements of his father, and he began new procedures which further enhanced the power and authority of kingship. In 1105 to 1106 he turned on his brother Robert and mounted an English conquest of Normandy, thereby reuniting Normandy and England.

Anglo-Norman Government

Most English administrative agencies were more developed than those in Normandy, and the Anglo-Norman kings retained them and expanded them greatly. The Anglo-Saxon writing office that prepared writs and charters acquired the new name of the Chancery and grew in importance as writs became important in law as well as in administration. A council of advisors was retained but was now called by the Latin name *curia regis* rather than the witan. The greatest Norman contribution to government was feudalism, with its contractual ties that bound the aristocracy to serve the monarchy. Now the curia regis was to consist exclusively of the king's feudal tenants-in-chief, but because there were nearly 200 of them most of the day-to-day advice to the king came from the council's members who held the major administrative posts.

Because the kings were often away on the continent to attend to Norman business, William II and subsequent monarchs established the office of justiciar to direct English affairs during their absence. Later the office was expanded to direct the administration even when the king was in England. William Rufus chose Rannulf Flambard as his justiciar, a man who worked with such a ruthless efficiency and an ability to make royal rights lucrative that the king had to remove him in order to placate a growing opposition. Under Henry I, Roger, bishop of Salisbury, held the office and expanded the judicial and administrative powers of government.

It was under Roger's direction also that the first administrative office went "out of court," ceasing to travel with the king and his royal court as they moved throughout England but instead settling down in one central location with a degree of independence. The Anglo-Saxon kings had entrusted the collection and dispersal of funds to the chamberlain in the royal household, and before Roger's time the members of the curia regis had superintended the sheriffs' accounting for the king's revenue. Roger developed a new office called the exchequer, which took its name from the checkered cloth upon which the sheriffs accounted after the fashion of an abacus. The cloth was marked in vertical columns to represent units of currency such as pounds and hundreds of pounds, and upon it were placed counters to represent the total revenue which the sheriff was expected to produce.

Because the sheriffs had been ordered many times during the previous year to make disbursements on the king's behalf, counters were removed from

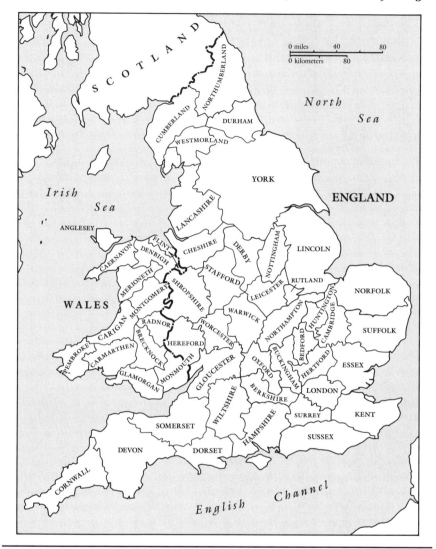

England and Wales

the cloth to symbolize these proper deductions, leaving a total to be paid into the exchequer as a result of a process which even the illiterate could follow easily. Pegs of wood shaped like modern tent pegs were notched to indicate the sums paid by the sheriff, wider notches for larger sums down to bare nicks for fractions of pounds, and then the wood (called a tally) was split lengthwise. If disputes arose, the sheriff was able to produce his half to match that kept in the exchequer.

Thus there was a growing number of administrative agencies—the curia regis, the justiciar, the chancery, the exchequer, and the royal court in which much was still done. The legal system grew more complex as well. The Anglo-Norman kings retained two existing systems of law, the Anglo-Saxon local courts with their Germanic principles and the system of royal pleas, and added a third with the introduction of feudalism. The feudal system of justice created many courts because each lord was obliged to hold a court for his vassals. A village might spread over several manors, and thus the duty of keeping order and other public duties were often assigned to the village—adding another layer of public justice which grew up alongside the private feudal jurisdiction. William I also separated the church's courts from those of his government. Although this merely followed the Norman practice, in time numerous conflicts would arise over the proper jurisdiction that each type might claim.

Anglo-Norman Society

Feudalism and the Upper Ranks of Society

When William I replaced rebellious English nobles with loyal Norman and French lords he affected nothing less than an aristocratic revolution. The new nobility differed considerably in their outlooks, attitudes, and values. These changes were evident above all else in their use of the French language which had supplanted English in high society, in their military attitudes which led them to mock the "softer" English with their long hair and finer clothes, and in their lack of interest in the arts and literature which many English nobles prized.

Because a much smaller number of new nobles replaced the substantially larger group of English aristocrats, the former tended to be richer and of more individual importance. In time they came to appreciate the more cultured English ways, as had William I. Growth in wealth had an important part in mellowing the Norman attitudes. As men of property, the new nobles began to devote more time to the management of their estates and less to military skills which had first brought them to prominence. At a later time the Norman kings capitalized on this attitude by allowing the nobility to commute the personal knight service that they owed into money payments, which sufficed to hire a smaller number of mercenary fighters.

The character of the knights who stood immediately below the nobility changed as well. At first a knight had been little more than a hired soldier, but once he received property through the process of subinfeudation he too wished to spend more time in managing his estates. As the gradual consolidation of the Norman Empire reduced the frequency of combat there were fewer opportunities for military service. Even the nature of warfare tended to change: the beginning of the Crusades to recover the Holy Land from non-Christians provided an idealistic motive for fighting, and the church promoted elaborate rules of chivalry in the twelfth century to mitigate the worst features of battle.

Soon it became more profitable to capture a knight, seize his expensive armor and horses, and then hold him for ransom rather than to kill him.

Because military preparedness was a necessity, a new style of architecture came to England. There were few castles from pre-Conquest days, but between 1066 and 1100 over eighty were built as strongholds to dominate and control the areas that the Normans conquered. Most of the early castles were of the motte and bailey type where a protective ditch was dug around the limits of some prominence, such as a hill, and then a timber fortification was built on top of the dirt heaped from the ditch within the enclosure. As the haste of the period of Conquest gave way to more settled times, these early castles were rebuilt in stone. When the style of building was fully developed in later centuries, there were a number of characteristics: castles' exterior walls were smooth with few openings through which an arrow could penetrate, there was but one entrance so that defenses could be concentrated, and the interior was of sufficient size to house a noble family in proper style, although such a damp, cold building with little light penetrating from outside was not comfortable. These castles were designed to enable a loyal force to hold out against an enemy for a considerable time until the royal forces could raise a siege.

Domesday Book and the Peasantry

In 1086, probably fearing a Scandinavian invasion and wishing to understand his realm's resources, William I sent commissioners throughout England to survey landholding and wealth. County by county, hundred by hundred, manor by manor, the commissioners recorded who had held the land before the Conquest, who held it in 1086, what obligations were owed, and what other resources there were such as plows and cattle. Men marveled that one could sooner escape the day of doom and judgment than the questions of the king's men, and so the name stuck to the results of the inquiry. Domesday Book helped the king be better informed, provided a record of landholding which was invaluable for settling later disputes at law, and showed clearly the extent of the aristocratic revolution. It also showed that the primary implications of the Conquest were restricted to the upper ranks of society and to a very small number of people.

Domesday Book was not a survey of population but rather of adult landholders; modern demographers who are interested in population studies have used the scientific aspects of their discipline, nevertheless, to attempt to estimate England's population from that unique survey. Granting that any estimate must be tentative, and that its accuracy depends on the proper selection of a multiplier by which one extends the known number of landowners to take account of the landless and of family size, it has been estimated that England's population in 1086 was about 1,600,000.

Domesday Book, page of entries for Somerset. Corbis-Bettmann.

Most agricultural workers—the landless for the most part—saw little more than the substitution of a new lord for the old and the requirement to attend the new manorial courts. Otherwise the rhythm of the seasons with the traditional sowing and reaping continued. English was used as a language on the nonaristocratic level, and at first the resentment at the conquerors spawned periodic violence which meant hardship for the common people.

The number of offenses that were considered to be a breach of the king's peace was expanded and reached thirty-seven under Henry I. The Normans had to introduce a murder fine to protect themselves. In English law the victim's family prosecuted someone who had murdered one of their kin, but the Normans usually had no family to avenge them and so there was a great temptation for the English to attack the invaders with little fear of retribution. The murder fine set by the Norman leaders was very high, and all the inhabitants of a hundred in which a Norman was slain had to contribute if the murderer went undetected.

THE NORMAN CHURCH

Religion and Society

The creation of new parishes made the church better able to serve people's spiritual needs but also created a number of problems. Parishes were often created when a wealthy patron donated land and other endowments sufficient to erect a church and support a parish priest. Because the patron reserved the right to nominate the next priest every time the office became vacant, the priest's primary loyalty was often to the patron. The training before a priest's ordination was usually inadequate so that many lacked the spiritual leadership demanded by the office. Since the priest farmed the land that was the parish's endowment he was subject to the same attitudes, trials, and temptations that beset the flock which he was to guide.

In spite of the problems, the reforms of the period kindled a great deal of religious zeal, and the stone churches which the Normans erected were the centers of both village and town life. These churches were erected in a style called Romanesque or Norman and are a testimony to the preeminence of spiritual aspirations. This was a massive style of construction limited only by the requirement that the walls and columns be strong enough to support the entire weight of the roof, so that the girth of the columns was usually the same as their height. The floor plan was usually of cruciform shape with the altar and choir on the eastern end to catch the rays of the morning sun, the nave to the west forming the remainder of the long part of the cross, and the north and south transepts making the shorter crossbar. The walls were usually constructed in three tiers with windows only at the highest level lest the wall be weakened, and the circular arch was characteristic of the style. The Norman cathedral thus mirrored the strength and even militant attitude that was characteristic of the feudal period. The cathedral at Durham is one of the finest examples in England of the Romanesque style.

Monasticism and the Spiritual Life

The clearest enunciation of the spiritual ideal of the time was to be found in the monastic life where men and women withdrew to live according to a rule of prayer and worship. A good example of early monastic fervor which came close to the ideal was the community at Fountains Abbey. A small number of Benedictine monks at St. Mary's Abbey in York had begun to yearn for a more ascetic and less comfortable life than was normal in their wealthy monastery, and so in the winter of 1132 to 1133 they left York to choose a remote site twenty-five miles away where abundant springs suggested the name Fountains. The following year the monks petitioned for adoption into the Cistercian Order, and under the direction of Abbot Richard endured winters of near starvation until at last their reputation for saintly lives brought both recruits and endowments. Within a decade there were probably 500–600 monks so that three times in ten years offspring monasteries were founded from Fountains Abbey.

Assuming that the daily routine at Fountains was similar to that at other Cistercian abbeys, the gray-clad monks would rise in the dormitories about 2 A.M. to go to the massive church built in the Norman style, where they would begin the first of an eight-part combination of prayers called the divine office—a blend of psalms, scripture readings, prayers, and hymns which complemented the two daily masses. About two-thirds of the day would have been spent in the church or in reading and prayer in the cloister, to which the monks added periods of manual labor in the fields. The business of the monastery was conducted in the chapter house and the one or occasionally two meatless meals of the day were taken in the refectory. Silence was maintained except for necessary business, and the rhythms of the seasons were seconded by the regular cycle of the liturgical year which represented Christ's life and held it up for the monks' imitation.

It was difficult to maintain such an austere life in full rigor, and many monasteries fell short of the ideal. The wealth that abbeys received from admiring benefactors often caused the monks to spend so much time in worldly management that it intruded on their otherworldly ideals, and ambitious building programs plunged some monasteries into debts and eroded the spirit of prayer. Nevertheless, the impact and attractiveness of the ideal were great, and the zeal of the reformed houses was an inspiration.

Religion and Education

There was a mutual dependence between the church and education: the church needed educated clergy, and the clergy were the only educated people who could staff schools. At the lowest levels were the "reading" or "song" schools, the closest equivalent to what today would be called elementary education, in which reading and singing were taught to boys primarily to meet the church's liturgical needs. In the twelfth century, as an intellectual renaissance swept across Europe, "grammar" schools grew up for students about 11 or 12 years old or older, usually as cathedral schools in major centers. The grammar that was taught was Latin grammar, the prerequisite not only for liturgical service but also for participation in the European intellectual world—one language common to all well-educated Europeans. Two Englishmen illustrate the mutual dependence of church and education—Anselm from the earlier part of the period and John of Salisbury from the later.

Before Anselm became archbishop of Canterbury under William II, he had been a monk at the great Norman abbey of Bec and had there established a scholarly reputation in philosophy and theology. He was well-known across Europe for his erudition. He set forth an argument to prove the existence of God with such intellectual force that his work still commands interest and debate among philosophers today. Anselm thus not only represents profound thought but exemplifies the central role of monastic schools in early education, especially in the eleventh century.

John of Salisbury was a contemporary of his friend and patron, Thomas á Becket, archbishop of Canterbury under Henry II, to whom he dedicated his two greatest books. In his early twenties he left England to go to the famous University of Paris, one of the earliest universities in northern Europe and by

Norman tower, The Tower of London.
Private collection.

far the most renowned in the entire Middle Ages. There he studied under its most famous early teacher, Abelard, and then John went to Chartres in France to complete his studies. He spent several years in the service of the pope and the papal curia, writing a history of the papacy. Because he served also in English government he had an idea of the state and of service to it, which animated his writings on that topic. He compared the political state to a human body: the priesthood corresponded to the soul, the king to the head, the judges to the eyes, the soldiers to the hands, and the tillers of the fields to the feet. John thus represents two important late twelfth century educational advances: the study at universities started to supplant monasteries as centers of learning and the employment of education in the service of both church and government.

ENGLAND AND ANJOU

War with France

The greatest threats to the English king's Norman possessions came from France which bordered Normandy on the southeast and from Anjou directly southward. William I and II had resisted their incursions, and Henry I by reuniting England and Normandy had increased his ability to resist. In Henry's reign the French King Louis VI began attempts to expand his territories beyond the areas immediately surrounding Paris and thus saw Anglo-Normandy as the principal obstacle to his plans. Although France was occasionally at war with the Anglo-Normans, Louis VI assisted Anjou and other more immediate foes in attacking Normandy. Henry I remained there over half the years of his reign after 1106 to meet the increased threats.

Matilda and Stephen

Henry feared that his realm's capacity to resist would be seriously crippled by the succession to England's crown. Of his numerous children, one boy and one girl only were legitimate and, thus, heirs to the throne. In 1120 his son drowned when a ship in which he and a number of equally drunk companions had embarked sank in the English Channel. Henry had no choice but to order his barons to swear to allow his daughter Matilda to become queen and reign after his death. A woman ruler was a novelty that few lords could anticipate without dread: Matilda was mismatched by a political marriage to Geoffrey, count of Anjou, a youth fourteen years old and eleven years her junior when Henry I died in 1135, yet the marriage offered Anjou the potential for dominating England. Furthermore, Matilda was extremely arrogant, fond of recalling that by her former marriage with the late German emperor she had been an empress.

Matilda never realized her claim because Henry's nephew Stephen seized the throne when the old king died. Stephen (1135–1154) was a popular man whose accession was greeted with relief by most of the nobility. As the grandson of William I through the Conqueror's daughter he was Matilda's cousin. Most nobles acquiesced in the extraordinarily hasty events of the first three weeks during which time he seized the treasury and had himself elected king, as had Henry before him. But this initial decisiveness and foresight were deceptive because for the remainder of the reign he was usually incapable of concentrated and sustained effort. Above all else he showed himself "soft" (as a chronicler put it), ever able to be prevailed upon and to make concessions to powerful forces in the vain effort to sustain an effective control over affairs.

Matilda's arrogance and Stephen's inability were a perfect match—Stephen lost effective control of Normandy to Matilda and neither could decisively win in England during the civil wars which lasted from Geoffrey and Matilda's invasions in 1139 until 1148 when they left England. Five years later an agreement was made between them which allowed Stephen to remain king as long as he lived and to be succeeded by the son of Matilda and Geoffrey, Henry.

Henry II and the Angevin Empire

Few kings have been as personally compelling as the twenty-one-year-old man who began to rule as Henry II (1154–1189). He was a bundle of energy, always on the move, able to spend the day in strenuous hunting and other sports and then the evening in conducting the business of his realms. He was up earlier than his ministers and retired later than they did—and he was so taken with nervous energy that his stocky body, which was topped with red hair, often trembled with uncontrollable rage and fury. Few could love a man of such intensity, but all respected him.

His inheritance was breathtaking: Anjou and other areas in what is now central France from his father, England as a result of the agreement with Stephen, and Normandy from his mother. When he married Eleanor of Aquitaine he assumed effective control over her territories which included most of the southwest of modern France. The total domain, often called the Angevin Empire (Angevin is the adjective derived from Anjou, his patrimony; the name Plantagenet is also often used for this dynastic line, from the devices on the family coat of arms), stretched 900 miles from England's border with Scotland to the Pyrenees which are the modern French border with Spain. Only the strongest of rulers could hope to hold together so many diverse territories, and then only if there was a strong government by which to rule. England alone offered the potential but first Henry II had to restore the powers of the monarchy that Stephen had frittered away. Within the first year of his reign Henry had regained the crown lands which had been alienated, had ridden the country of the hated mercenaries who had fought much of the civil wars, and had taken back the royal castles which the barons had occupied or erected without authorization as havens for resisting the royal power.

The barons' loyalties were won back by Henry's vigorous reassertion of his and their feudal rights. Officials wrote down in the *Cartae Baronum* (Charters of the Barons) the exact terms of feudal obligations. Henry reestablished the effectiveness of the royal administration, choosing the exceptionally able Ranulf de Glanville to direct the government and to fashion a staff of loyal administrators who oversaw the enforcement of royal policy. The greatest area of his achievements was in the development of royal law, and the greatest difficulty was in his dealings with the church.

Henry II and the Law

William I had retained English law and fused with it important Norman elements such as feudalism. Henry I, the "lion of justice," introduced a number of innovations which gave royal justices great flexibility. It was Henry II's regularization, systemization, and expansion of justice which made all that had gone before into a coherent and efficient whole. The curia regis heard important feudal cases and other important matters for the king, and the exchequer which by now had gone "out of court" heard cases over disputes on royal revenue. The great elaboration was the provision for hearing cases at royal law throughout England's many localities by the itinerant justices.

The name itinerant (from the Latin *iter,* meaning journey) was appropriate because the royal justices divided England into circuits composed of several counties in which they travelled several times a year. Their judicial sittings on disputes over property were called assizes (from the French *assis,* meaning seated or a sitting); on criminal matters, the trials over which they presided were called *gaol* delivery because they cleared the gaol (as the English spell jail) of all suspects whom the sheriff had detained to await trial. Property matters were heard before a jury (from the Latin word *jurati,* meaning "men sworn on oath"). Not until the thirteenth century were juries used in criminal matters. Men were not ready earlier to decide a neighbor's guilt when that might result in the death penalty and when God's judgment was able to be ascertained through the ordeal. The origin of the jury was the Norman inquest, the seeking of information from men under oath. William I used it to compile Domesday Book, and from 1176 onward it was used for informational surveys of local conditions which were called general *eyres.* The latter were very unpopular because men resented having to respond under oath to questions that were felt to be mere fishing for information to which the king had no right. In time the informational eyres were dropped, but the jury remained as a regular part of the judicial process.

A plaintiff began a case at royal law by purchasing royal writs. Some writs were jurisdictional, transferring cases from the feudal courts into the royal courts, while others provided means for determining the right to property or the lawful possession of it. The question of the right to property was the most important, and so the writ for this was called the Grand Assize (from the French *grand,* meaning large and implying importance). All parties to the suit had to present full documentation and proof about the ownership of the land, and the defendant was allowed many delays before the case was heard. Therefore, many plaintiffs decided to purchase writs that, without any delay, settled the more restricted question of rightful possession. These writs were called Petty Assizes (from the French *petit,* meaning small or of lesser importance). If through their processes a plaintiff was presumed to be entitled to possess the property, he was restored to it until the lengthy and final processes of the Grand Assize were completed. For example, he was restored to the property if the jury found him to be the heir apparent at the time of the "death of his ancestor" (hence the writ *mort d'ancestor*) or if he had been "recently dispossessed" by the defendant (writ of *novel disseisin*).

In time the system of writs was expanded to over 500 types. The king gained financially from the sale of the writs and from the fees for his justices who heard the cases, but more important he gained prestige as the protector of his subjects' rights. By the end of the Middle Ages the local courts in the shires and the feudal courts of the lords heard only the most minor matters, and royal justice had become the dominant system. The kings' subjects used the system because it guaranteed them the right to a speedy and relatively inexpensive trial by a jury of their peers, which was felt to be a far-superior process than in the feudal courts where the landlords were the judges.

Arundel Castle. Private collection.

Henry II and the Church

One area of conflict between the kings and the church was the proper relationship between the Papacy and England, but the settlement of the investiture controversy in Henry I's reign had cleared up most of these problems. The second difference was the degree of control that the kings could exert over the church in England, a problem which often concerned the proper spheres of jurisdiction between the separated ecclesiastical and secular courts for an offense such as murder. The church claimed that a spiritual person should be tried in a spiritual court; the monarchs argued that, because the church's courts did not inflict the death penalty but only penance and other spiritual punishments, the culprits escaped serious retribution. Many clerics were only in minor orders, the initial stages in the process toward ordination as priests and thus enjoyed full protection yet were not fully members of the clergy. Henry II hoped to solve this problem and all difficulties with the church by appointing as archbishop of Canterbury his loyal friend and Lord Chancellor Thomas á Becket. Surely together they could compromise the matter.

Becket surprised Henry and everyone else—from a cleric hardly renowned for piety, a carefree, pliant royal servant, Becket became the dedicated ascetic changed by a religious conversion and became devoted to defending every privilege of the church no matter how unimportant. When Henry II drew up in 1164 a codification of royal rights in the church called the Constitutions of Clarendon, matters came to a head. Becket refused to accept the Constitutions and in particular objected to the claim that clerics convicted before spiritual courts of a serious secular crime should be degraded by the church and handed over to the secular arm for execution. The conflict that ranged over the next years combined the personal bitterness of a former friendship gone sour with exaggerated claims of principles on both sides. Late in 1170 matters had gotten so bad that Becket excommunicated several bishops who had cooperated in a plan of Henry's, and in exasperation the king uttered the words "Will no one rid me of this troublesome priest?"

Taking him literally, four of Henry's knights went to Canterbury and murdered Becket in his cathedral. The effects of this act were profound. Although Henry disavowed the literal intention of his words he was made to do public penance for his carelessness. Becket was canonized in 1173, and the shrine at Canterbury of St. Thomas á Becket became a center of pilgrimage for Europeans. More important, the event forced Henry II and the Papacy to come to an agreement: Henry conceded that felonies of clergymen should be tried in spiritual courts while secular courts should retain jurisdiction over the lesser misdemeanors of clerics, and that appeals in some cases would be allowed from church courts in England to Rome. But in other matters that related directly to Henry's control over the church, such as nominating bishops and allowing papal orders to come into England only with his permission,

Henry retained the ancient rights of English kings. Because both sides had been forced to come to an explicit agreement, England was not to be subject to the same running disputes with the Papacy during the rest of the Middle Ages as were many other European kingdoms.

As marked as Henry's achievements were in so many areas, the seeds for undoing much of his work lay in his own family. Rule as he would throughout his lands, he could not rule Queen Eleanor, who was as formidable and cunning as he was, nor his sons, who spent much of their later years plotting against their father to increase their own inheritances. These family struggles were the more serious because they coincided with the accession to France's throne of Philip Augustus (1180–1223) who dreamed of driving the English out of France and who knew how to exploit the greed and rapacity of Henry's children. Henry II's Angevin Empire stood challenged.

SUGGESTIONS FOR FURTHER READING

Introductory surveys of the Anglo-Norman period can be found in Marjorie Chibnall, *Anglo-Norman England, 1066–1166* (1986) and M. T. Clanchy, *England and its Rulers, 1066–1272* (1983). The revolutionary impact on England of the Norman Conquest is revealed in R. Allen Brown, *The Normans and the Norman Conquest* (1985) and David C. Douglas, *The Norman Achievement, 1050–1100* (1969). Specialized studies of the Norman invasion and William the Conqueror are provided by David Howarth, *1066: The Year of the Conquest* (1981) and David C. Douglas, *William the Conqueror: The Norman Impact upon England* (1964). The military aspects of the Norman Conquest are carefully analyzed by C. Warren Hollister in *Anglo-Saxon Military Institutions on the Eve of the Norman Conquest* (1962) and *The Military Organization of Norman England* (1965). That the Norman Conquest degraded the status of Anglo-Saxon landholders and peasants is revealed by a close examination of the Norman land survey, *The Domesday Book*. The best studies of this document are by V. H. Galbraith, *The Making of the Domesday Book* (1961) and *Domesday Book: Its Place in Administrative History* (1974). Bryce Lyon explains feudalism and Anglo-Norman governmental institutions in *A Constitutional and Legal History of Medieval England* (2nd ed., 1980). The castles, which the Normans introduced to hold the Anglo-Saxons and, later, the Welsh in subjection, are described in N. J. G. Pound, *The Medieval Castles of England and Wales: A Social and Political History* (1990).

There are studies of important churchmen in R. W. Southern's *St. Anselm and His Biographer: A Study of Monastic Life and Thought* (1963), David Knowles, *Thomas Becket* (1971), and Frank Barlow, *Thomas Becket* (1986). The classic book on the religious orders of the medieval period is David Knowles, *The Monastic Orders in England* (2nd ed., 1963). For England's participation in the Wars of the Crusades, consult Christopher Tyerman, *England and the Crusades, 1095–1588* (1988), and Steven Runciman's classic *A History of the Crusades*, 3 vols. (1964–67).

Surveys of the social and economic history of this period include: J. L. Bolton, *The Medieval English Economy* (1986) and H. E. Hallam, *Rural England, 1066–1348* (1981). Helen Jewel, *Women in Medieval England* (1996) is a somewhat briefer treatment of the topic than the book by Leyser, cited in chapter 1. A weighty, but useful anthology of documents is available in David C. Douglas and George Greenaway (eds.), *English Historical Documents, 1042–1189* (1983). Besides chronicles and other literary evidence, it also reproduces the Bayeaux Tapestry depicting the Battle of Hastings.

CHAPTER THREE

High Medieval England
1189–1327

The thirteenth century was the high point of medieval culture in Europe, and England participated fully in its achievements. It was a century of aspirations, characterized by a religious revival led by the friars who called men to a life of simplicity and an imitation of the Lord's poverty; by the building of cathedrals in the new Gothic style which used height, light, and color to lift man's spirit heavenward; and by the flourishing of medieval philosophy which sparked such an interest in scholarship that universities were developed as centers of learning.

It was a century of change in many of the workaday aspects of life as well. Although rural life continued its traditional practices and rhythms, and agriculture was the way of life for most Englishmen, the countryside came to be dotted with flourishing walled towns whose newly won charters of privileges and new trade organization of the guilds made them ever more important centers for economic growth. As feudal society was broadened by these new styles of life, the century witnessed also a fuller development of England's own unique system of common law, a supplement to and at times a competitor with feudal justice.

It was in the years 1189 to 1327 that England became the first European power to work out a concept of government, the "community of the realm," which significantly broadened participation in government and altered relationships between king and subject. The king was both sovereign and servant of the kingdom, one with many privileges and also many responsibilities, the ruler *for* as well as *of* England. Should a king not satisfy the norms of good government, he could be restrained by the community—as Edward II learned in 1327.

The leaders in the struggle to realize this notion of community were the great feudal barons of England. They did not have a fixed theoretical goal toward which to work, nor did they attempt to wrest from the king his right to make policy and serve as England's leader. But through conflict and chance, through efforts at times inspired by great idealism and at other times merely by personal selfishness, they sought to define the king's and their own place in English life. In the process were forged many precedents and institutions that were unique in the European experience and which are at the heart of British government, most notably the Magna Carta and the beginnings of Parliament.

RICHARD, JOHN, AND MAGNA CARTA

Richard the Lion-Hearted

Henry II, great king and master of many lands, spent his last years in anguish, his sons fighting among themselves and even rising in rebellion against their father, each asserting his right to be the heir to England's crown. Richard, the eldest surviving son and the best fighter, sought the assistance of the king of France, the young Philip Augustus. Wily Philip knew that the expansion of France required winning back French provinces like Normandy, now under English control, and so he played many roles to Richard—confidant, supporter, perhaps even lover—and was rewarded when, in a particularly vengeful act of defiance to old Henry, Richard did homage to Philip for all England's French possessions. Should ever a pretext be found to allege that Richard or his successor was an unfaithful vassal, Philip now had the legal authority under the feudal system to declare those fiefs forfeit.

As King Richard I (1189–1199), Henry's eldest son became Europe's most formidable fighter; his chivalry and shining sword won him the title "Lion-Hearted" and the fear and respect of many. So consumed was he with fighting that he spent nearly all of his time in battle on the continent and only six months of his ten-year reign in England. England became merely his war treasury, with its offices, titles, and lands for sale to finance the costly wars. Because Richard was strong enough to prevent English discontent from erupting into a serious domestic rebellion, Philip Augustus had no opportunity to turn Richard's act of homage into any gain of territory for France. The machinery of government that Richard's father had developed was capable of promoting justice and good government, but it was also possible to use its capabilities for sinister purposes. Richard demanded more feudal service from his tenants-in-chief than could be justified by custom, exercised undue influence in the royal

King and Knight,
west facade, Exeter Cathedral.
Private Collection.

courts, and sought to wring every penny out of the system of royal administration. A less firm ruler would reap bitter fruit from his legacy.

King John

When Richard died from an infection of a minor wound, his brother John
came to the throne (1199–1216). John was a talented man capable of brilliance,
the favorite son of his father and as such pampered and indolent, a man who
hardly ever achieved anything because he could not sustain a course of action.
His secretiveness, moodiness, and intransigence provoked distrust, and he had
the uncanny ability to alienate almost everyone. John played right into Philip
Augustus' hands. While travelling through France, he fell in love with a young
woman, Isabelle, who was legally betrothed to Hugh the Brown, one of John's
vassals. When John married her, Hugh sought justice from Philip Augustus,
John's lord. When John refused to answer Philip's summons to appear at the

French court to answer for his actions, the French king declared all of England's French possessions, for which Richard and then John had done homage, to be forfeited.

John's efforts to win back the French territories by the sword failed. At the same time, he had run afoul of the most powerful pope of the era, Innocent III, over the choice of a cleric to be archbishop of Canterbury. As was traditional, John nominated a candidate, but another candidate was elected by the dean and chapter of Canterbury Cathedral. When the case was appealed to Rome, Innocent disallowed both procedures and installed his own choice. A series of retaliations on both sides followed, escalating finally to the point at which Innocent excommunicated John, a spiritual censure that denied the king any ministration of the church and forbade all from having any contact with him. John could neither withstand such a public reprimand, nor allow his barons the pretext for their continued opposition to him because of grievances, so he submitted to the pope and had the excommunication lifted.

The barons had come to feel more keenly a sense of outrage at the way in which John continued Richard's abuses and added his own. Not only did he pervert good government, but he was a failure. They agreed that the king should be forced to accept, in writing, a statement of the proper norms for government, articles that would spell out the proper relationship between the king and his feudal nobility. On June 15, 1215, John met a delegation of barons on the meadow at Runnymede near Windsor and put his seal to the document known as Magna Carta.

Magna Carta

Over a third of the sixty-three clauses of the "Great Charter" set out the exact feudal obligations of the king's vassals—these included the terms of wardship, the amount of reliefs, and the occasions when feudal aids were to be paid. Another third was directed against abuses in the royal courts, particularly at John's practice of seizing a defendant's property before judgment was made against him, and the remainder of the clauses dealt with a number of other problem areas, including a promise from the king to respect the church's independence. Magna Carta asserted that the king could receive more financial assistance than was already due him only if granted by the assent of the "community of the realm," that is, by the approval of his feudal tenants-in-chief. Although this document dealt primarily with the relationships between the king and his feudal barons, and only incidentally with other Englishmen, it was of fundamental importance to everyone. It stated a crucial principle—the king was not above the law but rather was subject to it. John's assent to this document was an acceptance of the principle that he and all Englishmen belonged to a community of law and that the law governed the ruler as well as the ruled.

Within a year John had repudiated Magna Carta, claiming that his assent was coerced and thus that his oath was not binding, and when he died in 1216 England was in the midst of a civil war as a result of his action. But every succeeding monarch reissued Magna Carta, and its role as a precedent was assured. Because tradition and custom were so highly esteemed in England, nothing made an argument more effective than to cite historical precedents to support a claim, but a precedent could be made enforceable only if the aggrieved party had the military or political power to insist upon it. Succeeding kings attempted to evade the law and repeat abuses that John or his predecessors had promised to reform; but in time the rule of law would prevail, and Magna Carta would be vindicated as the fundamental precedent.

HENRY III AND PARLIAMENT

The King and the Barons

Henry III, only nine years old when his father died, became England's first minor ruler (1216–1272). The regent appointed to look after Henry reissued Magna Carta in the young king's name. With the civil wars caused by John's repudiation of Magna Carta at an end, peace returned. The barons banded together to preserve the crown and kingdom for Henry, but, when he began to rule on his own, they increasingly felt that their trust had been betrayed. Although the king was cultivated, gracious, and generous in endowing fine new buildings, he was generally contentious in matters of state.

The barons particularly resented Henry's reliance on foreign favorites, kinsmen of his French mother and his queen. He refashioned his council, ignoring the barons who had a feudal right to give him counsel, and appointed instead the non-noble favorites who were bound to him by a special oath of loyalty. The king found it hard to control the day-to-day operation of the government because important administrative bodies had "gone out of court" (page 40), so he shifted many important financial and administrative tasks away from the exchequer and the chancery and into household departments of his royal court, such as the wardrobe and the chamber, which attended him daily. The growing resentments of the barons over the new council and the household government of Henry reached the breaking point in 1258. Henry sought to provide for his second son by accepting an offer of the pope to make him king of Sicily. But the pope did not control Sicily—to win the crown for his son, Henry would have to conquer it himself and pay all the debts the pope had incurred in his own unsuccessful wars of conquest. The barons, who would have to go to war in order to make these ludicrous terms work, had had enough.

Remembering how John had been forced to accept Magna Carta in 1215 when the barons acted together, and realizing that they would have to go fur-

Medieval England and France

ther now to regain their rightful share in the government of England, the barons framed a series of articles, the Provisions of Oxford, and forced Henry to agree to them in 1258. The provisions bound Henry to embark on a plan of reform, and gave supervisory control of the royal government to a council of barons. Henry soon rallied enough support to repudiate his acceptance of the baronial council, and, because the barons did not have a single leader capable of stiffening their resolve, the king's promise to reform bought him time. When it became clear that he was insincere, and when the brilliant Simon de Montfort stepped into the leadership of the baronial party, the barons began a civil war that ended in 1265 with Henry's capture. De Montfort had been born in France, had come to England to claim an inheritance, and then had married Henry III's sister. He served the king until they had a falling out. Although the motives of this mercurial man are as unclear today as they were to his contemporaries, he was shrewd enough to see that opposition by a small group would not suffice to counter the king.

The Beginning of Parliament

De Montfort realized that success in achieving governmental reform was possible only if the demand for it was broad based and not limited to a handful of baronial tenants-in-chief. In 1265 he called together a Parliament. This was to be composed not merely of the feudal nobility but also of representatives of England's shires and principal towns. The name "parliament" (from the French *parler*) was not new, because it had been used when the king met with his feudal advisors to discuss matters of state. The notion of representation was not new: the system of juries was based on the selection of men to act for their neighbors, and kings early in the thirteenth century had convened representatives of the localities—some who were even elected—to perform certain specific duties. The importance of the Parliament of 1265 was that it fused into one truly national body concerned with broad affairs of the kingdom the heretofore separate elements of feudal advisors and elected representatives. The two representatives from each county were called knights of the shire, and the two from each of the major boroughs were called burgesses. Although these representatives and the feudal barons might divide into smaller groups to discuss certain matters, they met as a unicameral (one house) assembly.

Later in 1265, Henry III's talented son Edward led the royalists against the barons at Evesham where he smashed their armies and killed de Montfort. But the notion of a truly national Parliament that had arisen out of the conflict was much too valuable to be lost, and Parliaments were frequently convened in the remainder of Henry's reign. At this early stage Parliaments were not legislative in character; after consultation the king could pronounce a law or statute in Parliament on his own initiative, as was done in 1267 when many of the reforms sought in the Provisions of Oxford were granted by the king in the Statute of Marlborough. The real development of Parliament as an institution lay in the future, and we shall see later in this chapter how important Edward was in the process.

The Common Law and Juries

The legal system fashioned by Henry I and Henry II came to maturity in the thirteenth century, primarily because it attracted a greater part of the litigation as a quicker and more impartial alternative to feudal justice. The procedures of the system of writs were uniform, the personnel were homogeneous because the same judges who sat in the royal courts at Westminster went throughout England twice a year on circuits to hear cases locally, and the principles that they followed were the same. This caused the system to be called the common law, based on the principles of *stare decisis*, to "stand in decisions" in earlier cases which were to be the precedents in similar matters later. This "judge-made law" based on the outcome of court cases naturally called forth a large body of legal literature to quote and comment on the precedents and required a learned profession of attorneys to plead in the courts.

In the thirteenth century the jury system was also applied to criminal cases. Previously it had been used only in disputes over property, according to the terms of the writs, and people were reluctant to judge a neighbor's actions in criminal matters where a conviction brought the death penalty. The notion of leaving the determination of guilt to God through the process of the ordeal had been severely compromised by the Norman practice of allowing a defendant to hire a champion to represent him in the ordeal of battle. The church recognized this and in 1215 ordered priests not to sanction ordeals any longer, significantly hastening the acceptance of juries.

There were two criminal juries, one for each stage of the process. A large representation was desired when accusations of criminal misdoings were sought, and so the name grand jury was adapted from the French *grand*, meaning large. The grand jury indicted offenders (from the Latin *in*, meaning against, and *dictum*, meaning speaking) or "spoke against" an individual. A smaller jury, called a petty jury after the French *petit*, meaning small, heard the evidence and determined whether the defendant was guilty or innocent. It was asked to "truly speak" about guilt or innocence, that is to render a verdict (from the Latin *vere* for truly and *dictum*). At this early stage the size of the petty jury varied greatly, but in time twelve became the accepted number.

NEW ECONOMIC GROWTH

The Towns and Trade

Perhaps 90 percent of England's population worked in agriculture with its traditional attitudes and techniques. But there were new economic developments that formed the prerequisites for a substantial and relatively sophisticated economic growth in the centuries to follow.

The importance of towns was out of proportion to their size. Only a few towns such as London, Bristol, and York had as many as 10,000 persons, and the average size of the slightly over 100 boroughs at the beginning of the fourteenth century was about 2,000. The towns became important for a variety of reasons. Some were important because they commanded a harbor or the confluence of two rivers or some other prominent geographical feature, and some were important because they were centers of administration, such as a shire, or were the seat of a diocese with its cathedral. In the latter case they were properly called "cities," regardless of size. Townspeople often helped with the harvest or farmed land within or near the town. The heart of a town's prosperity, however, was trade, and, when town became borough, the seeds of its trading growth were sown.

The transformation was made when a borough was chartered. A charter normally gave a town a degree of political independence from the shire's officers, conferred economic privileges such as markets and fairs, and enabled the burgesses to have legal rights that reflected their different style of life. Some towns were boroughs before 1066 and had traditional privileges, but the practice of granting written charters coincided with the great financial needs of Richard I. Officials often hoped to improve the terms in new grants that would let the town have prized privileges such as those enjoyed by London and Bristol. Important lords and bishops also granted charters for boroughs. If a borough prospered, it became a potential source of greater royal income, and kings developed new types of taxation. But a charter was no guarantee of success, and many boroughs languished or even disappeared.

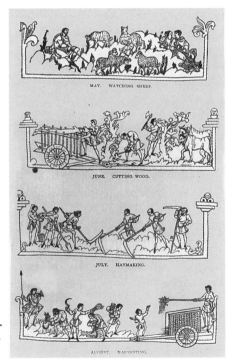

Medieval drawing of agricultural activities for the summer months. Corbis-Bettmann.

The political structure of the boroughs was rather uniform. If a borough was large enough, it was divided into wards, each of which elected an alderman. The aldermen formed the upper and most important of two councils, electing one of their members to serve as mayor for a year's term. The other council was larger, consisting of a number of representatives from each ward. The borough's officers enforced the laws, punished criminals, collected taxes, and kept "foreigners," as nonresidents were called, from usurping the privileges of the burgesses.

The economic control of the borough rested with the guilds. In smaller boroughs and in the early years of the larger ones, there was only one guild to control all economic activities—the guild merchant. It enforced the rules of the markets, supervised the quality of the products that were traded, and generally directed the town's economic life. If a town flourished, an economic specialization nearly always followed, and in time guilds for each of the crafts were organized, such as weavers, tailors, butchers, brewers, and goldsmiths. These guilds established regulations that governed the reception of apprentices and certified them afterward as journeymen (day workers) entitled to exercise the trade and, in due time, as masters. The transition from a single guild merchant to many craft guilds often involved acrimonious disputes as men fought for control of the economic life of the borough, but in time the craft guilds supplanted the guild merchant.

Although in theory the political and economic control of the borough were vested in different bodies, in practice the same men ran both; to this day, the buildings that house the governmental offices of English towns are called guildhalls. The town's lifeblood was the weekly or twice-weekly market; foreigners were welcome to buy or to sell at wholesale those specialized products not made in the town, but the borough's success depended in large part on restricting sale at retail to its own burgesses. A fair might be held once or twice a year, specializing in products peculiar to the area. There was entertainment and fun, but its success depended on drawing merchants from throughout England and the continent.

The Wool and Cloth Trade

England was the greatest wool-producing kingdom in Europe. From the vast numbers of sheep that dotted the hills of northern England came the fleece to make the wool cloth which most northern Europeans wore. Although it was possible merely to ship raw wool abroad, its value was considerably enhanced if it was made into finished cloth. So many stages were involved in the process that large numbers of persons were employed full-time on estates which specialized in making woolen cloth. Farmers everywhere worked at it part-time to supplement their income. In order to make cloth, shearers removed the fleece from the animals and sent it to carders who combed it so that the wool fibers lay parallel. Spinners fashioned this into thread, and weavers wove this into cloth. Fullers bleached the cloth, dyers added the desired coloring, and then it was stretched back into shape and trimmed to size. The cloth was sold either at fairs, or special marketing halls in England, or abroad.

In the early years the English were distinctly inferior to continental Europeans in making finished cloth, and the conduct of the market for the sale of the cloths was dominated by aliens as well. To learn to make cloth better, the English allowed aliens to enter and to teach the trade. By the beginning of the fourteenth century the English had begun to use the capitalistic method of controlling the manufacture of cloth. An entrepreneur gathered materials prepared at one stage of the process and delivered them to the next, and so assumed the responsibility of seeing the product through all its complicated preparation. In 1326 the English moved to gain control of the marketing stages as well. They forbade, as before, purchasers from abroad to travel throughout England to the various fairs to buy cloths and instead allowed them to buy only in a few regulated halls stocked with cloth gathered by English middlemen. With such a small number of set places for purchase, called "staple towns," the government was better able to supervise the trade, to collect a new type of tax in the form of customs duties, and to enforce the laws which controlled the quality of the products. Customs duties were also collected on the commodities that the English imported: wine from France, spices from Venice and other areas which traded with the Far East, and naval stores such as timber and pitch for building ships from Scandinavia. From these modest beginnings would develop an ever-increasing volume of trade, until in the eighteenth and nineteenth centuries England would be the greatest trading nation in the world.

Medieval York

Few towns better illustrate the importance of the new municipal government and the wool trade than York in northern England. On the moors and other hilly terrain to the north and west of this city grazed countless sheep, many on the estates of the Cistercian monks who had introduced the raising of sheep into England. York's location on the River Ouse gave it direct access to the North Sea and thus to continental markets. It was important militarily because it lay astride the only lowland route from England to Scotland and administratively as the center of Yorkshire and as the cathedral city of the diocese of York.

As the headquarters of the Roman garrison whose legions protected the northern frontier of Roman Britain (page 5), York had been laid out on neat military lines. The seventy acres within the walls housed barracks and other military buildings which had been built in rectangular fashion at right angles to the river. Medieval York was different in a number of ways. The neat pattern of streets was gone and was replaced by wandering lanes at helter-skelter angles, spilling out beyond the old walls to cover an area three times as great, even though the walls were kept as a fortification. The costly buildings were no longer military but ecclesiastical—forty-seven parish churches, several abbeys, and the jewel of the city, York Minster, the archbishop's cathedral with its captivatingly lovely gothic arches and windows. These churches were aligned not with the river, but with the morning sun in the east so that it spilled through the windows to illumine the divine services. There was a guildhall for the borough's officers and separate buildings to house the guilds of the various trades.

York was alive with activity. Food and drink were sold from dawn to dusk in the open market on the broad expanse of the center of town, called the Pavement, on Tuesdays, Thursdays, and Saturdays, while cloth and household needs were sold in another market on Thursdays and Saturdays. The areas in which the approximately sixty craft guilds were concentrated were revealed in the street names such as Tanner Lane and the Shambles, the latter where the butchers slaughtered animals in the street, letting the blood and offal ooze toward the Ouse. The narrow, paved streets allowed little sunlight or breeze to disperse the smells and sounds of trade, and, because the upper

Ruins of abbey.
Private collection.

stories of the houses extended further into the street than those on the ground level, the streets felt even more constricted.

York's burgesses were prospering. Aside from the laborers, the largest guilds were those of the weavers and tailors. The guilds and the religious confraternities of the city sponsored the mystery plays and pageants that provided much color and entertainment. The city's officers policed the markets to supervise quality and proper measures. The deceitful merchant suffered the ignominy and the appropriate punishment of having to drink his putrid beer in public or to eat the spoiled food he had attempted to sell. Urban problems and pollution know no bounds of time or place, but they arose in York to greater degrees because the fleece of the sheep and the success of trade brought increased population, prosperity, and plenty.

HIGH MEDIEVAL CULTURE

The Intellectual Revival

The late eleventh and the twelfth centuries were times of an intellectual revival in Europe. Some call it a "renaissance," a "rebirth," because the rediscovery of classical Roman and Greek writings had a major part. By the late twelfth and thirteenth centuries, the attitudes and institutions of this revival had become a mature part of English life.

The great rediscoveries that sparked the renaissance were in the fields of literature, law, and philosophy. Medieval scholars studied Roman literature to learn how to improve their own writing style and to discover the virtues and ideals which had let Rome dominate the ancient world. Medieval persons were especially intrigued by the study of law and philosophy because they found them highly amenable to synthesis, the drawing together into one coherent and organized system of a tremendous breadth of knowledge. The rediscovery in the eleventh century of the magnificent codification of Roman law made centuries earlier by the Emperor Justinian spurred medieval scholars to adapt this to the church's needs. The study of canon law flourished in England and helped provide the theoretical underpinnings for Henry II's legal innovations and for Becket's insistence on the church's privileges in his quarrels with Henry.

Theology was the most important medieval study: it placed God at the center of things and began with His revealed truths, which were the surest knowledge. The contribution of the intellectual revival was to make philosophy the handmaid of theology—to provide the tools of logic which would allow scholars to deduce useful knowledge from revelation. The Greeks had been the great philosophers of antiquity, but many of their ideas were unknown in the West. The conquest of the East by the Moslems put them into direct contact with Greek thought.

Eager Moslem intellectuals translated the works of Plato, Aristotle, and other philosophers into Arabic and incorporated them into Moslem thought. In the twelfth century translations from Arabic into Latin were the key to reopen a study of classical philosophy in western Europe. A Dominican friar at the University of Paris, St. Thomas Aquinas, "baptized" Aristotle, combining pagan philosophy and Christian dogma to produce a stunningly magnificent synthesis of theology. Before long the contents and techniques of this new learning had captured most European schools.

Universities

The broadened content of medieval knowledge demanded better facilities for study. Good teachers drew good students. However, it was easy for landlords and civic officials to victimize teenage students, and a teacher might collect fees and then not teach. The first reaction was for students to form a guild to protect themselves, and professors formed their own guild to ensure proper qualifications for instruction and to protect their interests. In time a single corporate body called a university developed, with specific privileges and responsibilities set out in a charter. The first English university was at Oxford, to which many of the English students came when called home from the University of Paris by Henry II in 1167 during his quarrels with Becket. Gradually a center of learning developed, interrupted by quarrels between the townspeople and the often rowdy students, called "town and gown" riots (the students' academic dress was a gown). These difficulties were overcome at the beginning of the thirteenth century by the bishop's supervision and control. A

King's College Chapel,
Cambridge University.
Private collection.

second university grew at Cambridge but was a good deal smaller than Oxford in its early years.

Oxford and Cambridge were in reality loose confederations of colleges, as the residential centers of instruction were called. A college was a corporation whose members, later called "fellows," were nearly always priests. Many of the students went on to become priests, and the students' day was much like that in a monastery. They arose before dawn for prayer and mass and returned for prayer at stated intervals during the day. In the usual three years it required to earn a B.A. degree, they studied the seven liberal arts of grammar, rhetoric, logic, arithmetic, geometry, astronomy, and music. Books were rare, so the students took notes during lectures, memorized them, and then formally disputed selected topics—all in Latin, of course.

Although most European universities were similar, Oxford did have some distinguishing features. Bishop Robert Grosseteste, who once headed the university, was interested in science and urged that the normal deductive process of learning be supplemented by observation, the forming of hypotheses, and experimentation. This uncharacteristic process was also advocated by a Franciscan friar interested in science, Roger Bacon. Another Franciscan, John Duns Scotus, was an influential philosophical thinker who was a critic of the accepted system of Thomas Aquinas.

The Friars and the Religious Revival

A spiritual revival was sparked by the creation on the continent of new religious communities, the friars. St. Dominic formed an order of preaching friars in Spain to teach true doctrine and to combat heresies, and on the Italian peninsula St. Francis of Assisi renounced his well-to-do heritage to embrace "the lady poverty" and teach his followers to imitate the humility and simplicity of the Lord. The Dominican and Franciscan friars did not live in monasteries but went among the people, especially in towns, to preach and teach by pious example.

Both communities of friars came to England in the 1220s. Because they believed in the importance of education and sound religious instruction they were well-prepared, especially when compared with the often inadequate training of the normal parish priest. Their emphasis on education led many to the universities; we have seen how important the Dominicans were at Paris, and the Franciscans at Oxford. The friars often aroused the jealousy of the parish priests, but their emphasis on preaching to the poor and unlettered made a significant impact on English spiritual life.

Gothic Architecture

The piety of the age was also expressed in stone and mortar, in new churches and in extensions built on the older ones. The Romanesque style of the tenth

*An example of fan vaulting and interior
height of the Gothic Norwich Cathedral.
Private collection.*

and eleventh centuries tended to be squat and massive because the walls had to support the entire weight of the roof. The emphasis was on the horizontal. The Gothic style which developed in the twelfth and later centuries utilized the discovery that the weight of a roof, if concentrated over a center of gravity atop a pointed arch, could be supported by slender columns in the walls. Since the walls proper were no longer supporting the roof, they could be considerably lighter and include large windows that were usually decorated with stained glass. Above all, the walls and the interiors were higher, the emphasis on the vertical.

The change was immediately apparent when one entered a gothic cathedral: with an interior height reaching and even exceeding 100 feet, the effect was to sweep the eye and, perhaps, the spirit heavenward. The ceilings were beautifully decorated in fan vaulting. The columns of the walls branched out in fingers along the roof to reach the center of gravity and to carry the weight downward. The stained glass windows became textbooks of Bible stories and pious legends to instruct the unlettered faithful. The airy and light effect of Gothic architecture was as refined and reflective of the intellectual outreach of the twelfth century renaissance as the massive Romanesque or Norman style was of the more military emphasis of the eleventh century.

E D W A R D I A N D E D W A R D I I

Edward I and Parliament

Edward I (1272–1307) was one of the strongest medieval kings, well-schooled by the difficulties of the reign of his father, Henry III. He was a tall, imposing man who commanded great respect, a talented administrator whose effective use of household government and of Parliament produced monuments to his energy and control. Domestic affairs flourished under his leadership, but wars in France, Scotland, and Wales caused no end of difficulty.

Edward had seen how useful a national Parliament could be; he called as many as two Parliaments a year. Although at first the representatives of the shires and boroughs were called infrequently, his growing need for revenue to finance his wars suggested that the representatives of his subjects who would pay the parliamentary taxes should be present regularly. In 1295 a Parliament met, which much later was to be called the "Model Parliament." It was not called this because its organization became a precedent to be followed invariably thereafter but because all the categories of membership were present. These would be included when the exact composition of Parliament would be fixed in the following century. It must have been a magnificent sight—twenty bishops and seventy abbots in their ecclesiastical robes, fifty earls and barons, representatives of the lower clergy from each diocese, and representatives of the shires and 110 towns, more soberly clad as befitted their common rank.

After the opening prayers and sermon, the king addressed the community of the realm and presented his needs. The burgesses withdrew across the way to Westminster Abbey to deliberate, the king and his inner council moved to a nearby chapel, and the others remained in the Great Hall of Westminster Palace. Over a period of about ten days, these various groups received petitions which protested grievances, considered the grant of taxes, heard cases of great importance, and counseled the king on important matters. This completed, all met together again in the Great Hall to hear the king promulgate as statutes the new laws he granted, which were based on some of the petitions, and thank the assembly for the grant of taxes.

Edward used Parliament very effectively to codify much of the law. "Judge-made law," with its reliance on precedents hammered out in numerous trials, had been the basis of the common law, but now Edward restated the laws on property, criminal offenses, and other matters succinctly in statutory form. Common law did not disappear—an offense could be punished at common law even if it had not been defined in a statute—but the principle gradually developed that the law could be changed only with Parliament's consent.

A crucial precedent for Parliament's future importance was won in 1297 when Edward was fighting to maintain control of Gascony, the area of southwestern France that was not included in Richard I's homage to the French king and was still one of England's possessions. So great was Edward's need for funds that Parliament resisted, asking that as a sign of good faith the king reissue many charters of privileges. Included in this Confirmation of Charters of 1297 was Edward's promise not to seek extraordinary funds without the consent of the "community of the realm." Magna Carta in 1215 stated that extraordinary feudal income could be granted only with the community's consent, but at the time the "community" meant the feudal barons; the Confirmation of Charters set conditions for grants of nonfeudal revenues, but now "community" meant Parliament—quite a broadening of the political nation in 82 years. Over future centuries, with much travail and long periods of reversal, these two precedents would give Parliament the control of finances, and eventually of the monarch.

Edward I and Scotland

Scotland had kept its independence by withstanding invasions attempted by the Romans, Anglo-Saxons, and Normans, but its separateness from England was gradually weakened as the Scottish royalty married into the English royal family. In 1173 Henry II had used a minor border clash as the first step in a full-scale battle with the Scots, and the defeated Scots king did homage to Henry for Scotland. Later, Henry III had improved relations by marrying his daughter to the king of Scotland, a minor. By 1290 the young Scottish king and all his direct descendants were dead, and the Scots saw no other way out of a complicated disputed succession than to leave the decision to Edward I as overlord. Edward insisted before hearing the case that the claimants and Scotland's leaders take oaths which explicitly reasserted his superior position. Even after choosing a new king of Scotland, Edward kept intervening in their affairs and Scottish patriotism was awakened.

The Scots began to ignore Edward I, and they sought an independent alliance with France. In 1296 Edward I deposed the king whom he had chosen and sent him into exile. Robert Bruce, the descendant of the unsuccessful claimant of the same name in the disputed succession case, then had himself crowned king of Scotland and began to rebel against Edward. Edward's military victories won him the title "Hammer of the Scots," but his opponents would not give up. Edward died in 1307 during a battle in the tenth year of the struggles.

Wales and Ireland

The Welsh had retained their independence from England longer than the other Celtic kingdoms on the British Isles. The mountains had been an effective barrier against invaders, but, because the Welsh leaders were continually bickering among themselves, they were really no threat to England. Llewelyn the Great (died 1240) was the first Welsh leader to succeed in uniting the Welsh against England, but Henry III had defeated him and conferred on his son Edward many Welsh lands to make an English presence felt there. Opposition to England began again in the 1260s, this time led by Llywelyn ap Gruffudd who took the title "Prince of Wales." His early victories especially humiliated Edward, whose estates were overrun. On his father's behalf (and then on his own when he became king), Edward completely defeated the Welsh. The statutes for Wales in 1284 symbolized the English domination, as did Edward I's gift of the title of Prince of Wales to his son, a title to this day born by the heir apparent to the English crown.

England had had far more success at an earlier date in Ireland, which Henry II had conquered with papal approval because of the sad state into which the church had fallen. Two-thirds of the island was under English control, and the remainder was the battleground of clan leaders who continually fought among themselves. Under later kings the English system of government and common law was introduced, but the fights of the Scots and Welsh against English control awakened Irish patriotism which in future centuries caused trouble for England.

Edward II

Edward I's son was unworthy of his father's legacy. Indolent and willing to seek any amusement rather than work at government, Edward II brought ruin upon England's military ventures and then upon himself. He scandalized his subjects because his foreign favorite, Piers Gaveston, was his lover and monopolized his attention. The Scottish situation was not attended properly, in part because of Edward's vacillation and weakness of character but more important because he was protecting Gaveston whom the English barons particularly wanted to remove. English forces in the north lost the military advantage, and Scottish victories such as at Bannockburn in 1314—which guaranteed the Scots a respite from English attacks—added to the king's ignominy. He refused to recognize Bruce as king, and only a series of truces kept the Scots from occupying even more of northern England.

The barons reacted to Edward by forcing upon him in 1311 a set of Ordinances that committed the king to reform and imposed a baronial council to control government. Edward was able to rally support and repudiate the Ordinances, as John had done with Magna Carta and Henry III had done with the Provisions of Oxford, but the defeat at Bannockburn led the barons to impose the plan of reform once again. Another precedent was invoked: just as Magna Carta had been reissued later, and the Statute of Marlborough granted much the Provisions had sought, so Edward II had to yield in a Statute of York in 1322 to many of the reforms sought in the ordinances. The barons did not stop there but captured Gaveston and had him executed, sparking the king to further vengeance and obstinacy. Later, Edward's wife took a lover, Roger Mortimer, and together they and others of the baronial party who were sick of misgovernment persuaded Parliament to debate how Edward had ignored his promises to govern justly and wisely. Edward was forced to abdicate and allow his minor son to rule as Edward III; within a year Edward II was murdered in prison.

SUGGESTIONS FOR FURTHER READING

Recent surveys of this period can be found in Richard Mortimer, *Angevin England, 1154–1258* (1994) and Michael Prestwich, *English Politics in the Thirteenth Century* (1990). One can read about the Angevin monarchs of this period in Caroline Bingham, *The Crowned Lions: The Early Plantagenet Kings* (1978) and in Ralph V. Turner, *King John* (1994). J. C. Holt studies the Great Charter in *Magna Carta* (1965) and provides a sympathetic portrait of King John. The custom of consulting the "community of the realm" began in the reigns of Henry III and Edward I and led to the practice of summoning parliaments, for which, consult G. O. Sayles, *The King's Parliament of England* (1974); Bertie Wilkinson, *The Creation of Medieval Parliaments* (1972); Margaret Wade Labarge, *Simon de Montfort* (1962); and John Chancellor, *The Life and Times of Edward I* (1981).

The involvement of the Angevin Monarchs in wars in Scotland, Ireland and on the Continent is examined in Malcolm Vale, *The Angevin Legacy and the Hundred Years War, 1250–1340* (1990) and Michael Prestwich, *War, Politics, and France under Edward I* (1972). The changing martial culture of English knights and barons is analyzed in Maurice Keen, *Chivalry* (1984) and Nigel Saul, *Age of Chivalry* (1992).

Surveys of economic and social history are provided in J. Z. Titow, *English Rural Society, 1200–1350* (1969); M. M. Postan, *The Medieval Economy and Society: An Economic History of Britain in the Middle Ages* (1972); A. R. Bridbury, *Economic Growth: England in the Late Middle Ages* (1975); and in Edward Miller and John Hatcher, *Medieval England: Rural Society and Economic Change, 1086–1348* (1978). Towns are examined in Colin Platt, *The English Medieval Town* (1979); John Schofield and Alan Vince, *Medieval Towns* (1994); Susan Reynolds, *An Introduction to the History of Medieval Towns* (1977); and Gwyn A. Williams, *Medieval London: From Commune to Capital* (1963). Eileen Power, *The Wool Trade in English Medieval History* (1941) and *Medieval Women* (1975) are classics which still repay reading. A more recent contribution to women's history can be found in Judith M. Bennett, *Women in the Medieval Countryside* (1987). A good selection of documents for the period is contained in Harry Rothwell (ed.), *English Historical Documents, 1189–1327* (1975).

CHAPTER FOUR

Late Medieval England
1327–1485

In these nearly 160 years, 1327 to 1485, if England is considered from the aspect of strong political power, or of peace and tranquility, or of military success in the wars against the French, then certainly England was in decline. The feudal bonds that had knit society together were unravelling, the Hundred Years' War gained neither territory nor the French crown, and the civil wars of the fifteenth century severely dislocated the political state.

Yet if the intangibles that give a country its unique character are considered, it was a period of transition and not of decline. In the early fourteenth century, the leaders of England spoke French and followed French ways. In the late fifteenth century, Englishmen spoke English and attended to domestic business, and distinctly English institutions such as Parliament became increasingly important. Even the political decline was arrested in 1485 when the Tudors captured the crown and revived royal power and ended the drift of the civil wars. The peace and prosperity that they brought were the preconditions of England's reassumption of an important place in European affairs.

THE FOURTEENTH CENTURY:
GROWTH AND DISRUPTION, 1327–1399

Edward III and the Hundred Years' War

Edward III (1327–1377) was a warm, cheerful, and inspiring leader, at once a practical man of affairs and an idealist. He had learned from his father's reign how deeply the barons resented their exclusion from the inner circles of power. As a valiant and generous warrior he led his realm to war and gave his nobility the sweet taste of victory and the comradeship of a shared mission—no aristocratic rebellion ever scarred his reign. In all of this he set a high moral tone: he made chivalry and pageantry points of policy and, by founding the Order of the Garter as an honorific society, he had the means for rewarding men of similar ideals.

The Hundred Years' War which Edward began lasted from 1338 to 1453, but in reality the war was a series of intermittent campaigns of limited fighting often interrupted by long years of truces. The war was distinctly new in several important aspects. When England fought in the thirteenth century it was to regain territories such as Normandy that John had forfeited to Philip Augustus, but in the fourteenth and fifteenth centuries the English king fought as a claimant for the crown of France. Edward's mother Isabelle was the sister of the childless French king (the last of the house of Capet) who died in 1328. The French had no intention of letting the end of the Capetian line result in their crown descending to an English king. By "inventing" the Salic law, which excluded descent through a female, the French denied Edward the crown; instead it passed to a French cousin, Philip VI, the first of the house of Valois.

The tactics of warfare changed also when the English began to use the longbow as a weapon. Before the Norman Conquest the English had relied on the militia of the shires and, after 1066, on the feudal host in which heavily armored knights acted as a cavalry. Edward III's bowmen were capable of shooting arrows with a force sufficient to pierce chain mail, so that when the French knights charged the English at Crécy in 1346 the English bowmen slaughtered the flower of the French nobility. This success was repeated in 1356 at Poitiers, when the French king was captured and held for ransom. It was impossible to convert these individual triumphs into total victory. The cost of sustained warfare was staggering, England lacked the financial resources, and France had a substantially greater area and population. Belatedly the French adopted new military tactics and erased the English advantage, and the capable French leader Bertrand du Guesclin began to wage a war of guerilla tactics that relentlessly destroyed the English forces. By 1377 England's military gains had evaporated and its original holdings in southwestern France had been severely curtailed.

The Growth of Parliamentary Powers

When Edward I promulgated the Confirmation of Charters in 1297 he established the principle that Parliament alone could grant the king extraordinary revenues; Edward's financial needs thus gave Parliament a tremendously increased importance. It was quickly agreed that the consent of the elected

The Battle of Crécy, August 26, 1346. English longbowmen were able to defeat the heavily armored French cavalry. Corbis-Bettmann.

representatives of the counties (two knights of each shire) and of the boroughs (two burgesses apiece) was needed to grant taxes. These representatives were present at every one of Edward's nearly annual Parliaments, and in 1339 these two classes of elected members met together to act jointly for the first time; these "men of the commons" were eventually to be the House of Commons. The secular and ecclesiastical lords formed the House of Lords. The representatives of the lower clergy ceased to attend Parliament but instead met with the bishops in a separate ecclesiastical parliament called convocation, which granted the king taxes on the church's wealth.

As Edward grew older his control of affairs lessened, tempting nobles and parliamentary leaders to wrest power. Edward's third son, John of Gaunt, duke of Lancaster, felt that he could grasp power by replacing the king's councillors with men loyal to himself, but by 1376 the king's eldest son, Edward the Black Prince, led a reaction. In the "Good Parliament" of that year the process of impeachment was used for the first time to remove John of Gaunt's "evil councillors," a process thus initially and henceforth directed at a king's advisors and never at the king. Even though John of Gaunt's faction was able to reassert itself a year later, the precedent had been set of Parliament's control of a royal minister.

Richard II and Absolutism

At Edward III's death in 1377 his grandson Richard II (1377–1399) was only ten (Richard's father, Edward the Black Prince, had died in 1376). This thoughtful boy had a goal, the restoration of the monarch's powers to the strength of Edward I's reign. He wished to reverse the loss of power wrung from Edward II and the voluntary losses Edward III endured to win taxes to pay for his wars. As a youth, Richard gathered about him a "court party" that shared his absolutist goals, but, as soon as his domineering uncle, John of Gaunt, went abroad in 1386, Richard was left unprotected and exposed to the barons who abhorred his absolutist views.

In 1386 Parliament impeached Richard's most able minister and imposed a baronial council to reform his government. Richard obtained judicial opinions that supported his views and that denied the propriety of Parliament's actions, but the latter had the power. In 1388 five leading lords, the Lords Appellant (they "appealed" against Richard's supporters and thus earned their name) removed Richard's supporters so thoroughly that it became known as the "Merciless Parliament." His powers temporarily eclipsed, Richard quietly bided his time to rebuild his court party.

By 1397 the king was strong enough to pack Parliament with his supporters, and this compliant assembly "appealed" against three of the five Lords Appellant and sent the other two into exile, including John of Gaunt's son Henry Bolingbroke. When John died in 1399, Richard refused to allow the normal succession of the Lancastrian lands and titles to Henry, so he returned to England with an army and rallied the lords to his cause. Parliament debated and then received Richard's abdication when he returned from a campaign in Ireland. Within a year Richard was dead, probably murdered. Although Parliament played a role in the abdications in 1327 and 1399, the precipitating cause in both cases was nonparliamentary military might. But in 1327 the normal heir apparent became king, whereas in 1399 there were cousins with better claims to succeed the childless Richard than Henry IV (as Bolingbroke styled himself). Royal absolutism had been stopped, but tampering with the legal descent of the crown would dictate much of the strife of the fifteenth century.

ECONOMIC AND SOCIAL STRAIN AND CHANGE

Economic Crisis

The early part of the fourteenth century was struck by economic crises. Most notable of these was the famine of 1315 to 1316, caused primarily by changes in the weather. The immediate problem was excessive rain which ruined the harvests; equally as important were long range weather changes, especially the lower than average temperatures (the period from 1309, when the Thames froze at London, to about 1700 is known by the exaggerated name "Little Ice Age"). Although the usual cycle of good and bad agricultural years continued, the overall trend was disruptive. England was relatively overpopulated in these years, perhaps with 5 to 6 million persons, and the suffering contributed to a general malaise.

The Black Death and the Peasants' Revolt

No generalized or particular crisis could ever approach the horror and magnitude of the "Black Death," which struck all of Europe at midcentury. The bubonic plague that destroyed so much of England's population in the first attack in 1348 to 1351 had begun fifteen years earlier in China and had travelled across Europe along the trade routes. Rats on the ships carried fleas that bore the bubonic plague. Infected persons suffered a grotesque swelling of the glands before death, and the asphyxiation and discoloration that often resulted from a buildup of fluid in the lungs contributed to the name Black Death. The number of lives lost, if not accurately measurable, was appalling.

Perhaps close to 40 percent of the entire English population died, reducing the population perhaps to around 3.5 million. Particular segments of the population suffered differently: nearly half of the clergy died, scores of densely populated settlements such as towns, villages, and monasteries were decimated, while those in the countryside who lived somewhat apart—notably the aristocracy and gentry—suffered much less. Even after the first attack had subsided, the plague recurred often in England for 300 years. The sense of personal tragedy at the horrible toll was profound and the fear evoked by such a visitation was gripping.

The immediate reaction of the propertied class was repression—a Statute of Labourers (1351) that attempted to hold wages to pre-plague levels. The agricultural workers felt deeply grieved by the Statute and by novel taxes. Previously, the wealthy alone had paid the taxes, but in 1377 a poll tax was levied, a flat tax on each person fourteen years or older. The combination of unrealistic wage regulation and taxes levied on the lower classes produced the first broad uprising in England, the Peasants' Revolt of 1381.

The Peasants' Revolt initially took place only in two English counties, Essex and Kent, but it was a major threat to the realm. From those localities the rebels marched on nearby London, which was the key to the kingdom's security. The initial strengths and actions of the rebels—the dynamism of Wat Tyler who led the forces, the freeing of men held in a royal prison, the burning of the palace of King Richard II's uncle, and then Richard's conciliatory meeting with the rebels—were lost when the rebels overstepped by pressing for wider and more revolutionary demands such as the abolition of lordships and a dispersal of church wealth. The mayor of London got into a scuffle with Tyler in which he stabbed the rebel leader to death. Quickly the king's forces took the initiative in dispersing and killing the rebels, not only in the London area but in other parts of England where news of the initial rebellion had spread.

Although the government relented in its taxing policies and the Statute of Labourers became a dead letter, the long-term consequences for society were far-reaching and revolutionary. Before 1348 England had been relatively overpopulated, and many peasants were in effect tied to the soil to render servile labor to their feudal lords on their vast demesnes. This system, known as "high farming," was characterized by vast labor forces working under the immediate supervision of the landowning class. Because the plague caused a severe labor scarcity, workers heretofore bound to the soil (the name "serf" had been used for those legally free but economically unfree workers) now had a valuable and avidly sought commodity. They could easily run away from a lord who did not end their servile status, and another lord who was desperate for help to harvest his crops would hire them, no questions asked. The king and aristocratic landowners were now unable to maintain the vast labor force that had made high farming possible. Lords instead began to lease out parts of their lands to independent laborers, and the nobility became collectors of rents rather than superintending estate managers. Serfdom became a thing of the past.

Changing Notions of Aristocracy and Gentry

There were other factors at work to change the notion of rank and class in the fourteenth century. Up to this time there were only two traditional ranks of the nobility, the barons and the earls. By the fourteenth century there was no clear definition of what set those in the lower rank of baron apart from many others in the class of those who bore arms. Earlier a particular type of land

Medieval town, Lavenham. Private collection.

tenure had distinguished them, but because of changing times and divisions of estates there was no certainty by the fourteenth century.

When Parliament started to sit, however, kings summoned certain barons to Parliament by individual summonses. Thus some who did not hold land by the traditional tenure were called and some who did were not called—the list that was developed throughout Edward I's reign became by Edward II's a definite list not only of who were summoned to Parliament but also of the extent of the peerage. In 1387 a man was made a noble by a specific grant in writing. Henceforth either individual summons or a particular grant in writing were the distinguishing characteristic of a noble.

In 1337 Henry III created a new rank of nobility when he made his first son a duke. This title, like that of earl, carried no office or special rights but did bestow prestige and precedence. A duke ranked right below the monarch and above earls; the first duke not of royal blood was created in 1351. In the fifteenth century two new ranks were created, marquess and viscount, so that then the order of precedence from highest to lowest in the peerage was duke, marquess, earl, viscount, and baron. All of these distinctions were social, not economic.

The rank of knight was the highest in that group called the gentry—a group as ill-defined in the early fourteenth century as the peerage had been. Knighthood was granted through a special ceremony so that it was relatively easy to distinguish them, but as with other titles it could receive a related but nonspecific use, as for country representatives to Parliament who were "knights of the shire" but who did not have to hold the rank of knight. The Hundred Years' War and other military employments kept the rank high, perhaps regularly in the range of 1,000 to 1,200 persons, but there was a serious decline in the number of knights in the fifteenth century.

As the ranks of knights contracted, there was a growth in the two other ranks, which with the knights constituted the gentry, the esquires and the gentlemen. A tax return of 1436 indicated there were about 1,200 esquires; it is more difficult to ascertain from that return exactly how broad the class of gentlemen was, but it was in the range of 1,000 to 2,000. There was such a fluidity about what constituted any group that exactness is not possible and was no clearer to persons of that time than to us today. When involved in public service, most of the gentry did so on the local level. Of all such employments, the most prestigious was to be a justice of the peace, an office arising in the fourteenth century originally as "keepers of the peace."

CHAUCER'S ENGLAND

Chaucer and the Revival of English Letters

English had remained the language of the lower classes after the Norman Conquest, the language of the towns and byways of rural England where wandering minstrels sang English ballads, versified narratives of heroic deeds such as wars against the French and Scots, and recounted episodes of chivalrous romance. Because French had been the language of the upper classes since the Conquest, there was no literature composed thereafter in English until the fourteenth century. The exact reasons for a revival of English in literature and in the common speech of the upper classes remain mysterious, but certainly the Hundred Years' War in which the French were the enemy provided a powerful psychological impetus.

Geoffrey Chaucer (ca. 1343–1400) led the revival of English letters. He combined an extraordinarily wide range of personal experiences with a keen eye for detecting the strengths and weaknesses of men and women and with a flair for setting down his characterizations in striking poetry. He was well acquainted with the world of business because his father and grandfather had been wine merchants in London, and he served later as comptroller of customs there. He had served with Edward III's army in France, had been captured and ransomed, and in later years went abroad on the king's behalf on diplomatic missions. He knew the nobility well and was befriended by the Lancastrians. He was a justice of the peace and sat in Parliament.

As one of the first major writers to use and prefer English instead of French, Chaucer allowed his countrymen to experience the richness and suppleness of their native language. One of his greatest gifts was the ability to portray vividly the ideals and prejudices of many different classes and walks of life. In *Troilus and Criseyde* he described the world of the king and court, and in *The Canterbury Tales* he immortalized a monk, a friar, a worldly prioress,

Canterbury Wall and Cathedral Tower. Private collection.

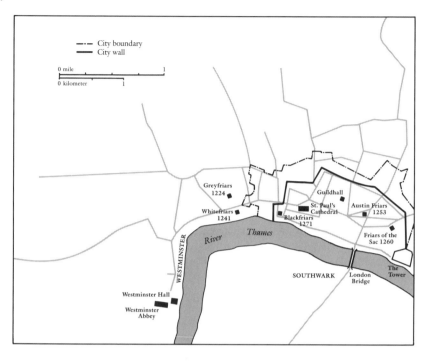

Chaucer's London

and other pilgrims who amused themselves by telling stories as they walked to the shrine of St. Thomas á Becket in Canterbury. Chaucer, the master story-teller, was strikingly secular in his approach to his characters.

Chaucer was the greatest of many writers who wrote in English, but other authors as well increasingly chose to use English rather than Latin, although there does not seem to have been a correspondence or exchange of ideas between any of them and thus no "school" of English letters. The legends of King Arthur were very popular, and the greatest medieval work in English in this vein was *Sir Gawayne and the Grene Knight,* written anonymously about 1370.

In addition to the more courtly works of Chaucer and those of the author of *Sir Gawayne,* there were writings in English on the life of ordinary people as well. The greatest medieval English work concerned with everyday people was William Langland's *Piers Plowman.* This work satirized all social strata but did nevertheless provide accounts of life on a level far removed from knights and the court. The lives of ordinary people also were reflected in the ballads, which sometimes reflected social discontent. The Robin Hood legends were in circulation by the time Langland wrote because he referred to them in *Piers Plowman.* In these legends a man of common stock and uncommon abilities harassed immoral sheriffs and kings. There is speculation today that the protests in the Robin Hood legends were in origin protests of the gentry who suffered from the legal system, but the stories gained a much wider audience because they touched on an exposed nerve of nearly universal discontent.

There were other means of popular instruction in English as well. The stained glass windows in churches, with their vivid colors, had long taught Bible stories to the illiterate flocks; now the church's drama spilled out into churchyards and towns in plays called mystery stories. These recreated Bible episodes and pious legends always taught a moral, but sometimes they upset stern officials because the moral lesson was often interspersed with stretches of broad humor which all too accurately portrayed the foibles of sinful man.

The Church and Wycliffe

There were problems within the church from many sources, some of which were satirized in literature, as noted, but others of far greater importance. The plague had a profound impact on religious life. Men analyzed it in terms of the divine wrath and began to conceptualize God as the God of judgment and retribution rather than of love and popular devotion. The death of so many clergymen curtailed proper religious instruction so that superstition increased. The prestige of the institutional church was hurt when from 1309 to 1377 the popes were French and resided in Avignon in southern France rather than in Rome. Their stay in France coincided with the Hundred Years' War and strained relations between England and the Papacy. For a short time in 1378 there were two popes, one at Avignon and one at Rome, each fulminating against the other and thus lowering the church's prestige.

There was no fourteenth century religious revival as there had been in many earlier centuries, and the uncorrected abuses called forth criticism and satire. The Oxford scholar John Wycliffe at first merely criticized these faults but then moved on to doctrinal heresy. He denied the efficacy of the sacraments as channels of divine grace and rejected Jesus' real presence in the consecrated Eucharist. In turn this led him to denigrate many of the church's roles and to insist that the Scriptures be translated into English to allow personal religious instruction. Wycliffe's followers came to be called Lollards. Although he died in 1384 of natural causes, the seeds of doubt that he had sown and that the Lollards nurtured in an underground movement had challenged the church's authority.

Chaucer's London

The 40,000 Londoners lived in the area of less than a square mile within the city's ancient walls, yet the city was alive with the sights and smells of the nearby countryside. There were signs of the ancient past now abutted by the commercial present, as in the wharves which lined the riverside. Although London was distinctly English, it did house many aliens who were part of the international trading community.

The ecclesiastical buildings were the most striking and most numerous—over a third of the city's area was occupied by church buildings. The cathedral of St. Paul was the largest. That massive building was 560 feet long and nearly 300 feet wide, with an interior height of nearly 200 feet and a spire reaching nearly 500 feet. (The medieval cathedral was much larger than the present cathedral built after the great fire of 1666). It was also the largest employer in London. The number of priests who staffed the cathedral chapter was about sixty. The size of the staff needed for the church's liturgy was very large. There were those to take care of the vestments, chalices, and other items needed for mass, seamstresses to make the vestments, men to light and replace the candles which were the only illumination, and a very large choir that included boys who sang the higher parts. The choir meant a school for the boys, not only to learn the music but also for their general education, and librarians to copy and prepare the music. Grave diggers were needed for funerals, archivists for the church's records, and estate managers for the vast lands held by the cathedral as its endowment, not only near London but throughout the realm. The size of the staff needed for expansion and repair was vast, including stonemasons, painters and gilders, carpenters, and a host of others in the construction trades.

The most numerous ecclesiastical buildings were the 100 or so parish churches within the walls, with another 20 in nearby areas—it has been estimated that there was a parish church for every 3.5 acres. London's parishes were not only centers of worship but also served particular craft guilds, whose members often worshipped as a group, and housed parish guilds that looked after the poor and cared for widows and orphans. There were also numerous abbeys and friaries that housed men and women of almost every religious order in England. Some abbeys served the city in ways other than prayer. The priory of St. Bartholomew was a hospital for the poor, and the Hospital of St. Mary of Bethlehem cared for lunatics—the name "Bethlehem" was pronounced "Bedlam," a name now popularly associated with irrational sounds and disorder. Because friars located in towns by preference, major houses existed for each in London, Blackfriars for the Dominicans and Greyfriars for the Franciscans, the names taken from the color of the capes worn by the former and the religious habit of the latter.

The many buildings dedicated to trade reflected London's position as the commercial hub of England. There were numerous markets to feed London's masses, and names such as Poultry, Ironmonger Lane, Fish Street Hill, and Honey Lane testify to concentrations of tradesmen. Small industry dotted the city, so that workshops and forges were a common sight. Over half of the wool exported from England passed through London, and Londoners also dominated cloth export. Foreign merchants such as the German Hanseatic League maintained massive trading complexes in London.

The craft guilds were so important that they dominated the city's government. A man was a citizen of London only if he belonged to a guild, and so less than a fourth of the city's residents were eligible to participate in government. Thus a trading oligarchy ruled the city, and the greatest guild had a privileged position—the Mercers and Drapers who dealt in clothing, the Fishmongers and Grocers who provided food, the Vintners who controlled wine, and a handful of other major companies. Power was further concentrated when major guilds absorbed smaller but related trades, as the Haberdashers did with the Capmakers. London had become so wealthy and important that after 1392 no monarch attempted to tamper with the city's government, but rather he courted it for the support and financial assistance his royal government needed.

The city's population also included a number of specialized and important occupations. The king's ministers lived in the western suburbs near Westminster and in eastern London near the military complex in the Tower of London and near the royal mint. Many lawyers lived in and near London because they pleaded cases in the royal courts, and students wishing to enter the profession prepared at the numerous Inns of Court and Inns of Chancery which were centers for legal education. These were concentrated just west of the city's gates. Chaucer's London was glittering—sumptuous pageantry and elaborate processions were frequent; there were many luxury shops that supplied jewels and the newly fashionable embroidered, colored clothing. The homes of the wealthy, larger than ever before, featured handsome furniture and tapestries. But London had the appalling problems common to all English and European cities—poor sanitation, overcrowding, and the threat of the plague and other diseases.

THE FIFTEENTH CENTURY: DISLOCATION AND STRAIN, 1399–1485

The Lancastrians and the War with France

Richard II had tried to deny Henry Bolingbroke his Lancastrian dukedom and lands when John of Gaunt died in 1399, and so Bolingbroke's forces had won for him not only the dukedom but the crown of England as well. Henry IV had the strength to face many difficulties. Richard II had been childless so that there was no line of descent through the first of Edward III's sons; Henry was the third son, and his seizure of the crown excluded the second son, Lionel, duke of Clarence. Not until 1410 did Henry IV put behind him the last of many rebellions raised by Clarence's descendants and their Welsh allies.

Meanwhile the French had seized the initiative in the wars and had landed raiding parties on the south coast of England. Henry IV's finances were so precarious that resuming a full-scale war was not possible. Luckily two factions of the French royal house, the Burgundians and the Orleanists, began in 1407 to feud among themselves. This gave Henry breathing space which stilled the mounting criticism in Parliament but increased the scheming of his son Henry. He was so anxious to press the seeming military advantage that he was willing to plot with his father's enemies.

Upon his accession Henry V (1413–1422) renewed the war immediately. He was an effective and self-confident fighter who insensitively dominated his friends and foes alike. The barons rallied to his side, and the English victory over the French at Agincourt in 1415 was so overwhelming that it evoked memories of Crécy and Poitiers nearly a century earlier. In 1420 Henry sided with the Burgundian faction, and together they controlled northern France. Henry and the duke of Burgundy made an agreement by which Henry would become king of France as soon as the present but insane French king died. It was while Henry was moving southward against the Orleanists that he died of dysentery a few months before the French king died.

It seemed that England was on the verge of its greatest achievements, but the reality was just the opposite: under Henry VI (1422–1461) the English monarchy reached its lowest point in foreign and domestic affairs. Henry VI became king of France according to the terms of the agreement between his father and the duke of Burgundy, but the Orleanists under the inspiration of Joan of Arc began a military effort that led to ultimate victory and the expulsion of the English from France. So convinced was the young peasant maiden Joan of the message which she heard from heavenly voices that she conveyed her sense of mission to the head of the Orleanists who was consecrated as Charles VII. As Joan rode in armor with his revitalized forces they swept to victory after victory. Even though the Burgundians captured and delivered her to the English who burned her as a witch, the duke of Burgundy recognized that English forces had lost the momentum to the French and allied himself with the Orleanists. By 1453 when the Hundred Years' War ended France was a unified country, and England had been left with only one town on the French mainland, Calais.

The domestic legacy of the Lancastrians was nearly as ruinous. Parliament gained many important powers because of the instability and military failures of Henry IV and because of the concessions Henry V made to secure funds for his wars. The House of Commons gained power in particular when it began to dictate to the king how taxes were to be spent and to examine his accounts to insure that he had complied. Parliament began to frame its own bills rather than to allow the king to dictate the provisions of remedies for grievances.

Henry VI was merely the puppet of his uncles during his long minority and was so inept as an adult that the government nearly collapsed. He had some personally attractive characteristics, such as a love for the arts and a generosity in founding schools, but his nearly total withdrawal from public affairs led to a breakdown in law and order and internal feuding between the different Lancastrian factions. This vacuum in political leadership coincided with severe economic depressions to make England's prospects grim.

The Yorkists and the Wars of the Roses

Since Henry IV had earlier repressed uprisings by the duke of Clarence's descendants there had been little further agitation over the Lancastrian usurpation of the crown. Meanwhile a female descendant of the Clarence line had married the duke of York (a descendant of Edward III's fourth son), and although their offspring bore their father's title they retained the superior theoretical claim of the Clarence line over the Lancastrians.

During the wars with France a Yorkist official had been removed from command, and gradually the relations between the two families worsened. In 1455 they fought the first of a series of battles in a civil war for the throne which centuries later was dubbed the "Wars of the Roses" because the Yorkists' coat of arms included a white rose and the Lancastrians' (a mistaken assumption) a red rose. The battles were intermittent and restricted for the most part to small armies, but many nobles were killed. This, and the collapse of government under the inept Henry VI, and the bickering of the different Lancastrian factions contributed to a Yorkist victory. In 1461 the mad Henry VI was replaced by the duke of York who became Edward IV.

Edward IV (1461–1483) was a strong, forceful man whose vision of kingship went beyond mere Yorkist dynastic ambitions. He realized that his subjects wanted an end to the civil wars and that England's renewal of the wars with France would squander the fragile kingdom's resources. He restored law and order and won confidence; by reviving household government, which placed important financial and administrative powers under his direct supervision in the royal court, he restored the prestige and effectiveness of the monarchy.

Parliament's exclusive right to grant extraordinary revenue had made it nearly indispensable in the Hundred Years' War and gained it many constitutional powers. Edward's refusal to revive the war obviated the need for frequent parliamentary taxes and allowed him to call Parliament less frequently. The king's greatest potential wealth was his vast holdings of land which now included not only the Plantagenet domains but also the Lancastrian lands added at Henry IV's accession in 1399 and the Yorkist estates added by Edward himself in 1461. By insisting on new techniques of land management he greatly increased the yield from the crown lands and thus reduced further his reliance on parliamentary grants.

Edward IV relied heavily on the abilities and strength of his brother Richard, duke of Gloucester; realizing that when he died his son would be a minor, Edward stipulated that Richard be regent for the young king. At the death of Edward IV in 1483 the family of Woodville, to which Edward IV's wife belonged, seized the regency and excluded Richard. Richard in turn argued that the marriage of Edward IV and Elizabeth Woodville had been illegal, and thus Edward V (1483) was illegitimate. Richard had himself crowned king, and no one had the strength to resist him.

Richard III (1483–1485) placed Edward V and his brother in the Tower of London. Nothing was ever heard of them again. There is no proof that Richard had any complicity in their disappearance, but contemporaries believed that he did, and that was part of his undoing. He attempted to purge the commissions of the peace in many counties of England, replacing justices of the peace who had long held that office with men more pliant to his ways, in an attempt to solidify his control over local as well as central government. These actions prompted a number of local rebellions—so that Richard had trouble in the localities as well as in his own administration. The time was ripe for revolt—and Henry Tudor, earl of Richmond, was waiting to step forward on behalf of the Lancastrians to do battle with Richard III and the Yorkists. In 1485, at the Battle of Bosworth Field, Henry defeated and killed Richard in battle. Few could have guessed what a turning point in British history that battle was to be.

A Stocktaking: England in 1485

Politics and Government

In the later Middle Ages a number of limitations on royal power had been imposed. It was clear that the law limited the king, a principle enunciated explicitly in the established convention that law could be changed only by the king acting in Parliament. It was also clear that the king's power tended to diminish in direct correlation to increased expenses in foreign wars, and so wise kings such as Edward IV freed themselves from parliamentary surveillance merely by declining to fight. The forum for holding a king and his ministers accountable was now Parliament, but in the depositions of 1327, 1399, 1461, and 1485 it was military power which made Parliament's role possible.

Yet any monarch who was willing to rule by law, to cooperate with Parliament and include the great feudal lords in the realm's policy and planning, and to avoid costly wars, possessed extraordinarily great powers of government. He controlled policymaking; directed an effectively organized and sophisti-

Ruins of Whitby Abbey. Private collection.

cated royal administration; provided a system of royal justice which with its writs and jury system protected Englishmen's rights better than did any other European monarch; enjoyed feudal rights; and in general presided over a kingdom protected from continental involvements by the sea. This potential royal power could reach even greater heights when combined with that all-important intangible, success.

Even in local affairs the king's power was great. Borough charters rested on the royal favor, the king's management of trade brought prosperity to merchants and port towns, and the office of justice of the peace which had been developed from the fourteenth century enabled the king to have royal officers close to local happenings. Local communities had been delegated important powers of self-government, not only in the institutional sense but in other responsible activities such as juries.

Society and the Economy

The aristocratic upper class had been the dominant group in society throughout the entire Middle Ages. In the early years of feudal England they were the indispensable military arm and the exclusive advisors of the monarchy, men who employed vast numbers of villeins (free peasants) in high farming. The Black Death had made these nobles landlords living from rents; the use of the longbow and the decline of the knights had made the nobles' military service less important, although their military leadership was still recognized; and the rise of the House of Commons lessened their political status but did not take away their predominant place in government. The greatest change was the bloodletting of the Wars of the Roses which left only twenty-nine surviving secular nobles.

In early feudal England the knights were immediately below the lords, but their military role had declined, and they had become socially allied with the aristocracy but politically allied with the burgesses in the House of Commons. The expansion of professions such as law and the royal administration had begun to create a nonagricultural middle class that was swelled by the merchants who managed England's expanded trade. Life in the cities was structured and sophisticated, temporarily diminished by depressions in the fifteenth century but soon revived in the sixteenth. London had become more than a trading center—like an octopus, its tentacles reached out to take away the economic importance of lesser port towns and to monopolize trade.

Many of the agricultural workers in the lower strata of society had been economically unfree in the early Middle Ages, but nearly all had been freed by the cataclysmic changes from the Black Death. This economic freedom did not, however, guarantee economic success. Most of the peasantry continued to live by subsistence farming, at the mercy of the weather which governed the crops and could in bad times send famine to decimate the countryside.

Religion and Culture

Although religion was certainly one of the unchallenged values in English life, the institutional church had suffered greatly and became a less effective force in England. The Black Death had swept away half the clergy and wreaked havoc on the monasteries and friaries that, in earlier centuries, had been the principal repositories of reformed religious ideals and centers of inspiration. The Papacy's prestige had been lowered by the Avignon "captivity," and Lollardy had first rent the doctrinal unity of English Christianity. From the time of the Conquest, French cultural values had supplanted the English in the upper echelons of society, so that in the cosmopolitan literate society and the intellectual community with its Latin learning England had been part of a truly pan-European world.

The flowering of the English language at the upper as well as the lower levels of society from the fourteenth century had reawakened an ancient heritage, and even in areas such as architecture the later Middle Ages had witnessed a separate, more austere native development. When considered together with the distinct political and governmental institutions, England was well on the way toward an appreciation of uniqueness that was soon to be assiduously cultivated.

SUGGESTIONS FOR FURTHER READING

An overview of the politics of late-medieval England can be acquired from Maurice Keen, *England in the Later Middle Ages* (1973); Michael Prestwich, *The Three Edwards: War and State in England, 1272–1377* (1980); and John A. F. Thompson, *The Transformation of England, 1272–1529* (1983). Recent studies of the reign of Edward III include W. B. Ormrod, *The Reign of Edward III: Crown and Political Society* (1990) and Scott L. Waugh, *England in the Reign of Edward III* (1991). The late-medieval wars in France may be followed in Anne Curry, *The Hundred Years War* (1993) and Robin Nellands, *The Hundred Years War* (1990). The dynastic civil wars of the late fifteenth century are the subject of John Gillingham, *The Wars of the Roses* (1981) and Anthony Goodman, *The Wars of the Roses: Military Activity and English Society* (1981). Recommended royal biographies include: Nigel Saul, *Richard II* (1997); Christopher Allmand, *Henry V* (1992); Charles Ross, *Edward IV* (1974); and Rosemary Horrox, *Richard III: A Study of Service* (1989). The late medieval aristocracy is examined in J. R. Lander, *Crown and Nobility, 1450–1509* (1976).

The fourteenth and fifteenth centuries were a period of social upheaval and demographic disasters as well as war. A good survey of rural society can be found in E. B. Fryde, *Peasants and Landlords in Late Medieval England* (1996) and R. H. Hilton, *The English Peasantry in the Later Middle Ages* (1975); while social unrest is examined in R. B. Dobson, *The Peasants' Revolt of 1381* (1970) and R. H. Hilton, *Bond Men Made Free: Medieval Peasant Movements and the English Rising of 1381* (1973). The disasters of the fourteenth century are described in Philip Ziegler, *The Black Death* (1969), while Maurice Beresford demonstrates the depopulating effect of the bubonic plague in *The Lost Villages of England* (1954). Popular heresy also contributed to the social unrest; for this, consult Margaret Aston, *Lollards and Reformers* (1984) and John A. F. Thompson, *The Later Lollards, 1414–1520* (1965).

The impact of civil war and social upheaval on one gentry family in East Anglia is described in Colin Richmond, *The Paston Family in the Fifteenth Century* (1990). Other aspects of family life are examined in Barbara Hanawalt, *The Ties that Bound: Peasant Family Life in Medieval England* (1986) and *Growing Up in Medieval London: The Experience of Childhood in History* (1993). London life is also looked at in A. R. Meyers, *London in the Age of Chaucer* (1963). The great flowering of Middle-English vernacular literature is surveyed in Boris Ford (ed.), *The Age of Chaucer* (1963) (vol. 1 of *The Pelican Guide to English Literature*), while Basil Cottle traces the rise of the vernacular tongue in *The Triumph of English, 1300–1500* (1969). A full collection of late-medieval historical documents is gathered together in A. R. Meyers (ed.), *English Historical Documents, 1327–1485* (1969).

CHAPTER FIVE

The Early Tudors
1485–1588

Richard III's reign was brief: his governmental actions had led to swift and violent reactions. More important, the action of which he was suspected—killing his nephews imprisoned in the Tower of London—caused the scandal that stirred others to rebel. Whether or not Richard ordered the killing of twelve-year-old Edward V and his nine-year-old brother Richard, duke of York, is still a lively matter of debate. Because Richard was widely suspected of the crime, it was the ideal moment for the Lancastrians to strike. When the nearest Lancastrian claimant defeated Richard III in battle in 1485, he set on the throne the Tudor dynasty (1485–1603) whose reign would be one of the most monumental England had ever witnessed.

HENRY VII:
CONSOLIDATION AND TRANSITION, 1485–1509

The Emergence and Triumph of the Tudors

Henry Tudor was the best Lancastrian claimant in 1485 as a result of a number of unusual links. Owen Tudor, a younger son of a Welsh gentry family, had married Catherine, the widow of Henry V, and thus became stepfather to Henry VI. Two children of Owen and Catherine's were ennobled, including Edmund, earl of Richmond. Edmund married Margaret Beaufort, a descendant of the line which traced itself back to a liaison between Edward III and his mistress, Katherine Swinford, and thus the Tudors assumed a tenuous potential link to royal succession. In 1471 when the Yorkists defeated a Lancastrian uprising, they executed Henry VI and his son, leaving as the nearest surviving Lancastrian claimant Henry Tudor, earl of Richmond, who had inherited the title from his father Edmund. Henry Tudor met Richard III at the Battle of Bosworth Field in 1485, and the victorious Henry placed on his head the crown of the slain Richard III and began to rule as Henry VII.

The Battle of Bosworth Field was the end rather than merely the continuation of the Wars of the Roses due to the ability of Henry VII (1485–1509). This tall, reserved, shrewd, calculating, aloof monarch was willing to spend long hours supervising every detail of government—consolidating, reviving, strengthening, expanding, searching for means to secure and develop English kingship and his own Tudor line.

Establishing the Tudor Dynasty

Henry's claim was tarnished. The children of Edward III by Katherine Swinford were illegitimate, and, although Henry IV had legitimized his cousins, he had forbidden any of that line ever to inherit the crown. Furthermore the claim of the Tudors to royal descent was not direct but was only as a result of Edmund's marriage to a female descendant of that line. In reality Henry had won by military might and thus was in a position to "convince" others of the truth of his theoretical claims. By sagacity and skill at government, he assured the maintenance of his line on the throne and also made royal power a present reality.

It took Henry ten years to secure the Tudor reign. He sought to merge the Lancastrian and Yorkist claims by marrying Elizabeth, the best female Yorkist claimant. He removed the males either by imprisoning them, forcing them into exile, or defeating them in real or imagined plots against himself. Several boys claimed to be the brother of Edward V, and Henry had to restrain these imposters and the men who attempted to manipulate them.

In order to insure the end of the civil wars, he dealt effectively with the "over mighty subjects" who had led the fighting in the aristocratic Wars of the Roses. He first took away from them the potential of gathering a rebellious army. Many lords had kept private armies of retainers, giving their supporters special clothing and badges known as livery. Henry had laws passed that severely reduced the number of persons a lord could retain, reducing a lord's entourage to a few honorific liveried servants much too small to be the nucleus of a private army. Henry then prohibited maintenance, a practice whereby lords often intimidated juries and local officers by appearing in armor when the lords' retainers were accused of law-breaking.

As a place to discipline "over mighty subjects" and others who might threaten the new Tudor regime, Henry VII revived the medieval Court of Star

*Henry VIII,
artist unknown, 1536.
By courtesy of
the National Portrait Gallery,
London.*

Chamber, a judicial arm of the council which gained its name from the painted roof in its chamber. Because this court was so closely linked with the king—its judges were the members of his council—the noblemen did not dare challenge its authority, and the "over mighty subject" could be held to account in it.

The Revival of Effective Government

Henry VII was one of England's most effective monarchs not because of innovation but because he revived those institutions and practices of strong government that kings before him had developed. In domestic affairs Henry continued to use household government, as Edward IV had done so effectively. Henry greatly increased royal revenues by insisting on the payment of all feudal obligations, including some that had long gone uncollected. He vigorously supported foreign trade and took steps, with varying degrees of success, to increase the competitive power of English merchants against foreign traders, increasing customs revenues in the process. He became the patron of the Genoan sailor, John Cabot; when that enterprising sailor led ships under the English flag across the Atlantic, Cabot discovered and claimed for England the eastern seaboard of America, even though his untimely death meant that the claim would not be exploited for many years. By the end of the reign Henry had nearly trebled the ordinary revenue of the crown. He left his son Henry a secure and wealthy kingdom, one which had risen from the internal divisions of civil war to a place of importance and respect in Europe. Henry VII had revived the medieval rights of kingship and made them effective once again.

Henry VII used traditional means, especially marriage, in his foreign policy as well. He named his eldest son Arthur to evoke memories of that legendary British king, and then married him to Catherine of Aragon, a princess of the Spanish house that was one of Europe's first powers. He married his eldest daughter, Margaret, to the king of Scotland to cement friendly relations with the other independent kingdom on the British Isles. Even after Arthur died, Henry attempted to continue the Spanish alliance by urging his second son, the future Henry VIII, to marry her. Although Henry VII seemed at times ready to forward his foreign policy by war as well as marriage, and even though he sometimes won parliamentary taxes to support the anticipated hostilities, he never really fought and thus conserved and augmented his own revenues.

HENRY VIII: THE EARLY YEARS, 1509–1527

A Renaissance Man

The young Henry VIII (1509–1547), who succeeded his respected but unloved father in 1509, was a magnificent specimen—an athlete who excelled in hunting, riding, and tennis and an educated prince with broad intellectual interests and the ability to speak Latin, French, and Spanish as well as English. He was a cultured Renaissance man who played instruments and composed music (he is thought to have written "Greensleeves"). He was also extraordinarily indulgent and vain, a boisterous lover of good times and carousing, a man who had been flattered all his life and had never had to work to achieve fame. He had a flaming and mercurial temper that quickly turned from pettiness into rage and vindictive cruelty.

Catherine of Aragon and the Imperial Alliance

Soon after his accession Henry VIII married his brother's widow, Catherine of Aragon. Lest there be any future question that the children of their union would be legitimate, Henry requested and received a dispensation from the pope specifically allowing the marriage to take place. Catherine, a well-educated Renaissance princess, was the daughter of Ferdinand of Aragon and Isabella of Castille, whose marriage in 1469 had been instrumental in the creation of Spain. In their early years a genuine love and trust grew between Henry and Catherine.

Catherine of Aragon,
1485–1536.
Corbis-Bettmann.

In 1516, Catherine's nephew Charles became king of Spain; in 1519 as Charles V he was elected emperor of the Holy Roman Empire. This monarch's domains were unprecedented: he ruled Spain, the Spanish Netherlands (modern-day Belgium and Holland), the Habsburg dominions (modern-day Austria, Hungary, and adjacent territories), and the new American territories opened by another Genoan sailor, Christopher Columbus. As emperor he exercised a nominal leadership over all of central Europe, particularly modern-day Germany. Because Henry VIII conceived of monarchy in the traditional manner and thus was eager to win glory in the customary way, through war, Henry became the willing partner of his wife's nephew in the latter's expansionary activities on the European continent.

Henry's early years were dominated by planning for English participation in warfare on continental Europe in support of Charles' actions. Henry was distinctly the junior partner in the enterprises, a king who had little part in the grand imperial strategy, whose battles were minor sideshows, and who had no part in the spoils of victory. Henry won occasional military glory, but his treasury was continually depleted.

Cardinal Wolsey

Henry VIII was unwilling to attend to the details of everyday administration as his father had, and so the burden fell on the willing shoulders of the king's chief minister, Thomas Wolsey. Because Wolsey was not of aristocratic birth, he entered the church where it was possible for a talented and bright young man to rise merely on ability, and after a budding career at Oxford he entered the royal service. Under Henry VIII he became lord chancellor, taking precedence over other ministers to head the legal system. In the church he was first a bishop, then archbishop of York, later a cardinal, and finally, at Henry VIII's request of the pope, a papal legate. In this last capacity Wolsey had the theoretical right to exercise in England certain of the pope's own powers, a grant made to allow him to reform the church.

Wolsey was generally unsuccessful as the king's minister. The aristocratic power elite were offended at his humble origins and resented his ostentatious display of the trappings of power. His arrogance ill-equipped him for the delicate tasks of managing Parliament and for the delegation of responsibilities which was the key to effective administration. In foreign affairs Wolsey substituted a pro-French alliance for friendship with Spain, risking England's wool and cloth exports that flowed through the Spanish Netherlands. He did serve well in the law, especially in the Courts of Star Chamber and Chancery where he acquired the reputation of being earnest in the pursuit of justice for ordinary folk.

His greatest failings were ecclesiastical. Although made a papal legate to reform its abuses, he was seen by his contemporaries to personify the very abuses in the Church that needed reformation. Priests were called to be chaste and celibate, but he had an illegitimate son. Priests were called to serve their offices faithfully, but he was a pluralist who multiplied office holding and was therefore nonresident in most posts. Priests were called to administer their posts faithfully and without gain, but instead he accepted bribes for favors.

Wolsey did leave his mark on Britain. He suppressed several religious houses and used the revenues to endow a new college at Oxford for the training of secular priests; after the Reformation its chapel was to become a cathedral for the new diocese of Oxford. He purchased a manor at Hampton and began a lavish building program that made it a showplace known as Hampton Court that evoked the envy of Henry VIII himself. He took the palace of the archbishops of York that lay just between the western edge of London and Westminster and began a massive rebuilding plan. In addition, he had two other magnificent country houses. Worse yet, he never visited York where he was the archbishop.

EARLY RENAISSANCE AND REFORMATION IDEAS IN ENGLAND

The Beginning of the English Renaissance

Early sixteenth-century England was starting to share in the flood of ideas and attitudes from continental Europe. The Renaissance that began in fourteenth-century Italy had been primarily cultural, philosophical, and artistic: writers such as Dante created early literary masterpieces in vernacular Italian, the thought of the Greek philosopher Plato was restudied, and artists such as Michelangelo and Leonardo da Vinci painted, sculpted, and designed magnificent palaces and churches in Florence, Rome, and elsewhere on the Italian peninsula.

The Renaissance in northern Europe beginning in the fifteenth century had a different character. It was more concerned with Christian than pagan scholarship, particularly in the study of the ancient biblical texts and the writings of the fathers of the Christian church in the second through fifth centuries. The most famous light of the Northern Renaissance was Erasmus of Rotterdam who researched and produced a more accurate text of the Greek New Testament. Erasmus and others also very interested in church reform wrote tirelessly (and bitingly) about its unreformed state. In both the Italian and the Northern Renaissances, the attention paid to the human condition produced the name by which Renaissance thinkers were known, "humanists." The development of printing in the mid-fifteenth century in Germany meant that the ideas of the humanists in the sixteenth century could be spread quickly and widely in a manner unparalleled in the western world.

Henry VII had invited Italian humanists to England, and during his son's lifetime Erasmus lived and worked in England, particularly at the University of Cambridge. William Caxton set up the first printing press in England, and from 1476 the English press played an important part in the Renaissance. John Colet, an Oxford-educated priest who had travelled three years in France and Italy, returned and became dean of the chapter of St. Paul's Cathedral. The statutes he wrote for the cathedral school about 1509 became one of the earliest documents of educational reform in the humanistic mold. Thomas Linacre, physician to the royal court, illustrated that well-rounded goal of learning which humanists so prized: in addition to his own medical studies and founding the Royal College of Physicians in 1518, he translated medical works from Greek and Latin into English and wrote on Latin grammar and composition.

The most renowned of the Tudor humanists was Sir Thomas More. The son of a London lawyer, the young More studied first in the household of the archbishop of Canterbury and then at Oxford. He thought first of becoming a priest but instead chose to devote himself to a legal career, to humanistic writing, to married life, and to public service. In time he rose to be speaker of the House of Commons and eventually lord chancellor, the highest legal office in the land and the titular head of the royal administration. Indeed, More was the first layman to hold that office which previously had been reserved for a bishop.

More was a close friend of Erasmus, and both wrote to forward humanistic ideas and the reform of the church. More's concern for his children was exemplary; in particular he wished his daughter to be as well educated in the classics and letters as any young man. His book, *Utopia,* describes an ideal city in profound contrast with the realities of the time; some have seen it as a frustrated admission that an ideal human state was an impossibility in his own time.

Early Reformation Ideas in England

Although the ideas of the Christian humanists were well received, the teachings of the continental Protestant reforms were officially suppressed. Martin Luther began his public confrontation with the Catholic church in Germany in 1517 and unleashed a flood of religious controversy and interpretation. Henry VIII showed his opposition to these ideas when he wrote an answer to Luther, a book entitled *Assertion of the Seven Sacraments.* For this display of orthodoxy he was rewarded by Pope Leo X with the title "Defender of the Faith." Wolsey, More, and other leaders in the royal government and the church worked to suppress Lutheran books, including William Tyndale's English translation of the Bible (1525) which had numerous Lutheran explanatory notes.

Queen Catherine of Aragon

Henry VIII's relationship with Queen Catherine was not without affection, but she failed to produce a male heir who survived infancy. The queen had numerous pregnancies and bore at least six live infants, but only the Princess Mary had survived childhood. Ignoring an illegitimate son which Henry could hardly foist upon his subjects, the only precedent in English history for a female heir was the example of Queen Matilda, whom Henry I had compelled the barons to accept as the royal heir in the twelfth century.* The consequence had been a disputed succession and civil war, and that was something that Henry VIII and his subjects did not wish to contemplate. The memory of the Wars of the Roses was still quite fresh.

Henry, who had a wonderful capacity for rationalizing whatever he wished to do, began to argue that the lack of a legitimate male heir was God's judgment upon an unwholesome marriage. At the age of eighteen, the Royal Council had pressured Henry into marrying his elder brother Arthur's widow, a relationship normally prohibited by Roman canon law. Catherine's sworn deposition that the marriage to Arthur, prince of Wales, had never been consummated, however, persuaded the pope to grant a dispensation for Henry's marriage to Catherine. Henry now asked another pope to annul the second marriage, which

*See chapter 2.

would have left the king free to marry again, whereas a divorce (a judicial decree that a valid marriage had been dissolved) would not, in canon law, allow remarriage. The chain of events which followed Henry's attempt to secure a legitimate male heir set in motion the Henrician Reformation.

THE HENRICIAN REFORMATION

The English Reformation

The English Reformation differed in a number of ways from the Lutheran and Calvinist Reformations, and was accomplished in several stages. It is useful to consider the differences before discussing the details. The first stage, from 1527 until Henry's death twenty years later, was initiated not by religious reformers such as Luther, but was carried out for reasons of state by the English government, by king and Parliament; the Henrician Reformation broke the jurisdictional ties between the Catholic Church and the Church in England. It did not alter doctrine or liturgy, and thus was not particularly Protestant, although a few Protestant reformers could be found within the English Church. The second stage of the English Reformation occurred during the reign of the son who was eventually to be born to Henry, the future Edward VI (1547–1553), and was more distinctly religious in character. During the Henrician Reformation, Henry's jurisdictional break was epitomized in the Act of Supremacy, which declared the king supreme head of the Church of England. The Edwardian Reformation brought a parliamentary enactment of a more distinctly Protestant liturgy and articles of belief. The protestantization of the English people was briefly interrupted by the official restoration of Catholicism under Queen Mary I (1553–1558), but was resumed under Elizabeth (1558–1603). On the continent, reformers such as Luther and Calvin led the break from the medieval Catholic Church and provided much of the initiative in effecting reforms; the English Reformation was led, not by religious reformers, but by crown and Parliament, and was effected by numerous Acts of Parliament.

The "King's Great Matter"

Cardinal Wolsey assured Henry that there were good precedents for obtaining an annulment of his marriage to Catherine, and a papal legatine court was established at the Blackfriars in London to gather evidence. Wolsey, however, was ill informed about foreign affairs, and what he and Henry did not reckon upon was that to ask Pope Clement VII to annul a marriage which rested upon a dispensation granted by a previous pope constituted a challenge to the exercise of papal authority. Moreover, an annulment of the marriage of the Emperor Charles V's aunt would diminish the honor and prestige of the Habsburg dynasty. Considering the fact that the emperor exercised military power in the Italian Peninsula and that the Imperial troops had sacked Rome as recently as 1526, that was an unlikely prospect. England was still a third-rate power in a backwater of Europe. That Wolsey's canon lawyers were able to cite recent precedents for papal annulments of royal marriages or to marshal favorable opinions from learned theologians was not significant.

Nor had Henry and Wolsey reckoned on the proud and stubborn resolve of the devout Catherine of Aragon who refused to allow so many years of her life to be cast aside as sinful and her daughter Mary declared a bastard. In the event, the pope recalled the case to Rome, and Henry and Wolsey were frustrated.

Wolsey's usefulness was clearly at an end. In vain he tried to recapture Henry's favor; he gave Henry his palaces and estates at Hampton Court and York Place in hopes that Henry would be content with these magnificent buildings which he coveted. Henry accepted the gifts but still determined to be rid of Wolsey. The means of Wolsey's removal was found in the fourteenth-century Statute of Praemunire, which had forbidden papal encroachments on royal jurisdiction. This law had been enacted when the popes lived at Avignon and were invariably French at a time when anti-French sentiment had been fanned by the Hundred Years' War between England and France. The law had seldom been enforced. Ignoring the fact that he had himself been a party to the application for an annulment to the papal legatine court at the Blackfriars, Henry charged Wolsey with violating the Statute of Praemunire by impinging on the king's jurisdiction. The usual penalty was forfeiture of offices, goods and estates and imprisonment during the king's pleasure. Unlike St. Thomas á Becket, Thomas Wolsey was not made of the stuff of martyrs and threw himself on the king's mercy. He retired to his cathedral city of York (his first visit there) and died a year later.

The Break with Rome

Henry summoned a Parliament in 1529 to gather support for his cause; it proved so cooperative that he kept it in existence for seven years. Because of the legislation which it enacted destroying papal power in England, it came to be called the "Reformation Parliament." Many of its members came to resent Wolsey's arrogant exercise of power, and anticlerical sentiment was always ready at hand. However, between 1529 and 1531 Henry and his advisors could think of little to do except to put pressure on the pope to grant an annulment to Henry by indicting the whole of the English clergy for violating the Statute of Praemunire and by withholding taxes customarily paid to the pope such as annates and Peter's Pence. By 1532, however, Thomas Cromwell had emerged as the king's chief minister and shaped royal policy to such a degree that some historians regard him as the architect of the Henrician Reformation.

Cromwell was an expert administrator and a superb parliamentary manager, and he had travelled and studied extensively in Italy, that hothouse of modern political ideas. The pre-Reformation Church in England had enjoyed considerable autonomy: it possessed its own system of courts, its own legislature known as Convocation, which enacted local canon law, and economic independence, based upon income derived from extensive estates and parochial tithes. Cromwell, who understood that sovereign rulers need not tolerate such ecclesiastical independence, proposed to destroy papal power in England and reduce the church to complete obedience to the king as supreme head of the Church of England.

The threats against the papacy together with Cromwell's plan for an independent English church under royal rather than papal authority were carried out after January 1533. Anne Boleyn, with whom the king had become enamored, was found to be pregnant, and Henry married her secretly in that same month. Thomas Cranmer, the first Protestant archbishop of Canterbury, had suggested to Henry the idea of having an English church court grant a divorce dissolving the royal marriage. This was done after Parliament passed a statute, drafted by Cromwell, called the Act in Restraint of Appeals, which prohibited any ecclesiastical case from being appealed to the Papal Curia in Rome. The same statute also declared that England was an empire, which meant that the king was a sovereign prince and not subject to any foreign power. The break with Rome was completed when the pope excommunicated Henry, who had violated an earlier papal order against his remarriage while the annulment case was still in litigation. To the king's dismay, his marriage to Anne Boleyn, purchased at so heavy a price, produced not a male heir, but another daughter, Elizabeth. The new queen became redundant, and in May 1536 she was executed for treason on apparently trumped-up charges of adultery.

The separation of the English church from Rome was only the prelude to its total subordination to the new sovereign state. Convocation had already surrendered its legislative independence by recognizing Henry as supreme head and acknowledging that a royal veto could nullify any canons which it enacted. It was understood that the church courts of bishops and archdeacons which operated in England now derived their jurisdiction from royal authority. Office holders and magistrates were obliged to recognize the new royal succession, which declared the Princess Mary a bastard. Finally, the Act of Supremacy of 1534 summarized the revolution in church and state, which had been proclaimed by the Act in Restraint of Appeals of 1533. The former provided the penalties of treason for those who refused to swear to uphold the royal supremacy in ecclesiastical matters and to recognize the new royal succession. Most accepted the new order, but a few individuals stood out in their protests: they included one single bishop, John Fisher of Rochester, the lord chancellor,

Sir Thomas More, the most eminent humanist scholar in England, and a few monks and friars of the more strict religious orders. All were executed.

The Dissolution of the Monasteries and Popular Resistance

Although all of the bishops of the English church but one accepted the Henrician royal supremacy, the abbots and priors of religious houses were viewed as men of divided allegiance. A few had actually spoken out against the religious changes. The vast amount of landed wealth possessed by the English Church—perhaps one-third of the arable land in England—was coveted by Henry, who always spent heavily, but had seldom asked the Reformation Parliament for taxes. Thomas Cromwell, whom Henry had appointed vicegerent and vicar general in spirituals to exercise the powers of the royal ecclesiastical supremacy, was authorized to investigate and reform religious abuses. There were certainly abuses, but probably nowhere near the degree depicted in Cromwell's lurid reports, which provided justification for legislation to dissolve the monasteries and friaries and expropriate their property.

The transfer of monastic lands and wealth to the crown doubled the value of the royal estates and constituted the largest real estate transaction in English history. However, Henry's involvement in wars in France and Scotland in the 1540s caused him to dissipate much of the confiscated monastic wealth. Most of the lands and buildings were sold to lay purchasers and helped to make the gentry collectively wealthier than the crown, the church or the ancient nobility. This conferred upon the gentry economic power and social status, and they soon turned that into political power through membership in the House of Commons. The monks and nuns were pensioned off and dispensed from their vows. Of the former, some became parish priests and some retired from religious life. A few of the more strict religious orders established convents and monasteries in exile on the continent.

In the parish churches the liturgy remained unaltered, and the mass continued. The dissolution of the monasteries provoked very limited protest in southern England. But in the North of England, where the religious houses were still valued as places of learning and hospitality, there was considerably more popular resistance. Agrarian grievances, dislike of Thomas Cromwell, and Catholic piety contributed to the Pilgrimage of Grace, a series of some five distinct rebellions, which spread across roughly the northern third of England during 1536–1537. Lacking a standing army of his own, the king was at a disadvantage when the Pilgrims mustered an army of 30,000 men. Henry resorted to deception: he promised to negotiate with the leaders, and when the Pilgrim army had disbanded, he hanged the leaders.

Opposition to Cromwell also led to factionalism within the king's own council. Cromwell and Archbishop Thomas Cranmer had been strongly influenced by continental Protestantism and wanted religious reform, while the faction led by Thomas Howard, duke of Norfolk, resented Cromwell's humble social origins and Cranmer's great influence on the king and wished to maintain traditional Catholic beliefs in the new English church. Henry had married a third time, gaining at last a son and heir but losing Edward's mother, Jane Seymour, soon after she gave birth. The Cromwell-Cranmer faction urged a fourth marriage to Anne of Cleves, a German Protestant princess. Henry's dislike of her plain appearance helped provide the lever for Norfolk's triumph over Cromwell who fell from power and was executed in 1540. Henry's fifth wife was Catherine Howard, Norfolk's niece, but her adulteries cost her her head and cost Norfolk his seeming ascendancy in Henry's favor. The sixth wife, Catherine Parr, was more acceptable to the Protestant party. Although Henry was able to master and control both factions, the unity of purpose that marked the earlier years of the Henrician Reformation was lost.

Early Modern Government

Cromwell had spent much of the 1530s in reorganizing the royal administration so that it would function for the king without his detailed supervision. In part this recognized that Henry VIII did not care to invest as much time in day-to-day affairs as his father had; in part it reflected Cromwell's vision of the state which looked beyond medieval traditional practices to newer roles of governmental service. In the place of the traditionally large advisory medieval council, Cromwell substituted a Privy Council of fewer than twenty. The council's function was not only to advise but also to act as an executive agency to supervise the royal administration. He then developed and held the office of principal secretary—receiving reports from royal officers and agents, preparing the Privy Council's agenda, and then drafting and issuing the letters and commissions needed to implement conciliar decisions.

The king's decision prevailed on important matters, but the Privy Council made lower-level decisions. Financial offices were created to handle the new revenues produced by the Reformation, but these were absorbed into the exchequer in Mary's reign and did not survive as permanent governmental institutions. Cromwell's dedication to the management of parliamentary affairs reflected the growing importance of Parliament in English government.

As the Tudor prosperity increased the wealth of the gentry and they came to see the House of Commons as a focus for their political energy, and especially as Henry VIII increasingly made the Commons partners in the Reformation, the lower house became more important. Thomas Cromwell, the commoner, sat there, bringing in government bills, attempting to keep the proposals intact as independent-minded members of Parliament considered them in the three readings and committee investigations, and keeping relations between the king and the House of Commons harmonious. The king and Parliament were both beneficiaries of this cooperation, a far cry from the acrimony not uncommon in the Middle Ages.

YEARS OF TENSION AND UNCERTAINTY: EDWARD VI AND MARY I

The Succession to the Crown

With Parliament's approval, Henry VIII had stipulated in his will that his son Edward would succeed to the throne and, were that young prince to die childless, then his daughters in the order of their birth, Mary first and finally Elizabeth. Henry had no illusions about the problems in store for the Tudor dynasty: Edward would be a minor at his accession, and, should a daughter reign later, there would be unprecedented difficulties. To forestall these problems, Henry ordered that a council and not an individual should serve as the regent for his son. But this precaution turned but to be in vain, and the next decade proved how prophetic his fears were.

Government on Behalf of Edward VI (1547–1553)

The provision for a council was quickly set aside by the nine-year-old king's uncle, Edward Seymour, who, as duke of Somerset, directed the government as his nephew's protector. Somerset was necessarily concerned with sustaining his irregular position, which meant he made concessions of power to court the House of Commons and tolerated Protestant dissent in the hope of winning men's minds and assent.

The duke of Somerset's power as lord protector depended upon the support of the landed aristocracy and gentry, and this group he quickly alienated. He displayed a sympathy for England's peasant-tenants and encouraged a royal commission to look into illegal enclosures of common pasture and arable lands by large landholders. Agrarian changes were proceeding rapidly and popular discontent focused upon the symbolic issue of enclosing hedges and fences, which excluded smallholders' animals from their traditional common rights of pasture. The result was an outbreak of armed rebellion in 1549 in Norfolk and several other parts of East Anglia and more violent protests against the introduction of the first *Book of Common Prayer* in Cornwall and Devonshire. Although the second set of rebellions was ostensibly directed against Protestant liturgical innovations at the parish level, all of these rebellions displayed popular ill-will against grasping gentry landlords. These popular protests of 1549–1551 extended into many other English counties and constituted yet another severe threat to the Tudor regime. Somerset bungled the attempt to suppress the rebellions, and foreign mercenaries, brought into England to fight a needless war against Scotland, had to be diverted to crush the rebels in Norfolk.

Somerset's inability to restore order provided the opportunity for another ambitious magnate to replace him as lord protector. Somerset was succeeded by a fellow Privy Council member, John Dudley, who was created duke of Northumberland, and subsequently had Somerset executed on charges of treason. Northumberland was a grasping, ambitious man, whose faults were magnified by the corruption of his followers.

England Becomes Protestant

The death of Henry VIII had removed the principal obstacle to the spread of Protestantism in England, and Archbishop Cranmer with Somerset's encouragement had begun gradual reforms. Early in 1549 Parliament enacted the first Act of Uniformity and the *Book of Common Prayer,* which introduced a Protestant liturgy, but was worded with some ambiguity in order not to alienate the Catholics. But there were unmistakable signs of changes, particularly when the chantries were suppressed just as the monasteries had been in the previous reign. Reformed Protestantism did not believe in a purgation after death from the effects of sin, and thus on theological grounds argued that the chantries in which masses were sung for the dead should be suppressed. The monasteries closed by Henry were usually rural, but the chantries were usually in towns and their priests often served as schoolmasters, so that the impact of the suppression caused considerable discontent. Under Northumberland a second Act of Uniformity and a revised *Book of Common Prayer* were adopted in 1552, which made a definite break with Catholic teachings on the mass, the real presence of Christ's body in the Eucharist, and many other beliefs repugnant to Protestantism. Priests were allowed to marry, and other changes were made, but Edward's early death ended further reform.

These monumental religious changes provoked reaction and rebellion, not only because of religious disaffection from Catholics and Protestants but also because of keenly felt economic and social grievances aggravated by economic distress (see pages 98–99). The insecurity of Northumberland's position as he faced a growing conservative opposition led him to side with radical Protestantism, which in turn became a test of political loyalty. But because young Edward, who had approved of this protestant emphasis, lay dying in 1553 of lung disease, all that had been begun was in jeopardy because the Catholic Mary Tudor was next in the succession. Northumberland's desperate plan was to avert this by proclaiming as queen a great-niece of Henry VIII, the naive young Protestant, Lady Jane Grey, to whom he married his own son, Lord Guilford Dudley. Such blatant self-interest awakened a nearly universal opposition, and within two weeks Mary and the forces of legitimacy had overthrown the plot, so that Lady Jane is not recognized as having sat on the throne.

Mary I (1553–1558) and the Return to Catholicism

Mary Tudor, the fiercely proud thirty-seven-year-old daughter of Catherine of Aragon, the woman whose childhood was scarred by the dishonor of her mother, the disinterest of her father, and the legal stigma of judicial bastardy, the ruler who was the focus of all the fears of the Protestant party, had few political skills with which to face England's mounting problems. She desired only to restore Catholicism, a policy that would be resisted by the governing elite. The accession of a reigning female monarch posed a dangerous issue: marriage. If she married an Englishman, she would marry beneath her rank. If she married a reigning monarch of another realm, the result would probably be to make England's policy subordinate to that of her husband's realm.

Mary decided to marry Philip of Spain, heir to his country's throne and an ardent Catholic. Although he was a willing participant, Philip did not care for his wife and her hopeless wish to bear a child, but rather he sought Parliament's recognition of the title "King of England" for himself and England's participation in Spain's wars against France. Mary's proposed marriage to Philip produced a multicounty plot, dangerously near London, led by Sir Thomas Wyatt. The rebellion was crushed, and the marriage was made, but Philip won the title of king that lasted only as long as his wife was alive. England did go to war as an ally of Spain, but the war was so unsuccessful that England lost its last possession in France, the town of Calais, which it had retained after the Hundred Years' War. Philip gained the hatred and distrust of his wife's subjects.

Mary's desire to return England to Catholicism involved two elements: the repeal in Parliament of the Edwardian Protestant statutes and the reconciliation of England with the Papacy. The first was made palatable to Parliament because Mary wanted a modified Act of Supremacy which would continue state control over the church, but especially because it was made clear that reconciliation would not require returning the lands seized at the dissolution of the monasteries. It is interesting that so doctrinally Catholic a queen was not willing to give up the power over the Church which had been won by her father and half brother.

With the legal preliminaries finished, the Papal absolution for England was pronounced late in 1554. Mary next tried to uproot Protestantism in England. With the queen's tacit approval, most of its leaders left England voluntarily to go to European Protestant centers such as Geneva and Frankfurt, but, while they drank at the pure springs of reformed Protestantism abroad, their fellow religionists suffered mightily in England. The government had reenacted the harsh medieval laws against heresy which Edward's government had repealed, and nearly 300 were martyred for their heresy by burning at the stake, many for radical Protestant views which were equally intolerable to

Death of Thomas Cranmer. From Foxe's Book of Martyrs, *published in 1563.*

Edwardian Protestants. Most were of lower social ranks, but a few had been notable leaders of the earlier movement, including Thomas Cranmer. Although Philip never hesitated to burn heretics in Spanish possessions, he had advised Mary not to persecute Protestants in England because he courted popularity among the English. The decision to begin ecclesiastical proceedings against the English heretics originated with Mary, who was determined to recatholicize England. Oral and written evidence of their sufferings was gathered together in the next reign by the clergyman, John Foxe, whose widely read *Book of Martyrs* depicted them as martyrs for the Protestant cause. The severity of the Marian persecutions were unprecedented in scale and caused the queen to be remembered as "Bloody Mary." However, had Mary enjoyed the longevity of her half-sister Elizabeth, and had she been able to organize a missionary movement based upon the Catholic Reformation, the attempted recatholicization of England might well have succeeded, as it did in continental countries such as Austria and Bavaria.

The Mid-Tudor Crises

Among the sources of political and social instability during the reigns of Edward VI and Mary I was the Price Revolution, an inflationary spiral of prices which plagued England for a century and a quarter starting about 1520. The production of wool—England's principal export during the late middle ages—was also declining as continental markets became less accessible.

Prices had been stable or declining during the fifteenth century, but in the years before Henry's death in 1547, prices had risen nearly 50 percent. In the troubled decade thereafter prices nearly doubled again. There were many causes of this inflationary spiral: the wars against France and Scotland were extremely expensive and led to large government deficits. The resulting shortfall of revenues tempted Henry's, Edward's, and Mary's governments into a policy of debasing gold and silver coins, which is called the "Great Debasement." But the main cause of the Price Revolution was the expansion of population which increased the demand for agricultural products. Ultimately, this stimulated the Agricultural Revolution, but, in the shorter run, it caused high grain prices and contributed to social unrest. The increased demand for food led to the technological innovations in agriculture, which led to the enclosure and consolidation of smaller farms into larger landed estates employing fewer agricultural hands than before. With the decline of the wool market, sheep grazing was no longer the main cause of the enclosure of agricultural land, rural depopulation, and unemployment, but popular opinion continued to blame enclosure for unemployment and economic distress. The governments of the time assumed that the resulting hunger was the sole cause of popular rebellion.

The social effects of enclosure wrought a major though gradual change in English life. The aristocrat who traditionally lived lavishly found it increasingly hard to maintain his economic standing when compared with the more industrious smaller landowner whose thrift and efficiency allowed him to buy land (much of it formerly monastic property) on the market. The monarch, as the largest and often the most inefficient holder of lands, was particularly vulnerable to this relative decline. Many small landowners were forced off their holdings through unscrupulous lawsuits and became leaseholders in a subordinate position to a landlord or perhaps became merely wage earners. The gap between rich and poor widened. To the extent that men forced off the land could not find another job, the number of unemployed and vagabonds rose, intensifying the already serious job of maintaining law and order. The extraordinary rise in English prices meant that the cost of English wool abroad continually rose and in 1552 reached such a height that it was priced out of competition, and the market collapsed. It was nearly thirty years before the exports rose to the pre-1552 level, and the unemployment that resulted in England was particularly severe. Governments of the sixteenth century, English and European, had no tools of economic analysis to discover the roots of the problem or to suggest remedies. In vain they attempted to treat the symptoms and to return to the days of stability by ordering that as many men be employed or that as much land be tilled as before.

A Legacy of Unrest

The short reigns of Edward and Mary left a legacy of unresolved problems. In addition to the major rebellions already noted, there were other spasmodic eruptions of violence so that governmental fears of insurrection at times bordered on paranoia. In Parliament the lack of leadership occasionally meant that private members dared to introduce bills on religion, heretofore the exclusive concern of the government. This precedent, when repeated in Elizabeth's reign, provoked a more confrontational style of politics. Both the Edwardian and Marian religious settlements were imposed upon the ordinary subject. The rapid changes and reversals bred confusion and suspicion, and hindered the spread of Protestantism. The intolerance of the times, which was both an English and a European characteristic, meant a legacy of enduring bitterness, and ultimately contributed to the revival of civil war in the 1640s.

Mary died alone in 1558, leaving a country repulsed by her religious policies, humiliated by unsuccessful war, and bereft of leadership. Her death probably resulted from a uterine cancer, the first manifestations of which suggested pregnancy and eventually led to ridicule of the pitiful queen when her term was up and she was still childless. England's first female monarch had been a failure as a ruler; the next, Mary's half sister Elizabeth, would completely reverse that experience.

SUGGESTIONS FOR FURTHER READING

John Guy, *Tudor England* (1990) provides an excellent narrative of political events, while Penry Williams, *The Tudor Regime* (1979) describes and analyzes the institutions of central and local government. J. J. Scarisbrick, *Henry VIII* (1968) is a detailed study of the life and reign of that monarch. The important changes in royal administration and Thomas Cromwell's influence upon them are discussed in G. R. Elton, *The Tudor Revolution in Government* (1953), although the author's argument is now thought to have been overstated. The troubled period from the end of Henry VIII's reign through the early years of Elizabeth I is the subject of D. M. Loades, *The Mid-Tudor Crisis, 1545–1565* (1992). The brief and tumultuous reign of Edward VI is covered in M. L. Bush, *The Government Policy of Protector Somerset* (1975). D. M. Loades, *The Reign of Mary Tudor: Politics, Government and Religion in England, 1553–1558* (1979) is an excellent study of that reign, but his biography, *Mary Tudor: A Life* (1990), is an unsympathetic portrait of the first Tudor queen regnant. The history of parliamentary institutions and politics is well served by Jennifer Loach, *Parliament under the Tudors* (1991) and M. A. R. Graves, *The Tudor Parliaments: Crown, Lords and Commons, 1485–1603* (1985). Two admirable studies of Henrician parliaments have been written by Stanford E. Lehmberg: *The Reformation Parliament, 1529–1536* (1970) and *The Later Parliaments of Henry VIII* (1977). A well chosen anthology of constitutional and legal documents can be found in G. R. Elton, *The Tudor Constitution: Documents and Commentary* (2nd ed., 1982).

The most detailed narrative of the religious changes of the first half of the sixteenth century remains A. G. Dickens, *The English Reformation* (2nd ed., 1989). Dickens assumed that the Reformation had run its course by the end of the reign of Edward VI, a view that is challenged by Christopher Haigh, *The English Reformation Revised* (1987) and *English Reformations: Religion, Politics and Society under the Tudors* (1993). A shorter survey is provided by J. J. Scarisbrick, *The Reformation and the People* (1984), and attention should be paid to Patrick Collinson, *The Birthpangs of Protestant England* (1989). The destruction of the monasteries and its impact is discussed in Joyce Youings, *The Dissolution of the Monasteries* (1971) and David Knowles, *Bare Ruined Choirs: The Dissolution of the English Monasteries* (1976). The reception of the various religious changes at the regional and parochial levels is studied in Susan Brigden, *London and the Reformation* (1989) and Eamon Duffy, *The Stripping of the Altars: Traditional Religion in England, 1400–1580* (1992). The important distinction between official religious doctrines and popular religious beliefs is brilliantly discussed in Keith Thomas, *Religion and the Decline of Magic: Studies in Popular Belief in 16th and 17th Century England* (1971).

A very good introduction to the social history of Tudor England can be found in Joyce Youings, *Sixteenth-Century England* (1984) (Pelican Social History of Britain), and economic history is well surveyed in W. G. Hoskins, *The Age of Plunder, 1500–1547* (1976) and in Christopher Clay, *Economic Expansion and Social Change: England, 1500–1700*, 2 vols. (1984). Peter Clark, *Crisis and Order in English Towns, 1500–1700* (1972) and *English Towns in Transition, 1550–1700* (1976) survey urban life and institutions. Studies of family history include: Ivy Pinchbeck and Margaret Hewitt, *Childhood in English Society, vol. I: From Tudor Times to the 18th Century* (1972); Ralph Houlbrooke, *The English Family, 1450–1700* (1984); Lawrence Stone, *The Family, Sex and Marriage in England, 1500–1800* (1977). For the history of women, consult: Retha M. Warnicke, *Women of the English Renaissance and Reformation* (1983) and Mary Prior (ed.), *Women in English Society, 1500–1800* (1985). The varieties of popular protest and disorder are described in Barrett L. Beer, *Rebellion and Riot: Popular Disorder in England during the Reign of Edward VI* (1982) and Roger B. Manning, *Village Revolts: Social Protest and Popular Disturbances in England, 1509–1640* (1988) and *Hunters and Poachers: A Cultural and Social History of Unlawful Hunting in England, 1485–1640* (1993).

CHAPTER SIX

The Elizabethan Era
1588–1603

The heir to the promise and problems of England's crown was its second reigning queen, Elizabeth Tudor, the twenty-five-year-old "Reformation child," the daughter of Henry and Anne Boleyn. Elizabeth's lengthy reign (1558–1603) was to be so successful and distinctive in so many areas that the "Elizabethan Age" is seen as the springtime of early modern England. The often overromanticized adulation of the period need not blind anyone to its serious problems, but the stability and progress that characterized the era arose in great part from the remarkable acumen of Elizabeth Tudor.

Elizabeth was popular, an indispensable element for success. She had impressive personal qualities that helped her fulfill the duties of the office. The policies of her government were successful, in part from her and her minister's sagacity and in part from the luck that all political leaders need. She often delayed making decisions, and her procrastination often worked to advantage when she was confronted with insurmountable problems. Also, she knew how to cultivate affection but could have retained it only because her subjects believed she cared for England above all.

Her subjects loved her, because they could see themselves in her. She mirrored their zest for the bawdy and bloody amusements of the day, attending with relish the cock fights, bear baitings, and plays. She reflected their extravagance, wearing ornately jeweled, outrageously ruffed and decorated clothing. Even in personal items—the reddish wig, the heavy white makeup, the blackened teeth—she was characteristic of the premedical age, hiding, as did many subjects, the ravages of smallpox, which left people hairless and pock-marked, and the indulgence of an excessive consumption of sweets.

In later years, when it became clear that she would not marry, the "Virgin Queen" claimed with sound reason and not a little hyperbole that she was married to the realm. Elizabeth was remarkably secular-minded in a century of religious passion. France was torn by religious civil wars, and the advancement of Catholicism was a principal motive of Spain's foreign policy; in contrast, Elizabeth made her church serve England first, then Protestantism.

THE ELIZABETHAN SETTLEMENT AND THE EARLY YEARS, 1558–1570

The Young Queen

When Elizabeth came to the throne of England conditions did not favor a female monarch. Neither Edward VI nor Mary had ruled long enough to unite the realm under one religion or the other, and England remained prone to factionalism and disorder. Her task was to unify the country and avoid the more extreme religious settlements of the previous two reigns. That she was able to do so and avoid civil war in an age of almost universal religious war is a tribute to her political skills, wisdom and judgment. She demonstrated an extraordinary ability to choose first-rate royal councillors who possessed administrative and fiscal talents and knew how to manage parliaments so as to minimize opposition. In an age when John Knox and other Protestant reformers thought that female government was "monstrous," Elizabeth knew how to intimidate male courtiers and master the factionalism which was always to be found in her Privy Council.

Perhaps the most notable of the queen's councillors was Sir William Cecil (1520–1598), whom she made principal secretary of state. Cecil founded a notable political dynasty and lined his pockets with the profits of office, but Elizabeth judged that he would always be loyal and steer a middle course. At the age of thirty-eight he was already a seasoned statesman who knew how to survive the vicissitudes of Tudor politics and factionalism. He always retained the queen's confidence and worked ceaselessly for political stability and fiscal responsibility.

The Elizabethan Settlement

Elizabeth sought a religious settlement which would bind the English people together in a national church and avoid the mistakes of the mid-Tudor period. She was mainly interested in reasserting royal control of the Church of England, and the Act of Supremacy of 1559 named her supreme governor of the

Queen Elizabeth I. Painting by Marcus Gheeraerts the Younger, 1592. By Courtesy of the National Portrait Gallery, London.

English Church. The Thirty-nine Articles enacted in 1563 were a more ambiguous statement of religious belief than the Edwardian Forty-two Articles, and were meant to conciliate the more moderate Catholics. However, a well organized group of Marian Protestant exiles in Parliament were able to compel the statutory enactment of an Act of Uniformity (1559), which revived something like the *Book of Common Prayer* of 1552, which prescribed a Protestant liturgy. The Act of Uniformity also imposed fines for not attending one's parish church, although this provision was not strictly enforced in the early years of the reign.

　　Closely related to the problem of the religious settlement and political stablility was the question of marriage and succession. Only a Protestant dynasty could secure these ends. Although there were a number of persons with plausible claims to inherit the throne should Elizabeth die unmarried and childless, they all possessed various defects. The most likely successor was Elizabeth's Stuart cousin, Mary, Queen of Scots, who was a Catholic, a foreigner, and closely linked to France. Elizabeth's personal preference for a husband probably would have been Robert Dudley, son of the duke of Northumberland, who had been the second lord protector in the reign of Edward VI. Besides being already married, Dudley was the son and grandson of convicted traitors and the patron of the Puritan faction. Although Parliament kept pressing her to marry or name a successor, knowing that the cause of Protestantism depended upon her fragile life as long as Mary Stuart lived, Elizabeth knew that marriage to a foreign prince would be unpopular and could lead to entangling alliances while marriage to an Englishman such as Dudley could provoke civil war. So she chose to procrastinate and remain a "Virgin Queen" until the problem went away.

Foreign Affairs and the Religious Settlement

England had always feared foreign interference or invasion by pretenders to the crown through the lands of its Celtic neighbors. The principality of Wales had been united with England in 1536. The kingdom of Ireland had long been, in theory, a possession of the English crown, but the Celtic Irish, distinguished by differences of language, culture and religion, continued to resist English efforts to conquer, colonize and protestantize their land. Remote from the Germanic heartland of Europe, the Protestant Reformation arrived in Scotland even later than it came to England. The Scots had preserved their independence from England, won at the Battle of Bannockburn in 1314, by allying themselves with England's traditional enemy, France. The presence of French troops in Scotland had helped to maintain this "auld alliance" while Mary, Queen of Scots (1542–1587) was minor and later while she lived in France, as the queen consort of King Francis II.

The beginning of the Protestant Reformation in Scotland dates from the arrival in 1559 of John Knox from Geneva, where the Scottish reformer had been the pastor of the English-speaking congregation and had sat at the feet of John Calvin. With the assistance of a faction of Scottish lords, and, without the assent of Mary, Queen of Scots, Knox had helped to impose a Presbyterian religious settlement upon the Kirk, or Church of Scotland. In 1560, Elizabeth intervened to support the Protestant party in Scotland, and by a combination of military and diplomatic means forced the French, by the Treaty of Edinburgh, to abandon the alliance with Scotland.

The return of the Catholic Mary to Scotland in 1562 not only threatened to undo the Protestant religious settlement in Scotland, but also posed a direct threat to Elizabeth. Mary was Elizabeth's cousin, descended from Henry VII, and viewed by many English Catholics and most monarchs of Europe as the legitimate claimant to the English throne. Mary's position as queen of Scotland was undermined by her bad political judgment, the scandals growing out of her choice of husbands and lovers and by the accusation of involvement in the murder of her second husband, Henry Stuart, Lord Darnley. Unable to extricate herself from this mess with any credibility, Mary abdicated in 1568 in favor of her nine-month-old son, James VI. She then fled to England naively believing that Elizabeth would allow her to go to France. Instead, Elizabeth placed Mary under house arrest. Mary continued to plot with Elizabeth's enemies until 1587, when faced by the threat of foreign invasion, Elizabeth executed the former queen of Scots.

A conservative faction of the English nobility had wished to marry Thomas, fourth duke of Norfolk to Mary, queen of Scots in order to secure the succession to the English throne for Mary. This was to have been a prelude to the restoration of Catholicism and involved a badly coordinated conspiracy which drew in the Catholic powers of Europe, a conservative faction at court and two Catholic and quasi-feudal members of the northern nobility, the earls of Northumberland and Westmorland. The premature unraveling of the conspiracy precipitated an armed demonstration known as the Rebellion of the Northern Earls of 1569. The rebels, motivated by religious conservatism and social and economic discontent, raised the banner that had been carried during the Pilgrimage of Grace of 1536, but were easily defeated. Westmorland fled abroad and Norfolk and Northumberland were executed. Their premature rising was to have been coordinated with the Pope's excommunication of Elizabeth, which did not come until 1570. The papal bull of excommunication effectively declared Elizabeth deposed, incited her subjects to rebellion and invited the Catholic monarchs of Europe to invade England. Elizabeth had survived a serious threat to her government and preserved the stability and unity of England. However, Catholics came to be viewed as persons of divided allegiance, and the English government began to persecute them more severely.

GROWING RELIGIOUS DISCORD, 1570–1585

Anglican, Catholic Recusant, and Puritan

The Elizabethan Religious Settlement, as enacted by Parliament in 1559, was intended to promote unity by compelling every person in the realm to attend Anglican services performed according to the *Book of Common Prayer* in every parish church. It was axiomatic to statesmen of this period that the ruler's sovereign authority could be maintained only by the establishment of a single, national church. The advocacy of toleration was equated with blasphemy and political disaffection, but during this period, growing religious discord and the revival of religious wars abroad made it increasingly difficult to include all English people within the Church of England.

Outwardly, the Church of England, legally established by Act of Parliament, resembled the medieval Catholic Church insofar as it retained episcopal government, or rule by bishops, who presided over territorial dioceses, which were further divided into parishes—the basic unit of both ecclesiastical and civil government. In the time of Henry VIII, royal authority had been substituted for papal authority, but the royal supremacy in ecclesiastical affairs was now shared with Parliament to a considerable extent. Elizabeth took the title "supreme governor" in deference to those members of Parliament, who objected to a woman being "supreme head" of the church as Henry VIII had been styled. She governed the church indirectly through the hierarchy of archbishops and bishops with occasional interference from Parliament.

The doctrine of the Elizabethan Church of England was Protestant but not yet distinctly Anglican. The liturgy of the church, prescribed by the *Book of Common Prayer* of 1559, looked Protestant to Catholics, but retained far too many medieval Catholic rituals and ecclesiastical vestments for Puritan tastes. The medieval Catholic Church's lands and revenues had been plundered by the Tudor monarchs and their courtiers, and numerous lands formerly belonging to monasteries, chantries and bishoprics had been expropriated by the crown and many sold into lay hands. Elizabeth continued to profit at the expense of the church, sometimes delaying the appointment of new bishops to dioceses where the previous bishop had died so that the crown could enjoy the revenues of that diocese in the interim, and sometimes forced church officials to exchange more profitable church lands for less remunerative royal lands.

The Elizabethan religious settlement placed Catholics in a difficult position. Some, known as "church-papists," compromised and continued to attend Anglican services in their parish churches. In some cases they were actually advised to do so by aging Catholic priests, who survived from the reign of Mary. But younger Catholic clergy, who had caught the spirit of the Catholic Reformation from abroad, dissuaded Catholics from attending Anglican churches. From their refusal to conform to the established church such Catholics became known as "recusants" [from the Latin *recusare*, meaning "to refuse"]. Many Catholic clerics from the Marian period—bishops, upper clergy, and professors of theology from the universities—had fled England at Elizabeth's succession, much as the Marian exiles, the Protestant leaders, had left the country during the Marian restoration of Catholicism and sought refuge in the continental centers of Protestant reform. So also, the Elizabethan Catholic exiles gravitated towards Catholic centers of learning such as the University of Louvain in the Spanish Netherlands. Taking advantage of a decree of the Council of Trent ordering the establishment of seminaries to train candidates for the priesthood, the English Catholic leaders in exile secured papal permission to establish the so-called "English Colleges" at places such as Douai, Rome, and Vallodolid to educate missionaries to send back to England. Without the continuing ministrations of these "seminary priests," Catholicism would have disappeared completely as it did in parts of Scandinavia.

While Catholic recusants wished to withdraw from the established church, Puritans emphatically wished to remain within the Anglican Church, but, at the same time, to reform it according to the pattern of the Calvinist Church of Geneva. The term "Puritan" was pejorative and was used by Catholics or more moderate Protestants to describe a wide variety of opinions, including proponents of moderate reform. While some Puritans were willing to accept government by bishops, most belonged to the presbyterian party and wished to replace episcopal government with rule by "classes," or councils composed of ministers and lay elders. Thus, presbyterian church government sought to reduce clerical influence in the church and to increase the influence of laymen drawn from the landed gentry and merchant oligarchies in the towns. Puritans disliked the Anglican *Book of Common Prayer* because it retained Catholic liturgical practices such as using the sign of the cross as well as requiring clergymen to wear the surplice when ministering the sacraments. Indeed, Puritans wished to abolish all practices, such as the observance of Christmas, for which no warrant existed in Sacred Scripture. Their beliefs were drawn exclusively from the Bible, and they wished to make sermons based on a biblical text the focal point of Anglican worship.

In the reign of Elizabeth there were no doctrinal differences between Anglican and Puritan; both shared the same Calvinist theology, and their differences grew out of matters such as church government, liturgy, and clerical dress. Thus, Puritanism should not be regarded as a deviant form of Protestantism; it remained well within the mainstream of English and European Protestantism. As such, Puritans are to be distinguished from separatists, those sects such as the Brownists and members of the Family of Love who did not adhere to the Church of England. What made the Puritans dangerous in the eyes of Elizabeth and the Anglican bishops was that they ultimately posed a threat to royal control of the Anglican Church and the monarchy itself through their attacks on church government by bishops. Many critics of Puritanism came to believe that if you scratched a Presbyterian, you would find a Republican underneath.

The Fear of Catholicism in the 1570s and 1580s

The popular fear of Catholicism became a permanent feature of English politics in the middle years of Elizabeth's reign and thereafter. It derived from two perceived threats. The first was the arrival of the first seminary priests in 1574 from the English Colleges on the Continent. These missionaries intended not only to minister to the spiritual needs of the English Catholic community, but also to reconcile lapsed Catholics and convert Protestants. Since the very act of being a priest, ordained abroad since September 1559, was defined by a parliamentary statute of 1585 as high treason, as was also the act of reconciling a lapsed Catholic, these seminary priests were obliged to enter the country secretly and in disguise. A traitor's death was almost certain if they were caught, so the missionary priests came psychologically prepared for martyrdom. Because the English Colleges were also located in Spanish or Papal territories, the seminary priests were perceived as being agents of hostile foreign powers which were actively planning an invasion of England during this period and were at war with England after 1585.

The most feared of all the English seminary priests were the Jesuits, the largest and most effective of the new religious orders founded during the Catholic Counter-Reformation. Like their rivals, the Puritans, the training of Jesuit priests emphasized learning and preaching, and they had already established a formidable reputation by their successes in recatholicizing parts of continental Europe, which had earier become Protestant. Although their numbers were never sufficient to pose such a threat in England, the seminary priests and Jesuits did stiffen the resistance of the English Catholic laity. Since the latter included a disproportionate number of peers and country gentry, their missionary efforts were always viewed as posing a political threat to England. This was especially true during the war years at the end of the reign, when the Spanish made several attempts to invade England and Ireland.

While Catholic seminary priests were branded as traitors, parliamentary legislation against Catholic laymen sought their financial ruin rather than physical punishment. The Recusancy Laws, especially that of 1585, intended to cripple the Catholic gentry by striking at their patrimony and eroding their social status. Heads of Catholic gentry households were subjected to crippling fines of £20 per lunar month (there were thirteen lunar months in a year) for failure to attend Anglican worship. Particularly stubborn individuals might be imprisoned and compelled to attend Anglican sermons; two-thirds of their estates might also be confiscated. Persecution, propaganda, and financial pressure did cause many Catholics to conform, at least occasionally, but the supply of missionary priests never ceased and, eventually, an irreducible hard core of the Catholic population emerged who could not be swayed by any amount of pressure. However, when the Spanish Armada of 1588 attempted an invasion of England, the English Catholics remained loyal to the queen.

The Threat from Puritanism in the 1570s and 1580s

Puritanism involved less of a confrontation but more of a sustained threat. Because the Marian Catholic bishops had fled on Elizabeth's accession in 1558, the new queen had had to rely greatly on those returning self-exiles who had spent Mary's reign abroad, the greater part in Geneva where they had become strongly Calvinistic. Equally as great a reason for Puritanism's success was that laymen as well as churchmen shared its leadership, so that its pressures for reform were made not only in the church but also in Parliament, where a disproportionate number of reformers were elected, and even in the royal court, where sympathizers such as Sir William Cecil and Robert Dudley were very influential.

The early efforts at reform in the 1560s had been piecemeal, seeking the removal of pre-Reformation religious practices. The reformers believed that the queen favored further reform, and they sought to hasten matters by making proposals in the church's convocation and in Parliament. They were surprised when she refused to let the proposals be discussed in the House of Commons, arguing that, as head of the church, its reform was her exclusive right. Some in the Commons recalled contrary precedents for parliamentary initiatives in the two earlier reigns, but Elizabeth refused to let a religious matter became a constitutional issue and promised to make reforms herself.

In the early 1570s Thomas Cartwright, a professor of divinity at Cambridge who came to Presbyterianism by an academic route, and other Presbyterian leaders who had learned at the feet of Calvin himself at Geneva, began to write and surreptitiously print books urging change. Not only Cartwright but even Archbishop Edmund Grindal lectured the queen on her religious duty to delay a "complete" and thoroughgoing reformation no longer. Elizabeth struck back by ordering the enforcement of religious uniformity against Puritanism.

Not unnaturally the movement went underground but resurfaced in the 1580s in more threatening guises. A clandestine Presbyterian organization was established in some parts of England, particularly in eastern England where Puritanism was strongest, alongside of and completely ignoring the bishops' authority. The pressure within Parliament to replace Anglicanism with Presbyterianism or at least a milder form of Puritanism was as unrelenting as it was unsuccessful. Elizabeth's counterattack triumphed when her anti-Puritan new archbishop of Canterbury, John Whitgift, made his own diocesan tribunal into a nationwide Court of High Commission in which Puritan churchmen were charged, tried, and removed from office and influence. Laymen who wrote books urging reform were branded "seditious," and thus, for example, John Stubbs, a Puritan author who wrote against the queen's consideration of marriage to a French Catholic prince, had his right hand cut off. More important, government agents sought out and suppressed the growing Presbyterian underground counter-church, so that by the late 1580s Puritanism was rendered less effective.

Meanwhile, three decades of internal growth had enabled Anglicanism to develop and enunciate its principles. The most mature expression was in Richard Hooker's *The Laws of Ecclesiastical Polity*, an argument that Anglicanism was a *via media*, a "middle way" between unreformed Catholicism and radical Protestantism. Anglicanism accepted as a valid norm for the church not only the Bible but also the tradition of the first five centuries of the church before the great growth of papal influence—thus it accepted the episcopal form of government, creeds, and practices, which had flourished in the early Christian church during and after the Biblical first century, and rejected the belief of Puritans and others that man's will was not free.

ELIZABETHAN SOCIETY

The Economy

In many respects Elizabethan society was shaped and changed by the continued importance of movements and trends previously considered. Inflation continued especially because of the rise of population; to counter inflation more and more persons converted leases to shorter terms to enable more frequent raises to keep pace, while inefficient landowners—the crown foremost among them—continued a relative economic decline. The flood onto the land market of former monastic and other church lands provided the opportunity for enterprising and well-connected Elizabethans to acquire the social as well as economic prestige of landowning. The movement toward enclosure continued unabated, although for a different reason: earlier there had been enclosure for pasture since owning sheep and selling wool provided a higher rate of return than growing crops; the advantage now slowly tilted back toward tillage of crops after the collapse of the cloth market in 1552.

But in the Elizabethan era there were newer sources of prosperity as well, such as overseas trading companies and new industries based on improved technology, whether in mining where coal was produced more efficiently from deeper mines or in boggy areas such as the fens in the east, which were drained for land reclamation. There were important social consequences of all these economic trends.

The Aristocracy and Gentry

Throughout the Middle Ages the small number of nobility had had a stunningly disproportionate share of power and responsibility: their military role had made them indispensable, their castles and vast estates dwarfed the landowning status of all except the king and the church, and they held the major positions in royal administration. The decline in the importance of the aristocracy was a constant in Tudor England, however. Henry VII and Henry VIII had not only been sparing in the creation of new nobles to replace those killed in the Wars of the Roses but had used many "new men" in administrative positions—had not Henry VII rewarded so many of his many wives' relatives with peerages, the number would have been even less. Elizabeth made only seventeen peers during her entire reign, and only two of these were from families that had not had a peerage earlier (Sir William Cecil was made Lord Burghley in 1571).

Meanwhile the size of the gentry grew strikingly. At Elizabeth's death there were perhaps 16,000 to 18,000 persons with a coat of arms, the greater number by far in the two lowest ranks of gentlemen and esquires. The entree into the ranks of the gentry was the possession of a coat of arms from the College of Heralds. Because land was now available—the market in lands arising from the dissolution of the monasteries assured that—the indispensable prerequisite of landowning which "qualified" one for a coat of arms was at hand. It was not surprising that an official from the College of Heralds could be induced for a price to search energetically and successfully for the gentle origins of a wealthy landowner's ancestors, provided of course that no official did violence to gentility by promoting manifestly unworthy persons.

The employment of the gentry showed their rising importance. There could be no question of menial work: the higher the rank, the greater the expected adherence to the principle that work was beneath their dignity. The gentry, like the aristocracy to whom they were often related, instead served in the public arena. The stepping stone to public trust was service as an unpaid local official—perhaps as a commissioner to collect the taxes voted by Parliament, or as a commissioner with special legal responsibilities for an important local case, or as a vice admiral who supervised the harbors

Longleat, an Elizabethan stately home. Private collection.

for commercial reasons and also to keep out unwanted persons, especially the seminary priests.

The epitome of local service was being selected as one of thirty to fifty men on the local county's Commission of the Peace. These justices of the peace regulated wages according to the Statute of Artificers, licensed alehouses and other places of amusement, committed those who broke the peace to prison until trial, enforced the laws passed by Parliament, served as the trial judges for important matters of royal justice, and otherwise controlled all aspects of local life. To be selected as a justice of the peace, a member of the ruling county elite, was a stunning show of prestige, and faithful service (aided by proper connections) marked a justice of the peace for preferment on the national level.

The most successful became courtiers, serving in the royal household or court or on the monarch's Privy Council. Many sat as members of the House of Commons; indeed, by the end of the century members of the gentry had come to fill the seats in Parliament theoretically allotted to town burgesses because the latter were honored to have such influential yet nonresidential representatives in Parliament.

Elizabethan Country Homes

Another sign of prestige was to engage in the Elizabethan building mania. The huge stately mansions of the nobility and upper gentry were monuments to the peace and prosperity of the era and symbols of the owner's importance. The new buildings ignored the irregular floor plans, ornate decoration, and gothic features which had prevailed early in the century, adopting instead cleaner classical lines, with symmetrical floor plans in the E- or H-shape and an extravagant use of glass. Lord Burghley had three mansions, the second largest of which (like many other new homes) was built out from a former monastic building at the east end. The interiors of these homes featured elaborate wood panelling, sculptured plasterwork ceilings, and tapestries hung on the walls to provide color and keep out the cold. The homes of the middle gentry had a distinctive new style called half-timbering, in which the darkened wood of the beams used in construction was contrasted with white exterior plasterwork.

The leisure activities of the aristocracy and gentry were prodigal. The brilliant possessions and pastimes of the Elizabethan era were thoroughly and gustily enjoyed although not widely shared, and the degree to which one participated in them depended on rank. A multitude of outward signs bore witness to gentle birth and its privileges: gentlemen could bear arms and amuse themselves at gambling while ordinary men could not; gentlemen wore hats and workers caps; and even within the upper ranks the gradations were apparent from whether one wore cloth-of-gold, silk, velvet, or more ordinary cloth in his apparel. Amusement in the country homes was extravagant: Elizabeth and her court of nearly 500 visited Burghley a dozen times, each time costing him huge sums (perhaps £5,000) in hospitality. Even the primary amusements of the country life, hawking and hunting, were restricted to the upper classes.

The Lower Classes

The enlargement of the ranks of the gentry and their increasing economic importance often cost lesser men dearly. The unemployed victims of enclosure tended to drift into cities, especially London, only to find endemic outbreaks of the plague, squalor, overcrowding, and a distinct loss of amenities. Crime was one possible solution, begging another. Even criminals and vagabonds lived according to rank, from the confidence man at the top down through levels of thievery such as "priggers of prancers" (horse thieves) to beggars— some of whom elicited sympathy with feigned wounds or intentionally maimed children. Living in close quarters in manifestly unsanitary conditions made the city poor particularly susceptible to the plague, which occasionally took its grim toll. The pockets of human misery, the stench of sewerless streets, and the many other hardships of city life were all-too-constant remainders that the poor had often left one type of misery for another.

In rural settings the lot of the poor was difficult as well. Most lived in hand-to-mouth subsistence dependent on the vagaries of weather and good crops. There were periods in the middle 1580s and especially in the late 1590s when steady rains for several years in a row left crops stunted and rotting in the fields. Prices for the inadequate supply of grain soared, and even those lucky enough to escape starvation suffered from severe malnutrition. In an act of 1597 and in its fuller elaboration in 1601, the Elizabethan government enacted a poor law which remained in its essence until the nineteenth century. It commanded that mandatory taxes be collected by local officials for the relief of the poor of the parish. Any poor person found away from his or her native parish was to be sent back there—a provision obviously aimed (and as obviously unsuccessful) at reducing the number of the poor who flocked to London and other larger towns. All of these conditions and the halting initial steps to remedy them are a pointed reminder that, although the Elizabethan age was glittering for the elite, the participation in the good things of life was yet very shallow.

The Attractions of the Sea

A major new outlet at this time was the rediscovery of the sea. Elizabethans came to realize that what the Mediterranean had been to the ancient world, the Atlantic would be to the modern, and that their location on it offered exceptional advantages. Henry VII had authorized the Genoan John Cabot to sail on voyages of discovery on behalf of England; that intrepid explorer had sailed across the Atlantic and down the American eastern seaboard, thus staking England's claim in the New World. No one followed up on his pioneering; all had been forgotten by midcentury, but now interest was reawakened, often through the writings of Richard Hakluyt who recounted *The principall Navigations, Voiages, and Discoveries of the English nation,* or urged colonization in his *The Discourse on the Western Planting.* In 1585 Sir Walter Raleigh began a colony at Roanoke Island on what is now the coast of North Carolina. When the first attempt failed a second was made, but locked among history's secrets is the fate of the first colonists who could not be found three years later when a relief ship arrived.

If the time was not yet ripe for sustained colonization, it was for other sea-related efforts. The navy was completely reorganized, and fighting ships were redesigned and armed with heavy guns capable of inflicting damage from a distance. The successes on the sea helped make naval heroes as important as soldiers in the national imagination. The most promising venture, however, was the development of the joint-stock company, a means for pooling the funds of many investors to finance sustained shipping trade with distant areas of the world. By 1588 companies existed to conduct trade with such far-flung places as Russia, the Barbary Coast of North Africa, and the west coast of Africa. A significant signpost to a later empire was the chartering in 1600 of the East India Company, and thus England's claim was made in that remote part of the world, the beginnings of a presence that would later blossom in India and the Orient.

THE ELIZABETHAN RENAISSANCE

Literature

Elizabethans knew their time was exciting, adventuresome, alive to new opportunities—a quickening time. But doubtless they would have been as hard-pressed to analyze its spirit as we are to describe our own. It was marked in part by a discovery of their own realm and of new horizons, and as always the printed word was often the key to discovering new experiences.

Caxton's world of printing a century before emphasized the theological, legal, and philosophical; Elizabethan booksellers also offered practical how-to books on better farming, navigation, correct manners for polite society, planning a garden, interpreting dreams, or being an effective justice of the peace. England itself was open to discovery in the pages of William Camden's *Magna Britannia,* written in Latin for the educated elite both in England and abroad. John Stow described the hub of Renaissance England in his *A Survay of London.* Freshly printed maps could be bought, often brightly colored by hand, awakening the imagination with sketches of sea monsters, the Indians of the New World, and strange animals in faraway lands. Elizabeth's tutor, Roger Ascham, argued for new teaching techniques in *The Scholemaster*, and Sir Thomas Gresham founded a college in London where merchants were taught mathematics, business, and science in English.

Elizabethan Poetry and Prose

One of the proudest proofs of the Elizabethan love of language and letters was the splendid outpouring of poetry and prose, mirroring the themes that fascinated the Elizabethan imagination: courtly and human love, violence and savagery, human emotions in turmoil, a search for national identity through the pageantry of past kings, and the confident realization of uniquely English values. The exclusive use of English and the predominance of secular themes distinguish this literary outpouring from the medieval.

The most polished literary expression was poetry in its myriad forms. Although the themes might reflect past times, the manner of composition pointed to the new. Edmund Spenser's epic poem, *The Faerie Queene*, was set in the medieval world of virtue personified, but the imagery was intended for Elizabethan ears hungry for sumptuous description. The original plan was for twelve books, each to set forth the adventure of a different knight of Gloriana, the queen herself. Another outstanding poet was Sir Philip Sidney. He had first served his queen as a soldier but added to that calling a literary career, using his artistry to express the soldier's ideal of chivalry. He wrote often in the new sonnet form that Elizabethans gave to the world: his *Arcadia* was a heroic prose romance, and in *Astrophel and Stella* he expressed his own unrequited love.

Shakespeare's family home,
Stratford-on-Avon.
Private collection.

Elizabethan Drama

The crowning glory of the Elizabethan Renaissance was drama. In medieval times drama had been religious and staged in the church or just outside it. Sixteenth-century drama was greatly different: the themes were rarely religious, and the use of language as the vehicle for vivid description was its greatest characteristic. Classical drama was emphasized in the universities: it demanded the keeping of the "unities," so that all the action occurred on the same day, in the same place, and in the same literary genre. It was unacceptable to mix tragedy with comedy. Drama written for the new playhouses around London often violated the rules, to the delight of the penny-paying audiences drawn from all ranks of society. James Burbage built the first playhouse in 1576, and before Elizabeth died a number flourished in the area of London— not in London itself because the Puritan officials of that great city thought the drama and the theater were immoral.

The second-most renowned Elizabethan dramatist was Ben Jonson (1572– 1637). This erudite man could write in majestic prose or in lyric poetry. He could describe the most amusing and slapstick of situations to delight the most unlearned theater goer, or he could bring into his works plots borrowed from Greek and Latin literature, or comments upon the state of scientific learning in his time. His career flourished to a greater extent in the reign of James I, Elizabeth's successor in 1603: in that time he produced the best known of his major plays, such as *Volpone* and *The Alchemist*, and entered into a partnership with the talented Inigo Jones to stage the masques which were the most prominent form of entertainment at the royal court.

William Shakespeare

The greatest literary figure of the Elizabethan Renaissance was William Shakespeare. He was an accomplished actor and wrote beautiful sonnets, but of course he was best known for the works he produced for the stage. The tragedies, histories, and comedies that he wrote rank among the greatest masterpieces of English literature. He had the uncanny knack of describing the complexities of human character: he brought alive ambition in *Macbeth*, the tragedy of young love in *Romeo and Juliet*, the panoply and triumph of English history from monarchs of the Middle Ages such as *King Henry IV* to his own century, frolicking comedic froth in *A Midsummer Night's Dream*, and the drama of the classical world in *Julius Caesar*. As a member of the Lord Chamberlain's Company (after the accession of James I, The King's Company or the King's Men) he and his troupe enjoyed aristocratic protection. Shakespeare's plays were as much to be heard as to be seen: the English language contains many words and phrases that he coined, among them "fasci-

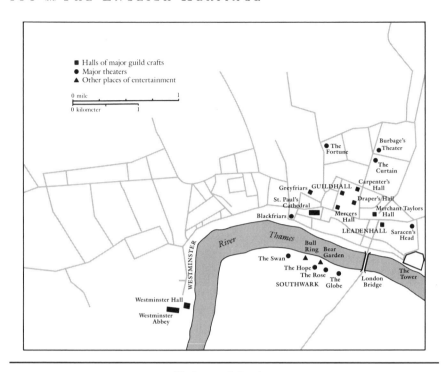

Shakespeare's London.

nate," "critical," "courtship," "dwindle," "primrose path," "flaming youth," "to catch a cold," and "hunchback."

The Globe (built in 1599) was the most important playhouse. It was patterned after the arrangement of tiered balconies overlooking an open courtyard, thus imitating the earlier practice of performing plays in the courtyards of inns. Little scenery was used and women did not act, so that the success of a play depended on vividness and the reality created by the spoken word. The acting company entertained a vast and varied audience: occasionally the monarch, always the "groundlings" who paid a penny to stand in the open floor of the playhouse before the stage, and the well-to-do who paid an extra penny to sit on stage—to see better and to be seen. Because all in the audience loved realism, an actor was expected to be an accomplished acrobat, wearing concealed bladders of red liquid which when pricked by a dueller's sword after a spirited fight on stage would graphically simulate death.

Elizabethan London

The stage for Renaissance England was the burgeoning city of London, swollen in size from the 50,000 of Henry VII's time to 250,000 at Elizabeth's death. It was a glittering Renaissance city for the upper ranks of society, the home of the Court and the hub of the legal world and the center of a social season with plays and amusements. For the merchants it was a place of exceptional opportunity, the largest and most lucrative market in all of Europe and the center of a fast-growing world of commerce. London also attracted the less fortunate—the unemployed agricultural workers no longer needed on enclosed fields, the ne'er-do-wells who wished to escape the tedium of country life, and the criminal who saw a golden opportunity. Slums grew quickly, especially when unscrupulous builders subdivided buildings into small, dark tenements into which the poor could be overcrowded. Plague and poverty were as much at home in Renaissance London as were opulence and entertainment.

London was still a city of half-timbered wooden buildings with thatched roofs along twisting and winding streets. There had always been much greenery in the city, and the countryside was not far away. The first growth was internal, filling up empty spaces and especially tearing down the former spacious monastic buildings to erect dwellings in their place. North of the walls the expansion was limited by poor soil and drainage, but the growth westward and eastward occurred for two reasons.

The movement westward was mostly residential. First there were the palatial buildings in the area between the river and the main road westward from the city gates to Westminster. The duke of Somerset, Edward's lord pro-

Westminster Hall.
Private collection.

tector, had erected Somerset House on the river, and closer to Westminster Cardinal Wolsey rebuilt his archepiscopal London home, York Place, until he "donated" it to Henry VIII (along with his fashionable palace outside London, Hampton Court) in a vain attempt to keep the king's favor. New and more opulent buildings north of the road and closer to Westminster housed those of high rank who wished to be near the Court. Near the western walls of the city there were slum areas. The movement eastward was mostly commercial. Docks and warehouses were required by the new overseas trading companies; the East India Company eventually built moorings and warehouses on ten acres of river frontage.

South across the river, there were the Globe and many other places of amusement, such as the place for the baiting of bears by English bulldogs. There were other new buildings besides the playhouses. Elizabeth's financial agent, Sir Thomas Gresham, built the Royal Exchange, a mart in which businessmen could display the wares so important in England's expanding trade, and then he endowed Gresham College, where instruction in English was tailored to the practical needs of the merchant class and the expeditionary trading voyages on the seas.

The vast overcrowding made London life exciting—and dangerous as well. Crime was endemic, fire was a constant danger because the structures were so flammable, filth was everywhere because the crush of people placed impossible demands on the manifestly inadequate sanitary facilities, and sickness and the plague spread rapidly through the teeming population. Richness and poverty existed side by side in gargantuan proportions in this Renaissance city.

THE WAR YEARS AND THE END OF THE REIGN, 1585–1603

Conflict with Spain

A state of war between England and Spain existed from 1585 to 1603. Its causes were long-standing: Elizabeth sent money and troops to help the Protestant Dutch who were fighting for their independence from the Spanish Netherlands; English seamen tried (unsuccessfully) to intercept the annual treasure fleets returning from the New World; English merchants attempted to break the Spanish monopoly on trade with America; and, most importantly, King Philip II sought the triumph of his cause over the Protestant queen.

The major campaign of the war was the attempted invasion of England in 1588, when the Spanish Armada, a fleet of about 130 ships, sailed to rendezvous with soldiers under Spanish command in the Netherlands and then to ferry them across for the invasion. The plan was beyond the capabilities of the time: communications were inadequate, there was no deep water in which the Spanish ships could anchor to pick up the soldiers, and the prevailing winds from west to east were likely to prevent the westward attack even if the troops reached the ships. The English seized the initiative by moving upwind, and with the wind at their backs they could harry the Spanish fleet, let the English heavy guns wreak havoc, and then even send unmanned fire ships into the moored Spanish fleet. Unable to retreat westward, the Spanish had to turn northward and circle Scotland, returning past Ireland. Philip had trusted God to overcome the obstacles his commanders had pointed out; the English felt the "Protestant wind" was their best ally.

The Spanish attempted unsuccessfully to mount armadas against England again in 1596 and 1597, and in 1601 actually landed a military force in the Irish port of Kinsale. Thus, the fear of hostilities and of the chance of an invasion colored English life in the last years of the queen's reign. The English knew that the likely route for another invasion would not be direct but would be from Ireland, where a native population hostile to Protestantism might eagerly contribute men to assist in an invasion of England. The queen therefore dispatched military commanders to "pacify" Ireland, first the ambitious and

Shakespeare's burial place,
Stratford-on-Avon.
Private collection.

mercurial earl of Essex and then the more dependable Lord Mountjoy. Essex botched his chance, failed to handle the situation, and in childish pique mounted an unsuccessful rebellion in 1601 against the queen who chafed at his failures—Essex paid with his head. Mountjoy succeeded just before the queen's death in decisively defeating the Irish forces, and thus he laid the foundation for England's later dominance of that island.

The End of the Reign

The last decade of the Elizabethan period was beset by crises. To the high costs of war in the Netherlands, Ireland and on the seas, together with the inevitable disruptions caused by discharged soldiers and sailors returning from the wars, was added a series of agrarian disturbances associated with four straight bad or disastrous harvests in a row in the late 1590s. As the queen aged and became less involved in the government of the realm, members of the Privy Council engaged in a factional struggle to determine who would inherit the power wielded by Robert Dudley, earl of Leicester, who died in 1588, and Sir William Cecil, Lord Burghley, who died in 1598. The earl of Essex was one contender, but his execution for treason following his rebellion in 1601 allowed Burghley's mantle of authority to pass to his second son, Sir Robert Cecil. A skilled politician like his father, Cecil became principal secretary of state and began a correspondence with James VI of Scotland, undertaken in secret because to the very end Elizabeth refused to designate a successor. Thus was effected a smooth transition in the government upon the death of Elizabeth and a personal union of the two crowns of Scotland and England which would eventually lead, in 1707, to a parliamentary union of the two kingdoms.

The Elizabethan Age

Although the political skirmishes left an unpleasant taste, the realities of the queen's reign could not be eclipsed. Her nation had avoided the religious wars which so decimated France, and Protestantism was safe for England. Political problems of greater magnitude she had simply left unattended, keeping her reign relatively peaceful but portending serious difficulties for James and his successors. The economic strife of the end of the century had been generally overcome and there was prosperity, although few realized the full extent of the social changes that the new economic realities had inaugurated. The first tentative forays on the sea were small: colonization had not worked and the new trading companies were not yet flourishing, but the foundations had been laid for an empire of trade, and the bold English mariner, Sir Francis Drake, had sailed around the world.

The English had left genuine triumphs: a triumph of spirit, a triumph of cultural achievement, the expanding of horizons in the minds of English sub-

Queen Elizabeth in Parliament. From D'Ewes Journal, *published in 1682.*

jects. Militarily a small nation, prostrate and unimportant after the civil wars of the fifteenth century, England had stood off the mightiest nation in the world, the political champion of the Catholic Counter-Reformation. There could have been no greater boost to English self-esteem. The trials of battle had proved that early-modern England was of age—flourishing, proud, successful. It was a remarkable heritage to pass on.

SUGGESTIONS FOR FURTHER READING

Penry Williams, *The Later Tudors: England, 1547–1603* (1995) (New Oxford History of England) provides an excellent narrative of political events. The best of recent biographies of the queen is Christopher Haigh, *Elizabeth I* (1988), although J. E. Neale's laudatory *Queen Elizabeth 1* (1934; rpr. 1961) remains a very readable classic. Antonia Fraser, *Mary, Queen of Scots* (1969) is a fascinating study of Elizabeth's cousin. Recent studies of the Elizabethan parliaments may be found in M. A. R. Graves, *Elizabethan Parliaments* (1987) and T. E. Hartley, *Elizabeth's Parliaments* (1992). J. S. Cockburn gives a description of the criminal justice system in a *A History of English Assizes* (1972). The best survey of foreign affairs remains R. B. Werham, *Before the Armada: The Emergence of the English Nation, 1485–1588* (1966), continued in *After the Armada: Elizabethan England and the Struggle for Western Europe* (1984), and *The Return of the Armadas: The Last Years of the Eliazabethan War against Spain, 1595–1603* (1994).

A comparative study of the two groups that opposed the Elizabethan religious settlement may be found in Patrick McGrath, *Papists and Puritans under Elizabeth 1* (1967). The important role of the Catholic gentry in the preservation of Catholicism is studied by John Bossy in *The English Catholic Community, 1570–1850* (1976). The Anglican clergy receive attention in Rosemary O'Day, *The English Clergy: The Emergence and Consolidation of a Profession, 1558–1642* (1979). The importance of Puritanism in shaping English Protestantism is demonstrated in Patrick Collinson, *The Elizabethan Puritan Movement* (1967), and *The Religion of Protestants: The Church in English Society, 1559–1625* (1982).

Useful surveys of social history are found in D. M. Palliser, *The Age of Elizabeth: England under the Later Tudors, 1547–1603* (2nd ed., 1992), and J. A. Sharpe, *Early Modern England: A Social History, 1550–1760* (1987). The world of the landed nobility is studied in Lawrence Stone, *The Crisis of the Aristocracy, 1558–1641* (1965); that of knights, esquires and gentlemen in Felicity Heal and Clive Holmes, *The Gentry in England and Wales, 1500–1700* (1994); while the impact of agrarian change upon those who tilled the soil is described in detail in Joan Thirsk (ed.), *The Agrarian History of England and Wales, vol. IV: 1500–1640* (1967). For London, consult Ian Archer, *The Pursuit of Stability: Social Relations in Elizabethan London* (1991).

The literary scene is surveyed in Boris Ford (ed.), *The Age of Shakespeare* (1982) (vol. 2 of *The New Pelican Guide to English Literature*). *Foxe's Book of Martyrs* was reputedly the most widely read book in the English language after the Bible for more than three centuries. A selection has been edited by Marie G. King (1968). There are various modern anthologies of the writings of Richard Hakluyt, that demonstrate the new interest in overseas exploration, navigation, and trade; one is Jack Beeching (ed.), *Voyages and Discoveries* (1982). The impact of the Renaissance in England is discussed in Arthur B. Ferguson, *The Articulate Citizen and the English Renaissance* (1965).

CHAPTER SEVEN

The Stuart Kings
and Their Parliaments
1603–1660

The accession of King James VI of Scotland as James I of England brought an end to the Anglo-Spanish War and removed the fear of foreign intervention in Scotland. By eliminating the threat of foreign invasion of the British Isles and inaugurating a long period of peace, members of the political nation, represented in Parliament, could focus their attention on domestic problems. Constitutional conflicts concerning the law and the royal prerogative, the government of the Anglican Church, taxation, and the responsibility of members of the Privy Council to explain their actions to Parliament, which had been suppressed out of deference to an aging queen, now came out in the open. At first these controversies were debated in the Privy Council, the law courts, and Parliament. As the disagreement between the Stuart monarchs and their subjects became more sharp, the possibility of compromise and reconciliation receded. Both sides resorted to arms to settle their differences. The resulting civil wars spread throughout the Three Kingdoms of the British Isles, and the victorious Parliamentarians executed one king and, for a brief time, established a republic, but were unable to settle the major constitutional and political problems. The continuing search for a solution led to the deposition of a second Stuart monarch and the assertion of parliamentary supremacy. Only then did political stability become possible.

James I,
painting by Daniel Mytens, 1621.
Corbis–Bettmann.

JAMES I OF ENGLAND

Political Ideas and Practices

Whereas the Tudor monarchs had based their claim to the throne on their effectiveness as rulers, James Stuart claimed his crown by divine right and asserted that as God's lieutenant he was answerable only to God for his actions. His appearance was awkward and ungainly, his Scots burr grated on English ears, and unlike the late queen who had been a consummate actress and knew how to charm her subjects, James scowled at or avoided his subjects. His homosexual preferences and the drunken orgies at court were morally offensive to those who remembered the decorum and learned discourse of Elizabeth's court. That James had survived plots to kidnap or assassinate him by the turbulent Scottish nobility after he came to the throne of Scotland at the age of nine months showed that he was not without political and military skills. James had received an excellent education from his dour Presbyterian tutors, and he liked to display his considerable learning. His continuing fear of assassination made him wary of military displays, and his refusal to be drawn into continental religious wars dismayed those who thought that he should have gone to the aid of the endangered cause of Protestantism during the Thirty Years War (1618–1648). Many subjects still believed that a king should project a martial image and were not prepared to accept a pacifist and a pragmatist instead. This monarch, who has been called "the wisest fool in Christendom," preferred to rule through favorites rather than choosing men of ability as ministers of the crown as Elizabeth had done. This inattention to affairs of state was exacerbated by the king's indolence and a tendency to waste much of his time on horse races and hunting.

James's Religious Problems

Because the new king had been raised and educated as a member of the Calvinist Church of Scotland, the English Puritans had hoped that James might be persuaded to eliminate certain liturgical practices in the Anglican Church that they found objectionable. In response to a petition from a group of Puritan ministers, James agreed to meet with them at the Hampton Court Conference of 1604. When he detected their Presbyterian hostility to the authority of the Anglican bishops he perceived that any attack on episcopal authority must inevitably lead to an undermining of royal authority. He told the ministers that they would do well to conform themselves to the Anglican Church or he would "harry" them out of the realm. James gave Richard Bancroft, the new archbishop of Canterbury, permission to proceed against their leaders, and Bancroft deprived nearly a hundred Puritan ministers from their benefices (or endowed religious offices).

James appointed bishops with an anti-Puritan bias, and expected them and the Anglican clergy to preach sermons upholding the divine-right theory of kingship and reminding his subjects of their Christian duty to obey the king as they would obey their God. Wishing to replace the Geneva Bible with its highly political marginal commentaries, the king authorized a new translation of the Bible, the strikingly beautiful King James Version of 1611, which became the most widely read book in the English language and did much to shape that language throughout much of the English-speaking world.

James's reputation for tolerance had also encouraged Catholics to look for relief from the Recusancy Laws when he came to the English throne. They, like the Puritans, were also to be disappointed. A group of Catholic conspirators, including a Catholic gentleman named Guy Fawkes, planned to blow up the Houses of Parliament in November 1605 when the king would be present to open Parliament. A relative of one of the conspirators revealed the plot to the government and Fawkes and the others were caught, tried, and executed. The discovery of the "Gunpowder Treason" exacerbated the popular fear of Catholicism and gave rise to a major Protestant holiday, now known as Guy Fawkes Day. Parliament enacted more stringent penal laws against Catholic recusants, but James's lax enforcement of these statutes led Puritan leaders in Parliament to perceive that the king was harsh towards Puritans and indulgent towards Catholics. Increasingly, the relations between king and Parliament deteriorated.

James I and Parliament

James was at a disadvantage because he did not understand the politics and constitution of England as well as he did those of Scotland. Nor was he one to seek good advice. The extravagance of his court and his gifts to favorites doubled the indebtedness that he had inherited from Elizabeth. He frequently called Parliament to vote taxes, but he failed to undestand the need to conciliate and manage Parliament. He lacked the judgment to select able Privy Councilors, and few of them sat in Parliament. One of the few men of ability who was able to manage Parliament effectively, Sir Robert Cecil, was created earl of Salisbury and removed from the House of Commons to the House of Lords, and, consequently, the initiative in drawing up new legislation passed from the crown to the House of Commons. As a result, Parliament never voted the king sufficient taxes and the financial problems of the crown worsened.

Instead of reducing expenditure, James turned to methods of raising revenue which Parliament found objectionable. He sought an alternative source of funds by increasing customs duties and justified this action by saying that the purpose of the increase in customs duties was to regulate foreign trade, which power came under the royal prerogative and was none of Parliament's business. James resorted to other extraparliamentary means of raising revenue, which the royal judges, who served at the king's pleasure, usually upheld. The king's attempt to lecture the members of Parliament concerning the theory of divine-right monarchy and to justify his actions in terms of the powers of the royal prerogative created an atmosphere of distrust. Members of Parliament replied by making extravagant claims about Parliament's ablility to limit the royal prerogative which English law had long recognized was nothing more than the legitimate exercise of royal authority. When, in 1610, Sir Robert Cecil, earl of Salisbury proposed to Parliament the forward-looking Great Contract, by which the king promised to abolish the unpopular Court of Wards and to rescind certain extraparliamentary taxes in exchange for guaranteed annual subsidies from Parliament, the atmosphere of distrust prevented a compromise which might have avoided some of the future conflicts between king and Parliament concerning extraparliamentary taxation.

The conflict between James I and Parliament raised the question of whether the king was subject to the law or was, as he claimed, the very source of the law. In this James's most formidable opponent was a judge, Sir Edward Coke. As attorney general under Elizabeth and James, Coke had been a staunch defender of the royal prerogative. Upon his appointment as chief justice of the Court of Common Pleas in 1606 and, subsequently, King's Bench in 1613, Coke took up the cause of the common law and the independence of the judiciary with equal ferocity. Coke argued against James's exercise of the royal prerogative, asserting, for example, that the king did not possess the right to legislate by means of proclamations in an emergency situation pending a meeting of Parliament, nor could kings remove judges from office. In his zeal to champion the the common law Coke used his great learning but also resorted to the disreputable practice of inventing historical and legal precedents when he needed to clinch an argument. James dismissed him from his judicial office in 1616, but Coke was elected to the house of Commons in 1620, where his leadership of other common lawyers elicited opposition to royal policies and practices.

James's Reliance upon Court Favorites

The king's relations with Parliament were aggravated by his predilection for choosing ministers for reasons of personal affection rather than reasons of state. His choices were invariably disastrous, and the revelation of scandals caused the king to disavow several court favorites before his affections finally led him to select a young knight from Leicestershire named Sir George Villiers. After the death of Sir Robert Cecil, earl of Salisbury in 1614, James governed through these favorites while his Privy Council grew so large as to become unwieldy. James alienated many potential supporters when he bestowed upon Villiers the highest rank of the peerage with the title of duke of Buckingham, and allowed him to gather all the choice plums of patronage into his hands. The inability of Parliament to resolve differences with the king concerning religious and foreign policies, the management of royal finances, or the granting of unpopular monopolies to court favorites, led Parliament to revive the medieval judicial procedure of impeachment. The process of trial by Parliament was employed in an attempt to make the king's ministers accountable to Parliament. Among the first to be impeached and removed from office was the brilliant philosopher, Sir Francis Bacon, the lord chancellor.

James's foreign policy of avoiding entanglement in the continental reigious wars was viewed by Parliament with dismay. After the king's son-in-law, Frederick, elector of the Rhenish Palatinate, was elected king of Bohemia, a Habsburg possession, by that country's rebellious Protestant subjects, Catholic Imperial forces overran both Bohemia and the Palatinate. Thus began the Thirty Years War, and many of James's subjects felt that he was bound in honor to go to the aid of his dispossessed daughter Elizabeth and her husband. Others felt that James should become the Protestant champion against the political and military forces of the Catholic Reformation. His favorite, Buckingham, urged upon James a marriage alliance between the Spanish Infanta and James's heir, Charles, prince of Wales, as a peaceful means of recovering the Palatinate for his son-in-law. The journey to Spain undertaken by Charles and Buckingham to woo the Infanta turned into a humiliating fiasco. Upon their return to England, Charles and Buckingham urged a war of revenge against Spain, and James took the unusual step of allowing Parliament in 1624 to discuss foreign policy after having told Parliament earlier that foreign policy pertained to his royal prerogative and was none of their business. Before James died in 1625, Parliament voted taxes for a naval war against Spain in the tradition of the Elizabethan privateers, but refused to fund the military expedition that was to help recover the Palatinate.

CHARLES I: THE EARLY YEARS

Charles and His Parliaments

Charles was a shy and reserved man, and was less intelligent, articulate and confidant than his father. Unlike James I, his private life was above reproach, and his court displayed the decorum that was lacking in the time of his father. Even his nemesis, Oliver Cromwell, was forced to admit that he was a model husband and father. But he did nothing to cultivate the affection of his subjects, and he lacked the political skills to be a ruler. Unable to communicate his needs to Parliament, he became even more dependent for advice upon the duke of Buckingham than King James had been, and Buckingham gave him consistently bad advice.

The war with Spain and the Holy Roman Empire which Charles had inherited from his father led him into actions that caused relations with Parlia-

Equestrian portrait of Charles I
by Anthony van Dyck.
Courtesy of the Royal Academy
of Arts, London

ment to further deteriorate. Charles and Buckingham, now responsible for a war which Parliament had urged but was unwilling to finance properly, proved to be inept military leaders. A joint naval-military expedition that raided the Spanish naval base of Cadiz was mismanaged and regarded by Parliament as a disgrace to English arms. A second military expedition to relieve the French Protestants at the siege of La Rochelle, which involved Charles in a separate war with the king of France, was also bungled. In order to raise the revenues which Parliament would not vote, the government began to extract "forced loans" from subjects with no intention of repayment. Those who refused to pay on the grounds that extraparliamentary taxation was illegal were imprisoned or impressed as soldiers. While awaitng transport overseas, the government quartered soldiers in the homes of citizens in port towns, and then had to resort to proclaiming martial law to restore order among the ill-disciplined soldiery. Perceiving illegal taxes and martial law as manifestations of arbitrary government, the Parliament of 1628 presented the king with the Petition of Right, demanding that he cease these arbitrary measures. Although Charles gave his assent to the Petition, which thereby became a statute, he refused to honor it. When Parliament began impeachment proceedings against Buckingham, Charles dissolved it. In the meantime, a disgruntled naval officer assassinated Buckingham.

The king's attempts to raise extraparliamentary taxation continued to irritate members of Parliament. Because of resentment of James I's action in increasing the rate at which customs duties were levied, Parliament had refused to grant Charles the authority to collect customs duties for life as had been traditional, but, instead, proposed to authorize them for one year only, renewable each year by Act of Parliament. After 1628, Charles began to collect customs as if they had been granted for life, and he also began to revive a number of old feudal taxes. The mood of the Parliament of 1629 was so hostile that the king quickly decided to dissolve it. Before the speaker of the House of Commons could rise from his chair to read the royal message, several members of the Commons sat on him and held him down in the speaker's chair while another read a resolution branding as a traitor anyone who supprted the king's extraparliamentary fiscal measures or the recent innovations in the Anglican Church. Thereafter, Charles resolved to rule without Parliament.

The Period of Personal Rule

Charles I persisted in his policy of ruling England without a parliament for eleven years (1629–1640). By bringing the unsuccessful wars to an end, he was able to find sufficient funds to pay for his government from the income of the royal estates and by imposing further extraparliamentary taxes. Two royal ministers were particularly associated with Charles's personal rule. Sir Thomas

Wentworth effectively governed two areas which had hitherto been difficult to control, first as president of the Council in the North, and then as lord deputy of Ireland, in reward for which he was raised to the peerage as earl of Strafford. William Laud, made archbishop of Canterbury in 1633, imposed upon the Chuch of England a distinctive theology and liturgical practice called Arminianism. So-called after Jacobus Arminius, a Dutch theologian who had led a revolt against orthodox Calvinism in the Dutch Reformed Church early in the seventeenth century, Arminian theology repudiated predestination and advocated free will. These theological doctrines were deeply offensive to all orthodox Calvinists and especially the English Puritans who regarded such ideas as indistinguishable from popery.

Charles consistently supported Laud and the other Arminian bishops who insisted upon strict adherence to the *Book of Common Prayer,* decent and reverent decorum in church, the wearing of prescribed ecclesiastical vestments, and the use of the sign of the cross in baptism. All of this outraged Puritans in Parliament and clerical allies who still retained benefices in the Church of England. Laud also insisted upon higher educational and professional standards for the Anglican clergy. A generation of royalists, who would later fight

Ceiling by Peter Paul Rubens in the Banqueting Hall, Whitehall, designed by Inigo Jones.
Corbis-Bettmann.

in the civil wars, acquired their strong attachment to Anglicanism during this period. But the cost was the complete alienation of those Puritans who persevered within the Anglican Church in the hope of reforming it on the Genevan model.

The perception that the Laudian church was veering in a Catholic direction was reinforced in the minds of Puritans by a distinctive Caroline court culture. Charles's French queen, Henrietta Maria, introduced the French style into her court and brought Catholic priests and friars with her, which required the king to dispense them from obedience to the Recusancy Statutes. Charles collected paintings and sculpture and patronized artists with the unerring good taste of an Italian grand duke. The official architecture of the Caroline court was based upon the strict classical models of Renaissance Italy. That the new artistic style in buildings, paintings, and scenery for the elaborate court masques were introduced by Catholic artists such as Inigo Jones and the Flemish Sir Anthony van Dyck did nothing to reassure Puritans that Charles could be trusted as the guardian and supreme head of the Church of England. Since the dominant style of the court was Italian or French rather than English, critics of the court were led to believe that Charles intended to rule in the French fashion, i.e., without consulting a representative assembly.

Charles could dispense with Parliament if he could find sufficient extraparliamentary sources of revenue. The crown attorneys plundered the past to find feudal precedents for levying taxes without the consent of Parliament—a practice called fiscal feudalism. Crown estates were sold off to courtiers; royal tenants subjected to increased rents. The boundaries of the once vast royal forests, which had been shrinking since the thirteenth century, were once again extended. The whole of the county of Essex was made a forest and subjected to forest law rather than common law, and the inhabitants fined in the Court of Star Chamber and other prerogative courts for trespassing on royal lands. The most striking example of the practice of fiscal feudalism was the levying of ship money. It had long been accepted that the crown had an undisputed right to require residents in maritime counties to contribute money in time of war for the building of new ships which would provide an added and immediate means of defence. Charles's innovation was to levy ship money in inland counties and in time of peace. When John Hampden, a wealthy country gentleman and leader of the opposition to extraparliamentary taxation, refused to pay the ship money assessed upon him, he brought a court case against the crown, but lost by a 7-to-5 verdict among the judges who heard the case. Charles was notorious for dismissing judges who disagreed with him; that a substantial minority risked their careers by dissenting from that verdict was a moral victory for Hampden.

It was rebellion by his Scottish subjects that precipitated a political crisis in England. Believing that Anglicanism was more conducive to reverence for monarchy than Presbyteriasm, Charles sought to impose an episcopate and the English *Book of Common Prayer* upon the Church of Scotland. The governing General Assembly of the Kirk resisted, and drew up a Covenant by which many Scots promised to resort to arms to defend their own religious settlement, if necessary. The Scots raised an army, called the Covenanting Army, and invaded England in 1639. This war, called the Prayer-Book Rebellion, was the first of the Wars of the Three Kingdoms, which spread throughout the British Isles during the next two decades.

King Charles possessed no standing army and no funds with which to raise one. The trained bands of the county militias were called out, but fled the field when they met the Scots. The king realized that he could put an effective army into the field only if he could find the money, and he was advised to call a Parliament. The meeting of the new Parliament on April 13, 1640, ended the eleven years of personal rule during which the atmosphere of mistrust between the king and many of his subjects intensified. Once again, Charles revealed himself to be inept in his efforts to secure the cooperation of Parliament in making war against the Scottish rebels with an administrative machine and finances unequal to the task. Within two years, unable to resolve his differences with Parliament, the king broke off relations with that body, and civil war and rebellion broke out in England and Ireland as well as Scotland.

Ideas and the Challenge to Authority

Science and Practical Learning

Medieval thought was characterized by deductive reasoning that used logic to draw particular conclusions from general truths. Sir Francis Bacon, a royal official to James I, wrote to urge a reorientation: one should begin with the particular, and by repeated and extensive observation form a hypothesis expressing a general truth, capable of proof by experimentation. Bacon was sure that this scientific method would expand knowledge and produce many practical applications. Obviously the old was not instantly displaced (Oxford and Cambridge continued to teach the traditional curricula in Latin and many were suspicious of change), but the ideas of Bacon and many like-minded Europeans found fertile ground in the English emphasis on the practical. At Gresham College in London the instruction was conducted in English and emphasized scientific matters and applications in the business world, such as in navigation and shipbuilding. When Sir John Napier published his discovery of logarithms in 1614, a professor of astronomy popularized it and provided useful tables.

Scientific reasoning captured the imagination of the learned. In 1628 William Harvey set forth his theory that the blood circulated through the body, a major anatomical discovery. Navigational instruments like the telescope were widely produced, and the emphasis on mathematics awakened an interest in statistics and resulted in more reliable and accurate maps. By midcentury many of the upper classes had laboratories in their homes, even if just to be fashionable. An indirect result of the scientific method was to make authority and tradition less important and to emphasize the things of this world. When scientific discoveries proved wrong some of the clergy's scientific orthodoxy, it impugned their credibility in religious matters as well. The full impact of all of this was felt fully only toward the end of the century, but seeds of disruption had been sown alongside those of scientific advances.

As well as pioneering studies in science there were similar endeavors in the humanities. The Society of Antiquaries had been founded near the close of Elizabeth's reign in 1586. In the Jacobean period, the Society could count a number of distinguished members whose studies in the primary materials of manuscripts were essentially the introduction of scientific method into historical studies. Much of what they wrote was polemical. But the desire to discover historical precedents to support political arguments, a practice raised to a fine art by Coke, also advanced knowledge about the past and the evolution of English society. Foremost among the antiquaries was Sir Robert Cotton, because his famous library was made freely available to all applicants and provided the stuff from which the tracts and books were made. In the next century the library was acquired by Parliament for the nation and became one of the cornerstones of the British Museum. Bolton, Camden, Speed, Ussher, and D'Ewes were among the more important of his friends and fellow scholars, historians whose work still has value today.

The Social Ethic of Puritanism

Puritans saw themselves as agents of Divine Providence, sent into this world to do God's work. Hence, Puritans intended not only to carry through a complete reformation of the church, but also to remake the state and society in a more godly image. Preaching the word of God was important to Puritans because they understood that this was the usual means by which God imparted his saving grace to individual souls. Moreover, regular preaching also inculcated the virtues of selfdiscipline and industriousness. The Puritan understood that God bestowed outward signs of inward grace, such as success and prosperity, on the elect. Labor thus became a social duty and idleness a religious evil. This aspect of Puritan ideology appealed to merchants and skilled artisans living in the ports and towns, for whom frugality and hard work were necessary for economic success. The profits of the industrious Puritan became capital ready for investing, and the business contacts they formed throughout the realm came to constitute a network of economic interests.

Idleness was much condemned by the Puritans, which explains the harshness with which they treated vagrants, vagabonds, and beggars. They launched an attack on traditional calendar customs such as the Twelve Days of Christmas and parish festivals such as churchales, and sought to ban many traditional sports. Some Puritans questioned the social dominance of the nobility and gentry, and after 1640 a number of radical sects separated from the mainstream of Puritanism and espoused political, social, and economic ideas that threatened social revolution. Other radical groups rejected not only the authority of the Anglican clergy but also that of Puritan ministers as well, and claimed to be in possession of interior revelation and divine inspiration. All of these tendencies sharpened the social conflict of the years of rebellion and civil war.

Capitalism in Agriculture, Commerce, and Industry

Most Englishmen continued to work in agriculture, although improved methods of husbandry required fewer hands while increasing productivity. Only large landowners could afford the capital improvement which the new agricultural methods required, and, increasingly, peasant farmers were forced to sell their ancestral lands and to find employment as agricultural laborers and workers in rural industries. The profits of large-scale commercial agriculture were an important source of capital investment, which was directed into industry and commerce where most of England's future economic growth occurred. Increases in the scale of operation were often more important than technological innovation and invention at this stage, and thus considerable capital investment was required. In particular it was realized that England's vast coal resources were exceptionally valuable as the supply of wood for fuel and timber for building dwindled. Seams near the surface had long been mined, but capital was needed for digging deep shafts and for the pumps to ventilate gasses, to remove water, and to help raise the coal. As production grew eightfold in a century, the coal from centers in the northeast such as Newcastle-upon-Tyne came to be valued as important for England as Peru's silver had been for Spain a century earlier. The iron industry grew apace, and the huge increase in the production of iron benefited both older industries, such as foundries making cannons and nails, and newer fabricating trades.

Traditionally, wool and unfinished cloth had been England's principal exports, shipped almost exclusively from London to a few continental markets such as Antwerp, and thus subject to vicissitudes outside England's control. Attempts were made to produce newer types of cloth such as worsteds and to finish cloths before export, but neither succeeded, and trading depressions continued into the seventeenth century. The opening of non-European trade revived English commerce. The highly capitalized joint-stock trading companies traded with the new colonies in America and with parts of Asia and Africa. More ships were needed, and a new rivalry was thus created with the Dutch, a powerful maritime nation determined to dominate the seaborne carrying trade.

Capitalists became important in domestic trading also. Middlemen were needed to bring foodstuffs from distant counties to feed London's burgeoning population, and to put out the wool to spinners and weavers and then bring the finished cloth to the market. The increased demand for food encouraged a vast engineering project, the draining of the boggy fens of eastern England. Before the end of the seventeenth century nearly 400,000 acres had been made fit for farming.

The crown supported many of these ventures—the manufacture of gunpowder was important militarily, the new trading companies had royal charters, and Charles invested in draining the fens. But the more common royal attitude was indifference and even hostility. Capitalism was feared because of the new concentrations of wealth it created, for the social unrest that often followed, and because it was often unregulated. The Stuarts sought to control trade, as the Tudors had earlier, and they often exploited the wealth of the trading companies. The monopolies so freely granted to increase royal revenues often stifled economic development. Although most Englishmen were untouched by the new economic activities, the new economic entrepreneur came to resent the crown's attitude.

A distinction may be made between the merchants whose main interest was in foreign trade and those who managed domestic concessions—internal monopolies, patents, licenses, and the like. It was those dealing in foreign trade who were most estranged by the failure to protect shipping, the compromising of charters, and the increasing financial demands of the Court. The domestic concessionaires also had cause for disquiet from the Londonderry Plantation, incorporation of suburbs, royal commissioners, and arbitrary taxation. The latter received even worse treatment at the hands of the Long Parliament and were drawn back into the support of the crown in 1641 to 1642. A good deal of the military geography of the coming civil war was determined by the degree to which merchants and traders had welcomed or resisted royal interference in the economy.

COLONIZATION

The First Settlements

The English began colonizing near home by establishing fortified settlements in Munster in south-eastern Ireland. Later, Protestant settlers were dispatched to Ulster in the north of Ireland. The English regarded the Irish as rebels who were beyond the pale of civilization, and so assumed that soldiers must always accompany colonists. Thus, a pattern of colonization was established before the first English colonists ever set sail for the New World, and it is not surprising that they regarded the American Indians as savages and established a military presence from the very beginning. Religion motivated some colonizing efforts, the hope of economic profits spurred others, but in every case the impetus to colonize was of private and not royal initiative. The desire for profit led the Virginia Company to send settlers to Virginia, where the first colonists to arrive in 1607 named their settlement Jamestown after the king. Half of the settlers were gentlemen, who in proper English fashion did not intend to work but rather sought to find precious metals or the route to the orient. There was no room in the harsh and hostile new land for such an attitude, and not many survived the early years of starvation and Indian massacres; success came only when tobacco cultivation became the colony's economic mainstay.

The landing of religiously motivated "Pilgrims" at Plymouth in 1620 was an indirect result of James I's anti-Puritan sentiments. A congregation in Scrooby, Nottinghamshire, left England for Holland to practice their religion freely, then relocated in the New World. They had no legal authority for the move, but as a close-knit community in a relatively unimportant location they were able to practice their religion without interference. In later years a great level of maturity in appreciating the difficulties of colonization was manifested by the Massachusetts Bay Company whose settlers first arrived at Boston in 1630. Everyone was equipped to be self-sufficient through early lean years, and the insistence on living in towns gave a degree of success and independence not to be found in Virginia. The settlement in Maryland, which began in 1634, had yet a different authority and motivation. Charles I granted Lord Baltimore and his fellow Catholics the territory as a proprietary colony to be

Colonization and Trading Companies.

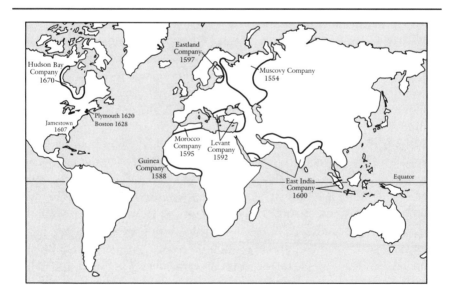

held by feudal tenure. As important as these mainland settlements were, the English colonies in the West Indies such as Bermuda and Barbados were more economically beneficial to England.

In each of these instances the actual management of affairs proceeded independently of the king. If abuses arose and the aggrieved petitioned the king, then James or Charles might revoke a concession and nominally take control, but this was more theoretical than actual. The Stuarts had neither a plan for encouraging colonization nor a policy of political management of those which others began. The substantially larger migrations in the 1630s arose from the royal anti-Puritan policies. Only in 1651, when the Commonwealth and not the crown ruled, did an imperial commercial policy begin. The Navigation Act of 1651 required colonists to ship their produce exclusively to England, on English ships manned by English sailors, so that the mother country might monopolize the fruits of its colonies. This measure would help to lay the foundations for English maritime and naval power in the next century.

CONFLICT AT ARMS:
THE CIVIL WARS AND CROMWELL

The Long Parliament

Charles called Parliament in April 1640 to demand taxes for fighting the Scots, and as soon as the session opened the able parliamentary leader John Pym rose in the Commons to list years of grievances against the Stuarts and to win approval for debating these issues first. After three weeks and no grant of taxes, Charles angrily dissolved this Parliament (later to be called the Short Parliament); but that summer the Scots invaded and occupied two northern English counties, and to meet the crisis, Charles had to call a new Parliament in November (the Long Parliament). Pym realized that even though two-thirds of the Commons was bent on reform, the proper tactic to keep together the majority was first to focus on removing hated royal officials. Accordingly he sought to remove from office Strafford and Laud, the ministers most closely associated with Charles's period of personal rule. Strafford was the key figure, and Pym tried to remove him first through the process of impeachment, a trial before the House of Lords. When that faltered he resurrected the ancient process of attainder by which, through simple majorities, without any requirement to prove guilt, Parliament could legislate Strafford's death, thus ignoring the rules of equity and justice. Pym's intimidating tactics succeeded, and the king was persuaded to give his consent, thus sealing Strafford's death sentence. His trial, attainder, and execution on May 12 had a profoundly and permanently divisive effect on the realm and its leaders. Thereafter there could be no trust, no accommodation.

Even as Strafford was condemned to death, both Houses passed a bill in May 1641 which stated that Parliament could not be dissolved without its own consent. Then Parliament passed bill after bill to be rid of many institutions and practices that it despised. It abolished the Court of Star Chamber, which had coercively enforced questionable royal policies; the Court of High Commission, which had stripped Puritans from church offices; and the two regional councils in the North and in Wales. It granted the king customs for two-month renewable periods only, declared ship money illegal, and ended financial expedients such as enlarging the royal forests. It passed a Triennial Act, which required Parliament to meet once every three years, so that the king could not once again refuse to call it into session. Charles gave his assent to every bill in order to gain time. His subjects began to wonder why he had allowed his faithful ministers to be executed, his government to be stripped of crucial powers, and Parliament to gain a potential permanence. Late in 1641 Charles began to rally his supporters, claiming that he alone was able to save the Church of England from a minority who would displace it. He requested an army to put down a fresh rebellion in Ireland, and many Parliamentarians feared to accede lest an army under royal control would become the instrument to reverse the hard-won reforms.

Fears about the king's sincerity were heightened when on January 4, 1642, he burst into the House of Commons to arrest Pym and four other leaders, but they had been forewarned and had escaped. Soon Charles left the hostile mobs of London for the more loyal North. Long months proved that an accommodation was not possible, so in August 1642 war broke out between the king and Parliament. Each side justified its actions: Charles claimed to fight to preserve the balance of the constitution and to keep the Commons from assuming all powers; Parliament insisted on a distinction between the office of kingship and the person of the king, asserting that it sought to preserve the office from the unworthy Stuart tyrant.

The Civil Wars

The king's forces, the Royalists or Cavaliers, advanced in 1642 to the outskirts of London and won a major engagement at Edgehill, but neither then nor in the proposed triple offensive of 1643 were the royal forces able to convert occasional successes into a conclusive victory. In the interim Parliament had to learn to govern the areas under its control. In such a novel situation there was much freedom in discarding traditional but inefficient practices, and gradually Parliament developed effective administrative and taxing procedures.

The war's turning point was Parliament's reorganization of the army made up of Parliamentarians, or Roundheads, in 1644. By passing a Self-denying Ordinance, Parliament excluded its own members from military offices, thus removing men for whom social rank and birth but not ability had meant leadership. The result was the creation of the New Model Army which was open to Puritans with military skills, an innovation as novel for Europe as were the striking new red coats in which all the soldiers were uniformed. An exception was made for an extremely capable Parliamentarian, Oliver Cromwell, a member of the gentry powerfully motivated by his Puritan faith and a man who kept himself ready to serve God by diligent prayer and self-examination. Cromwell was a major proponent of the role of cavalry in battle, and the flair with which he led his mounted soldiers to rout the enemy in disciplined and perfected charges soon made him one of the highest ranking generals and an inspiration for the soldiers. In 1644 the military tide began to shift in Parliament's favor, and at Marston Moor that year and at Naseby in 1645 the Royalist forces were soundly defeated.

From the time that Charles surrendered in 1646 the central political issue was the terms of negotiation. Two factions in Parliament were seriously divided by religious and constitutional attitudes. The majority party, the Presbyterians, wished to make the long-delayed religious settlement along the Scottish Calvinistic lines while the Independents wanted to allow a great deal of doctrinal latitude to each individual congregation and to restrict the national church to matters of public policy such as repressing blasphemy. The Presbyterians were constitutionally more moderate, wanting to place no restrictions on the monarch beyond those enacted in the Long Parliament, while the Independents felt that further restraints were absolutely necessary.

The Presbyterians were the more powerful faction in Parliament, but the New Model Army, England's first professional standing army, had become highly politicized and demanded a role in determining any new political and religious settlement. Refusing to be disbanded, as the parliamentary Presbyterians wished, the army asserted that it had been called "to the defense of our own and the people's just rights and liberties." Its officers prepared a plan of negotiations which strongly supported the Independents in Parliament, and the soldiers, through elected spokesmen called agitators, presented their own constitutional scheme based heavily on the philosophy of the Levellers, a radical group comprised mainly of Londoners of lower social rank. The Levellers went beyond an insistence on religious toleration for Protestant dissenters to demand more democratic participation in the political nation. This was to be achieved by granting the right to vote to all male heads of households. The agitations of the Levellers and the other radical sects threatened army discipline and gentry rule and raised the spectre of social revolution. Cromwell and the senior officers responded by restoring military discipline and suppressing the Levellers.

Meanwhile the king contrived to escape, and Parliament and the army buried their differences; within a year they fought a second civil war against

Charles and the royalists, and won another victory. When negotiations resumed, the Presbyterians did not budge from their earlier position of seeking a settlement with the king. The Independents regarded it as folly to negotiate with a king who would not keep his word and broke the peace. Colonel Pride led a company of soldiers into Parliament to purge the Presbyterian majority, and the fifty or so Independents remaining established a court to try the king for treason—a novel application of the legal doctrine which had originally defined treason as levying war against the king. Charles behaved with dignity and put up a good defense, but his conviction was a foregone conclusion. On January 30, 1649, a few days after the office of monarch was abolished, Charles was beheaded, and then the small remnant of Independents, now called the Rump Parliament, also abolished the House of Lords and office of bishop. Thus, James I's prophecy of "no bishop, no king" had come true. There followed an eleven-year period called the interregnum (1649–1660), a time of political experimentation during which a stable alternative to the traditional monarchial form of government was vainly sought.

The Commonwealth

The earliest experiment was the Commonwealth (1649–1653), in which the Rump was the legislature and the executive functions were shared by a forty-

Oliver Cromwell, painting by R. Walker, c. 1649. By courtesy of the National Portrait Gallery, London.

member Council of State composed of thirty-one Parliamentarians and some generals. The psychological wrench of abandoning so many traditional practices was a severe problem. The army was kept busy suppressing Royalist uprisings and crushing rebellions in Ireland and Scotland, while the navy was kept busy fighting the Dutch in a mercantile war over the supremacy of the sea and the control of colonies. Little progress was made in the issue of religion, still unsolved since 1642. A diluted form of Presbyterianism was enacted but found little support outside of London. In default of an enforceable plan, all forms of worship were allowed except Anglicanism and Catholicism.

The most important political tension was between the Rump and the army. The latter wished old grievances settled and insisted that the Rump keep its promise to dissolve itself and call new elections. Cromwell had become the leading general as others died or retired, but he was unwilling to dispense with the Rump lest the last link to the traditional form of representation be broken. When in April 1653 the Rump declared itself permanent, Cromwell finally intervened to dissolve the Rump. He then tried an utterly novel and totally unsuccessful experiment. The army asked the Independent congregations to nominate God-fearing Puritans to enact reforms. The 129 members of the Nominated Assembly proved so radical that it acquired unpleasant nicknames such as the "Assembly of the Saints" and the "Barebones Parliament." The latter nickname was a word play on its member, Praise-God Barbon or Barebone, whose low social rank seemed to epitomize the perceived danger of entrusting government to others than the wellborn elite. Cromwell quickly ended the experiment.

The Protectorate and the End of the Interregnum

Cromwell and the army were ready with another plan, a written constitution called the Instrument of Government. As Lord Protector, Cromwell assumed executive control with sweeping powers such as the right to issue ordinances which were to have the force of law until Parliament should meet. It was the exercise of these powers that caused unrest. Cromwell realized that the army's power had to be reduced and civilian control extended, and this attitude dissatisfied the army, while Parliament was stunned by his use of ordinances to collect money and even settle religious matters. No Stuart king had ever enjoyed such power and independence.

To correct some of these problems, in 1657 Parliament drafted a new written constitution, the Humble Petition and Advice. Cromwell rejected that part of the proposal which offered him the title of king yet accepted most of the rest, including the right to name his successor. But the constitutional dilemma continued, and only the extraordinary skills of Oliver Cromwell kept the political state together. Even that had its limitations. The war against Spain was an expensive failure. It further alienated the merchant and financial interests of London, who were vital to the survival of the Commonwealth. When he died on September 3, 1658, and was succeeded by his son Richard, the Protectorate Government was near collapse.

Richard Cromwell was ineffective—his nickname was "Tumble-Down Dick"— and many of the army's leaders grew increasingly arbitrary in opposition. The commander in Scotland, General George Monck, took the initiative to end the stalemate by marching his army southward and capitalizing on the public sentiment which called for a permanent solution. Monck was well suited to the task. He shared the conservative views of the gentry from which he sprang. These included the belief that the army should be the servant and not the master of the civil authority. First, he called back the Rump Parliament, then he added all the others purged in 1648. The restored Long Parliament called for new elections and dissolved itself, and the newly elected body issued an invitation to the son of Charles I to return as king. In May 1660 Charles II arrived back from exile to inaugurate the Restoration—a restoration of the monarchy, of the Church of England, and of traditional government.

A STOCKTAKING: ENGLAND IN 1660

Society and the Economy

The size of the aristocracy had grown greatly in the seventeenth century, but its importance had diminished. The twin pillars of aristocratic preeminence in the Middle Ages had been military service and the nobility's wealth and influence. Most of the military responsibilities had been lost in the sixteenth century, and the eclipse of the House of Lords temporarily by the Commons had diminished their political role. More important, the aristocrats' land ownership was severely curtailed by the Civil Wars. Most had fought for the king and, although those whose estates had been confiscated were entitled to sue at law for recovery, the nobles who sold their estates for any reason whatsoever were not able to regain them.

The early-modern state had opened up great opportunities for the gentry. What the dissolution of the monasteries had done to enlarge the land market of the sixteenth century, the confiscation of the nobles' and bishops' lands had done in the seventeenth. Many became newly landed gentry in time to rise to the new nobility. The merchants who formed a nonagricultural middle class and the professionals such as lawyers had all grown in importance. Success in any endeavor produced capital ready for investment in myriad new economic adventures at home and in trade.

The economic restraints imposed by the monarchy were removed. Gone were regulations governing the quality of manufactures and the rates of wages; gone were feudal tenures which had disinclined landowners to invest to improve their crop yield; gone were the royal monopolies and the Star Chamber which hindered the free marketplace. The removal of restrictions primarily benefited the well-to-do. But many of the "lesser sort" had been politicized, allowed to speculate freely along with others in a time of constitutional experimentation and allowed to have access to printing presses to propagate sincere reform ideas such as the Levellers or the outlandish ideas of religious fanatics. Many of these movements had been suppressed either in the interregnum or at the Restoration, but politics was not likely to remain the close precinct of the upper classes alone.

Religion and Ideas

Sixteenth-century religion was based on the premise that truth was certain and discoverable and that dissent and diversity were literally intolerable. By 1660, Catholicism was effectively eradicated, but Puritanism had temporarily come to supplant Anglicanism. The varieties of religious dissent had multiplied, and no longer was it possible to substitute one set of practices and form of church government for another. Although Anglicanism in the Restoration would bring an end to the period of practical toleration, the memory endured. Puritanism had indeed triumphed in many urban settings as a social ethic. Long after the specific religious teachings had been lost, the lessons of industriousness and discipline in work remained to influence many in the middle ranks of society. New directions in thought emerged, especially the humanism of the sixteenth century and the scientific inquiry of the seventeenth. The how-to orientation of many books reflected the practical, this-worldly bent of Englishmen. Many of the old orthodoxies were crumbling as much in the world of religion and ideas as in society and politics; the next quarter century gave a firmer shape to the new.

SUGGESTIONS FOR FURTHER READING

Recent surveys of the seventeenth century can be found in Mark Kishlansky, *A Monarchy Transformed: Britain, 1603–1714* (1996) and David Underdown, *A Freeborn People: Politics and the Nation in Seventeenth-Century England* (1996). Royal biographies include: Christopher Durston, *James I* (1993); Maurice Lee, Jr., *Great Britain's Solomon [James I]* (1990); Pauline Gregg, *Charles I* (1981); and Charles Carlton, *Charles I: The Personal Monarch* (1983). The royal favorite of both James I and Charles I is dealt with in Roger Lockyer, *The Life and Political Career of George Villiers, First Duke of Buckingham, 1592–1628* (1981). The early-Stuart parliaments are less thoroughly covered than those of Elizabeth, but see D. M. Hirst, *The Representative of the People?* (1975), Mark Kishlansky, *Parliamentary Selection* (1986), and Conrad Russell, *Parliaments and English Politics, 1621–1629* (1979). The attempts to make ministers of the king responsible to Parliament are explored in Clayton Roberts, *The Growth of Responsible Government in Stuart England* (1996). The eleven years of personal tyranny between parliaments is treated in detail in Kevin Sharpe, *The Personal Rule of Charles I* (1992). For the influence of court culture on politics, consult Linda L. Peck, *Court Patronage and Corruption in Early Stuart England* (1993) and R. M. Smuts, *Court Culture and the Origins of a Royalist Tradition in Early Stuart England* (1987). J. P. Kenyon provides a useful selection of constitutional and legal documents in *The Stuart Constitution, 1603–1688: Documents and Commentary* (1966).

The intellectual, political and social origins of the civil wars and rebellions are touched upon in J. P. Sommerville, *Politics and Ideology in England, 1603–1640* (1986) and in Christopher Hill, *Society and Puritanism in Pre-Revolutionary England* (1964) and *The Intellectual Origins of the English Revolution* (1965). Christopher Hill also studies the origins and development of political, religious and secular radicalism in *The World Turned Upside Down: Radical Ideas during the English Revolution* (1975). Developments in the Anglican Church are studied in Nicholas Tyack, *The Anti-Calvinists: The Rise of English Arminianism, 1590–1640* (1987) and in the works by Patrick Collinson cited in chapter 6. The importance of sermons within the Puritan movement is discussed in Paul Seaver, *The Puritan Lectureships: The Politics of Religious Dissent, 1560–1662* (1970).

The events of the English Revoultion, or the "Great Rebellion and Civil Wars" as they are called by contemporaries, are surveyed in Robert Ashton, *The English Civil War: Conservatism and Revolution, 1603–1649* (1978), but the student should also dip into that great historical and literary classic, Edward Hyde, earl of Clarendon, *The History of the Rebellion and Civil Wars of England*, 6 vols. (1888). A fascinating narrative of the civil wars, as they spread throughout the British Isles, is provided by Charles Carlton, *Going to the Wars: The Experience of the British Civil Wars, 1638–1651* (1992). The politicization of England's first standing, professional army is examined in Mark Kishlansky, *The Rise of the New Model Army* (1980). Biographies of the great parliamentary military leader and lord protector have been written by Christopher Hill, *God's Englishman: Oliver Cromwell and the English Revolution* (1970) and Antonia Fraser, *Cromwell: The Lord Protector* (1973). The politics of the commonwealth and protectorate periods of the Interregnum are analyzed in Blair Worden, *The Rump Parliament* (1974); and in David Underdown's *Pride's Purge* (1971) and *Royalist Conspiracy in England, 1646–660* (1960).

Peter Laslett gives a fascinating and provocative introduction to the social and demographic history of seventeenth-century England in *The World We Have Lost: England before the Industrial Age* (3rd ed., 1984). The social origins of divided allegiances within county communities during the civil wars are explored in David Underdown, *Revel, Riot and Rebellion: Popular Politics and Culture in England, 1603–1660* (1985). Aspects of women's history are examined in Susan D. Amussen, *An Ordered Society: Gender and Class in Early Modern England* (1988) and Sara H. Mendelson, *The Mental World of Stuart Women* (1987). Antonia Fraser looks at the lives of individual women in *The Weaker Vessel* (1985). For the important role that London played in politics, consult Valerie Pearl, *London and the Outbreak of the Puritan Revolution* (1961) and Robert Ashton, *The City and the Court, 1603–1643* (1979). A useful suvey of literary history during the seventeenth century is contained in Boris Ford (ed.), *From Donne to Marvel* (1963) (*The Pelican Guide to English Literature*). An introduction to developments in science will be found in A. G. R. Smith, *Science and Society in the Sixteenth and Seventeenth Centuries* (1972).

CHAPTER EIGHT

Restoration England
1660–1688

When Charles II (1660–1685) set foot on English soil at Dover on May 25, 1660, he returned amidst general rejoicing and relief. Charles II appeared to be well cast for his role. He was dark and swarthy, but not handsome; his young, athletic appearance, his stature (he was six feet, four inches tall), and his easy manner, sharp wit, and shrewd intelligence made him an instant success. His faults, though evident to his close associates and advisers, took longer to be revealed. Lazy, with little interest for business (though he unquestionably had the ability), insincere and gifted at dissembling (a trait he had been forced to acquire in his struggle for life and throne), overly fond of pleasure, women, and gambling, he cut the figure of a king but lacked the substance. Perhaps his most important trait, if hardly the most admirable, was an instinct for survival.

THE RESTORATION

The Political Settlement

Charles left to the Parliament the settling of such vexatious and difficult matters as the arrears of pay of the army, a general pardon, and the forfeited estates of the Royalists. Parliament rather than the king thus bore the odium of the disappointed. The Cromwellian army was reduced to a few regiments; the rest of the troops were paid what was owed them and retired from active duty. The Act of Indemnity, which forgave all but fifty named individuals, was a gracious and healing measure. The land problem was a more complex one, and

Charles II. After Sir Peter Lely.
By courtesy of the National
Portrait Gallery, London.

any solution was bound to create opposition. The compromise was sensible if not wholly equitable. Crown lands and those of the church, together with confiscated estates, were returned to the original owners. Those properties sold by private individuals during the Civil Wars could only be repossessed through court action and then only in the case of abuses of the law not exempted by the Act of Indemnity.

The nature of the king's own authority was perhaps the most important long-range consideration. It seemed clear to most people that a return to the old constitution, shorn of the Commonwealth innovations, was the common desire. The Long Parliament, which called for the election of the Convention Parliament, had itself shown the way by resolving that the House of Lords "had and have to be a part of the parliament of England." When the new Parliament assembled the Lords participated fully and equally without any reference to their dissolution in 1649. Their presence and that of a substantial number of Royalists insured that the prerogatives of the monarchy would be preserved. The restoration was not complete. The acts passed by the Short Parliament and the Long Parliament until 1642 that had received the assent of the king remained on the statute books, including the acts that had abolished the prerogative courts. The most important changes were left unstated. Parliament had executed one king; now it had restored another to the throne.

Though it supported Charles II by restoring the bishops to the upper House, by vesting sole command of all the armed forces in the king, and by repeal of the Triennial Act of 1641, the fact that these measures were done on the authority of Parliament and king and not the king alone was not lost on the participants.

The Financial Settlement

The adequacy of the financial settlement made to support the king's honor and government has long been a subject of debate. The radical innovations enacted by the Long Parliament in the 1640s had substituted a whole new series of internal taxes to maintain the army and navy and to replace those hereditary sources that had been abolished. These new taxes, especially the excise, an internal tax levied on commodities in general and on liquor in particular, were not popular with the general populace. For some months the Convention Parliament attempted to establish a tax on land to replace the feudal revenues that had been taken from the king. Direct taxes were regarded as an extraordinary rather than a regular source of revenue. When the Commons failed to agree on a land tax, court members in the Commons successfully moved an excise tax on liquor. The usefulness of this tax, which could be expanded to innumerable other commodities, was evident to the government. The most recent estimate of various taxes voted by the Parliament at the beginning of the reign show that they yielded approximately £980,000 per annum, short of the £1,200,000 that the Parliament projected. Additional taxes voted during the course of the reign brought the average up to £1,170,000, and if the king had managed his affairs wisely they should have sufficed. That they did not is an indictment of the king, not the Parliament.

The Religious Settlement

The religious settlement, like so many other aspects of the Restoration, proved to be an interim arrangement. While still in exile, Charles II had promised liberty of conscience to his subjects. During the Commonwealth, Presbyterians and Independents had been introduced into church livings, and both groups had expectations of remaining in an established church. The Anglicans were hardly unanimous in their attitude. That party identified as Laudian or high-church strenuously opposed any relaxation of the forms of the church to please the Presbyterians and other Dissenters. Others were disposed to define the church broadly so that it would be possible at least to comprehend the Presbyterians. The king and Clarendon were both disposed to moderation, though for differing reasons. The king was most interested in toleration for the benefit of the Catholics. Clarendon favored a church that was national and Protestant, and to achieve that he was prepared to and did incorporate many of the clergy who had accepted the Cromwellian settlement.

A conference was held in the spring of 1661 to reach an accommodation between the Presbyterians and the Anglicans. Unable to agree among themselves, the Presbyterians, who were poorly led and overconfident, prolonged the proceedings with the consequence that the Cavalier Parliament, which met on May 8, took the matter into its own hands. In league with the bishops, the Parliament ruled against an accommodation with the Presbyterians. The Anglicans now employed the same tactics of prohibition and persecution against Dissenters that had been used against them in the previous two decades. By the Act of Uniformity nearly 1,000 incumbents were purged from the church in 1662 for their refusal to accept the restored church's liturgy and doctrines. The Corporation Act denied Dissenters the right to hold office even at the local level, though the Act was never completely implemented. The Five Mile Act of 1665 and the Conventicle Acts of 1664 and 1670 placed penalties on Dissenters' meetings and ministers. An intermittent and not always effective persecution lasted until the Glorious Revolution of 1688, but the civil disabilities under which the Dissenters suffered were not removed until the nineteenth century.

The Diplomatic Settlement

Peace was an essential prerequisite to buy time to consolidate and secure the king's government. The fear of a Puritan insurrection made essential an alliance with a strong continental power that could supply troops in time of need. There were not many choices. Portugal, anxious to obtain allies to confirm its independence of Spain, was the most eager to conclude an alliance with England and offered Charles a bride—Catherine of Braganza—a handsome dowry, and the cities of Bombay and Tangier. Although the offer of Portugal was accepted, the most important link was forged with France. In part the ties of family impelled Charles. His French mother lived in retirement in her native country, and his sister Henrietta was married to the brother of Louis XIV. The views of Louis XIV on the nature of kingship were congenial to his English counterpart. Above all it was the offer of French gold that persuaded Charles to conclude a treaty for the sale of Dunkirk in 1662.

RESTORATION ENGLAND

Society

The social structure of Stuart England was a well stratified one. One can identify hierarchies in the cities and in the country; the two are roughly parallel though not identical. The whole was characterized by a very small upper layer with family incomes well above £1,000 a year, and middling groups with incomes ranging from £100 to £1,000 a year. These families controlled the wealth and political power. They and their immediate dependents totaled less than 10 percent of the population. All the rest fell below this level. The principal basis for wealth and political power was property, as in the House of Lords, whose members' titles and affluence reflected landed estates; the House of Commons, the majority of whose members were landowners; the law courts, where both the English common law and the litigation arising from it were all based on matters involving real property; the electorate both in cities and in the country, where the franchise was generally based on a property qualification; or the principal commodities of English commerce, especially wool. The society was firmly tied to the land.

An analysis by the pioneer statistician Gregory King, made at the end of the Restoration period, estimates the total population of England at 5,500,000 people. It is now known that his calculations were based on very limited and fragmentary sources. Moreover, King—a conservative, a divine right Tory working in the mid-1690s—projected his estimates back to 1688 to demonstrate the disastrous impact on the economy of William III's continental involvement. But even if his figures are deliberately conservative underestimates, his social categories are valuable for the manner in which one traditional but perceptive Englishman conceived of the social order of his country.

At the head were the nobility, some 160 lay lords and 26 spiritual lords, who were the leaders of the society, both because of their great wealth and their social status. Next in rank were the gentry, also possessing great landed wealth and often holding minor honors, baronets or knights. These were the men who filled the House of Commons and acted as the justices of peace in their counties. Gradations must be recognized within this class. The wealthiest rivaled the loftiest peers in holdings and political power. The lesser gentry were barely distinguishable from the small freeholders or farmers. Though numbered in the thousands, they still formed a small and discrete class. Small freeholders and farmers comprised the largest number in the country, according to King, and nearly six times that when their families were counted. They inherited the role of the yeomen of former times. Good husbandry and economic independence distinguished them. The lowest orders were the cottagers and paupers, who eked out a bare subsistence living by tilling small parcels of soil, grazing livestock on the common, and hiring out as day and seasonal laborers while their families supplemented their income by spinning and weaving. Some 20 percent of the population, essentially this group, received some form of public assistance or relief.

The leading residents of the cities were the wealthier merchants who controlled the moveable wealth of the kingdom and accounted for much of England's growing prosperity. Below them one found the shopkeepers, tradesmen, artisans, and craftsmen, which included some 5,000 substantial innkeepers. The middle and upper classes were sustained by a vast army of more than 300,000 laboring people and outservants, nearly 90 percent of them in rural employment, who with their families comprised some 1,275,000.

London: The Great Plague and Fire, 1665–1666

England was visited by two great natural disasters in the early years of the Restoration. The Black Death struck England in 1665 for the last time. It lasted into the next year, and before it was over some 70,000 had lost their lives out of 460,000 in London alone. The court and the Parliament fled to Oxford in hopes of escaping the pestilence. In order to maintain communication with those left behind in the capital and to allay fears throughout the country, the secretaries of state inaugurated a newspaper, the *Oxford Gazette,* to be renamed the *London Gazette* upon the return of the Court. For twelve years it was the sole newspaper permitted in the country, and though rivals began to appear in 1679 the paper itself has continued down to the present day, a unique publication record.

London had not recovered from the plague when it was struck by a second disaster, the great fire. In the space of four days in September 1666, the fire destroyed 40 percent of the old city within the walls. The city of London was a maze of wooden buildings and houses, each story built further out into the narrow street so that the roofs almost touched those opposite. The city was dank, crowded, dirty, and fetid, and land in it was dear. Merchants and artisans wanted to live close to their businesses if, indeed, both home and shop were not on the same premises. Restrictions on new construction outside the walls tended to retard development in the suburbs and concentrate the population within the walls. To the west the upper classes were building their houses; the earl of Clarendon, the lord chancellor, put his up in Piccadilly shortly before his impeachment in 1667. But in the city proper and in East London living conditions were poor and crowded, with a density as high as 40.3 households per acre. Brick and stone were rarely used in construction until required by proclamation in 1661. The rapidity with which houses were put up is one testimony to the poor quality of the structures; some houses were built in a night. Frontages were narrow, as little as eleven or twelve feet, and buildings were deep, with the consequence that there was little light within them. The average house was a small, two-storied dwelling with a square footage of about 1,200 in the poorer parishes, on the average with four to six rooms each. Bed, chairs, and tables were the staple furnishings. After the great fire, standards improved and the density of housing declined as some of the people moved out of the city to avoid the congestion and the high costs.

So much of the old city was swept away that an opportunity for a whole new start existed, and the heart of the commercial capital could be laid out on a scale and plan that befitted one of the great centers of Europe. But the hurry to restore the business and commerce of the trading center, a necessity doubly important with the losses in revenue suffered because of the plague and the war, and the reluctance to trade building space for broader avenues and parks, limited the planners. The network of streets at least was regularized to some degree, and new building codes reduced the fire hazard for the future. But the main consequence was the opportunity given to Sir Christopher Wren and his assistants and successors to design and build a new cathedral of St. Paul and many churches that still survive as the great glory of the city of London.

The development that marked London, economic and material, intellectual and artistic, was not exclusive to the metropolis. The Restoration ushered in a sustained period of general urban prosperity. Initially the growth was not so much in population as it was in commerce. Trade and social traffic burgeoned, perhaps in part as a reaction to the restrictions and sobriety of the Commonwealth. Industrial growth was an essential component. Many towns developed specialized industries, fueled by the rise of real wages in the countryside. Middle-rank towns not only served as market centers but also as the focus of occupational regions. The stocking trade, with its heart at Leicester, or the metalware trade, with its epicenter at Sheffield, are two examples. The growth of overseas trade was also an important spur. But sustained growth depended on expansion of the home market for manufactured goods. Migration to the towns, though at a lower level than earlier in the century, provided

Christopher Wren's monument
to the Great Fire of London.
Private collection.

labor, especially women who sought employment in the growing service and market trades.

A notable example of the renewed vitality of the provincial towns after the Revolution was Norwich. By 1700 it was the second largest city in England, growing during the century from about 12,000 to 30,000 people. Its achievement was the more remarkable as it was the largest inland town in the country (it was also atypical in the strength of Dissent in the city). External trade and ports were characteristics of its competitors. Immigration, mainly of individuals or families from Norfolk and Suffolk, was the basis for its increase. The principal employment was in textile manufacturing. By the end of the century the weavers jostled the merchants for power and prestige. The mayor elected in 1693, reputedly the wealthiest man in the city, came from the former rather than the latter group, heretofore dominant in the town. The market for the cloth was mainly domestic, and the product was mostly light and brightly colored textiles. The cloth was bought variously for apparel, linings for more expensive fabrics, and home furnishings. Competing chiefly with imported goods, the Norwich weavers shrewdly devised and introduced innovations in finish and design to maintain their competitive edge, especially in London, their principal market. Increases in duties on foreign cloth and peri-

Wren Tower, St. Mary-Le-Bow
Church, London.
Private collection.

odic bans on French goods also proved important stimuli. In addition to its role as a principal market town, one with an increasing number of permanent retail outlets, and as a center for wholesale trade and distribution, Norwich waxed so prosperous that by the end of the century it began to emulate London in its winter season with theaters, shows and assemblies, the summer assize, and other entertainments.

RESTORATION CIVILIZATION

The Royal Society and the New Science

The mid to late seventeenth century was a pivotal time in the intellectual and technological history of western Europe. England was at the heart of what is now recognized as the scientific revolution. The country was alive with a ferment of ideas, artistic, philosophical, religious, political, and scientific. The Royal Society, founded in 1662, was one focal point for the interchange, discussion, and development of these ideas. It was a circle of virtuosos, dilettantes, practical men of business, wealthy aristocrats, and new professional men, all inquisitive and interested in keeping abreast of the new developments in the natural sciences. Sir Christopher Wren typified this new breed of men. A student of great brilliance, he shone both as a Latin versifier and a mathematician of distinction. Praised by no less an authority than Sir Isaac Newton as a geometrician, Wren was a professor of astronomy and engaged in scientific experiment and study until he became assistant to the surveyor-general of works and devoted the greater part of his life to architecture, a field in which he was largely self-taught. Newton, who joined the Royal Society in 1672, was the greatest mathematician of his time and made contributions to mathematics, physics, astronomy, and optics. Associated with Wren and Newton was Robert Boyle, who made important contributions in chemical analysis. His work is remembered to this day by the law to which he gave his name on the relation between the volume, density, and pressure of gases. Yet one must not make the mistake of assuming a too sudden and complete modernity by the standards of our own time. We must also remember that both magical and apocalyptic ideas continued to hold great currency, even in the circles of the Royal Society. Throughout his life Newton displayed a strong interest in biblical chronology and a consuming commitment to alchemy.

The fellow of the Royal Society who has given us the most vivid picture of London in the 1660s when it passed through the two great catastrophes was the diarist Samuel Pepys. As a key civilian official in the navy from the Restoration to the Revolution he was the perfect bureaucrat—industrious, knowledgeable, always protecting the interests of his office and the navy. He illustrated how a young man of ability and connections, though lacking a large fortune, could rise to a position of great responsibility. He lived a rich and varied life. An indefatigable worker, he put in long hours at his office or in attendance on his superiors. As a young man he already had cultivated tastes and was a competent musician and an ardent book collector. He was also a man of pleasure, enjoying the many divertissements of the metropolis, the taverns, women, musicals, and the stage. London was the center of his life and he rarely left it.

Political Theory and Literature

One of the founders of the Royal Society, Sir William Petty, pioneered in yet another branch of knowledge, political economy. He came to the field after a term as a professor of anatomy and then physician-general to the army in Ireland. He undertook to make a survey of Ireland for the Commonwealth government in order to map the forfeited estates. He went on to make a complete map of the whole island, a task not finished until 1673. His skill and accuracy set new standards for cartography. After the Restoration he wrote a pioneer work on vital statistics and treatises on finance, the growth of the city of London, taxes, the origins of wealth, and a host of related topics. Another physician, John Locke, the most important political philosopher of the age, did not see his magnum opus published until after the Revolution. Locke joined the entourage of the earl of Shaftesbury and employed his pen in defending his patron and his political views. In the early 1680s he wrote his classic *Two Treatises of Government* to refute the *Patriarcha* of Sir Robert Filmer, the latter published posthumously by the Tories in 1680 to support the king's authority. Hounded into exile with Shaftesbury, Locke published his *Treatises* in 1689 as a justification of the Glorious Revolution. Such was the conservatism of his countrymen that his view was not accepted until decades after his death.

The reopening of the theaters in 1660 made possible a rebirth of English drama. The theater was heavily patronized by the court, the men of letters establishing that connection with the great aristocrats and politicians which was to reach its fullest flower in Queen Anne's reign. However, the greatest products of English writers were in forms other than drama. John Milton, a vestige of the Commonwealth, blind and out of favor, ennobled the English language with his great epic poems *Paradise Lost* and *Paradise Regained*. Another Puritan, John Bunyan, who found only adversity in the Restoration, wrote the *Pilgrim's Progress* while in prison. The finest literary representative of the Restoration and the poet laureate to the royal brothers, Charles II and James II, was John Dryden. Though a prolific contributor to the Restoration theater, he is best remembered for his poetry, his translation of Vergil, and his satires. It is not surprising that the prolonged political heats of the Restoration spawned a profusion of polemical works. Dryden's *Absalom and Achitophel*, a satire on the duke of Monmouth and the earl of Shaftesbury, was the supreme example and was singularly effective in reducing the Whig cause to ridicule. The full flower of this literary outpouring, however, was to be found in the Augustan Age, which followed the Revolution. While the circle of educated readers these writings reached was limited, literacy itself was not limited to the upper classes. Husbandmen and laborers had gained elementary reading skills even before the Civil War. Popular educational improvement continued into the Restoration period and beyond as the abundance of cheap printed literature—primarily ballads and chapbooks—attests.

ENGLAND, FRANCE, AND THE DUTCH REPUBLIC

Clarendon and the Second Dutch War, 1665–1667

The first ministry of the reign was nominally headed by Edward Hyde, raised to the peerage as earl of Clarendon and made lord chancellor. Its record was not a happy one. Clarendon refused to act as a chief minister in the traditional sense by coordinating and supervising the other ministers, and he lacked the suppleness and flexibility to manage the Parliament successfully. He lasted in office until 1667 when he was brought down by the failure of his foreign policy and by discontent arising from the plague and the great fire. Relations with the Dutch, never good since the first Dutch War (1652–1654), had steadily deteriorated until war broke out again in 1665. Trading disputes had already led to armed conflict between the two nations in India and Africa. The war finally reached America in 1664 when an expedition from New England seized New Amsterdam and renamed it New York in honor of the king's brother, the duke of York. The war in Europe opened with an English attack on a Dutch convoy at Bergen the next year. The English were able at first to withstand the challenge of the Dutch, who were supported by an alliance with France. By 1667, however, their diplomatic isolation told against them. The low estate of the English military and naval power was revealed in that year when a Dutch fleet sailed up the Thames, destroyed half the English navy, and towed away the flagship, the *Royal Charles*. The ignominious failure of English diplomacy and arms toppled Clarendon from his post. Made the scapegoat for the disasters, he was impeached by the Parliament and forced into exile to France, where he lived until his death in 1674. The king and his other advisers negotiated the two treaties that brought hostilities with the French and the Dutch to an end. By the Treaties of Breda (1667), England regained the islands in the West Indies taken by France but ceded all rights to Acadia (Nova Scotia) in North America. England kept th Dutch colonies in North America but gave up Guinea and most of the outposts in West Africa, except for Cape Coast Castle on the Gold Coast.

The Cabal

The ministers who succeeded Clarendon in the main offices were an ill-matched group. The fact that the combination of initial letters from their last names—Clifford, Arlington, Buckingham, Ashley, and Lauderdale—spelled CABAL was accidental, but the appellation when defined as a small body of persons engaged in private machination or intrigue is not inappropriate. Arlington alone seems to have demonstrated both a consistent and well-considered policy in his field of expertise, foreign affairs. All the ministers were overshadowed by the king, who now undertook the principal direction of affairs of state.

Even as the negotiations for peace at Breda were being concluded, Louis XIV undertook a new diplomatic initiative. Through his ambassador he suggested a defensive league or a joint expedition against the Spanish West Indies. He further implied that if hostilities were to break out again between the Dutch and England, France would no longer intervene on behalf of the Dutch. While negotiations dragged on, Arlington and his supporters sought to achieve the opposite, an alliance with Holland against France. Jan De Witt, the grand pensionary of Holland and chief official in the United Provinces, responded positively to the English overtures. The French seizure of a series of fortresses along the Spanish Netherlands had impressed upon him his nation's vulnerability to French military might and the need for allies. The Triple Alliance (1668) negotiated by Sir William Temple was the consequence, a treaty to which Sweden was also a signatory. In addition to mutual support in case of an attack by a third party, the Protestant powers hoped to lay the foundation for a larger alliance to prevent further French aggression. The alliance met with a positive reception in England. Parliament voted the improvident king a new tax on wine and spirits. More important, it marked the first stage in the rapprochement with Holland that was ultimately to unite the two great Protestant powers in arms against the ambitions of a Catholic France.

Despite a shared concern by England and Holland over the growth of French power, the Anglo-Dutch rivalry for colonial trade and European markets continued. Charles, chafing from the tedious and irksome necessity of having to persuade a recalcitrant and obstreperous Parliament to give him sorely needed funds, was encouraged to accept a French subsidy. His response to the French overtures was further encouraged in 1669 when his brother and heir, James, duke of York, decided to avow Roman Catholicism. Charles was also inclined to embrace the Roman Catholic faith as one in harmony with his notion of the monarchy and the state. Urged on by his sister Henrietta, by his mother, by Buckingham, and, belatedly, by Arlington, Charles broached the terms of a new alliance to France. He would announce his own public conversion to Catholicism and the instigation of war against Holland if France in turn would provide him with the financial support he so desperately needed.

The Secret Treaty of Dover, 1670

Charles II's financial resources were so depleted that he could not await the results of the inevitably protracted negotiations required for the alliance. He recalled Parliament in October 1669 to seek additional subsidies. Instead of granting him a supply, the Commons proceeded to investigate the king's ministers in England and in Ireland and even threatened impeachment. Angrily the king prorogued the Parliament in December; when the members reassembled in February, the needed supplies were forthcoming and the threats against his ministers were dropped. The king now concluded the secret Treaty of Dover with France on May 22, 1670, in which he subordinated his country to France in order to satisfy his own needs. In so doing he put his country's independence and constitution in jeopardy. In order to allay the suspicions of Buckingham and his other Protestant ministers, the king openly negotiated a second "bogus" treaty, identical to the first except that it omitted the king's avowal of Catholicism. Though the cynicism of the king's designs has left an indelible stain on his record, the treaty made it possible for the English to win commercial advantages over their Dutch rivals in the important trade with France. Even the Parliament seems to have recognized this advantage in the articles made public; when they were recalled in October they provided an additional subsidy estimated to be worth £800,000 in new taxes for the king's support.

In April 1671, Charles chose to prorogue, or dismiss, the Parliament by royal prerogative and embarked on a disastrous course of personal monarchy. Although he did not announce his conversion to Catholicism, he made a bold demonstration in favor of both Roman Catholics and Dissenters (1672), when he issued his Declaration of Indulgence, which suspended the execution of all penal laws against noncommunicants of the Church of England. It was an audacious move, a resumption of regal authority that if followed successfully in other areas would have changed the nature of the English constitution. It did not succeed because Charles was undone by his own ineptness in the field of finance and by his misadventures in diplomacy. On January 20, 1672, his acute financial distress resulted in another, more desperate gamble, the stop of the exchequer. Unable to meet his obligations he called a moratorium on all repayments of sums owed by the crown. He consigned his fortunes and those of his government to the long-planned war with Holland, which he declared two days after the Declaration of Indulgence.

The Third Dutch War, 1672–1674

Only success in war could save Charles's plans. But the Dutch seized the initiative and inflicted a defeat on the English fleet, and the French pushed to the Rhine and into the Dutch Republic itself with nothing to prevent their advance. De Witt was overthrown and executed by his own people. The Dutch installed the young William of Orange, Charles II's nephew, in the long-vacant stadtholdership of their country as their last hope to preserve their independence from the French. With Charles's gamble having failed and the Protestant strongholds of Europe in mortal danger because of his surrender to France, the king was forced to recall Parliament. Meeting in February 1673 they withheld supplies until the king cancelled the Indulgence. Not content, Parliament passed a Test Act that required officeholders to take communion in the Anglican Church and to disavow the doctrine of transubstantiation, a clause inserted specifically to eliminate Catholics. The duke of York was forced to resign the admiralty. He was followed into retirement by Clifford, another convert to Catholicism, and was replaced by a staunch Protestant, Sir Thomas Osborne, best known by his later title, earl of Danby. A second disastrous campaign abroad in 1673 only added to the king's troubles. When Parliament reconvened in winter it criticized the Treaty of Dover, the war, and the duke of York's recent marriage to a Catholic princess, Mary of Modena. Parliament refused any funds until peace was made. Charles quickly concluded a peace with the Dutch that restored the status quo, and he left control of domestic affairs for the most part to Danby for the next four years.

DANBY AND THE EXCLUSION PARLIAMENTS

Danby as Lord High Treasurer

Danby proved equal to his task. He provided a personal direction and control to the ministry that was without parallel in the reign. Assuming the office of lord high treasurer from Clifford in 1673, Danby was faced with substantial debts, weak public credit, and mounting war expenses. By maximizing income sources and by curbing government expenditures he turned around the Treasury's near insolvency and slowly restored public confidence. He was aided during his ministry by the rise in customs receipts following England's withdrawal from the war on the continent in 1674. As a neutral and active trading nation England enjoyed commercial advantages. These advantages continued until anti-French sentiment in Parliament forced Danby to place an embargo on trade with France in 1678. Charles vacillated between his pro-French advisers and Danby, accepting French subsidies in 1675 and 1677 in exchange for prorogations of the Parliament. Danby pressed the king to make common cause against France with his nephew, William of Orange. In November 1677, Charles agreed to the marriage of James's eldest daughter Mary with William, hoping thereby to propitiate Parliament and to encourage Louis XIV to make peace with Holland. When Louis resisted, Charles recalled Parliament in 1678 and signed an offensive alliance with Holland. His initiative failed when the Parliament turned against him and Louis came to terms with Holland. Danby's Protestant, anti-French policy enabled him to convince Parliament to grant further subsidies in 1677. But all his efforts were nullified by his inability to curb royal expenditures. A renewed mobilization for a potential war against France in 1678 resulted in a growth once again of the floating debt. On his retirement Danby bequeathed to his successor a debt more than twice that he had inherited. To block an impeachment, the king pardoned him for any offenses he might have committed.

When Danby assumed the direction of the king's affairs, he realized that cooperation with Parliament was essential. To insure a compliant Commons he began to organize a government party in that house through a careful and judicious use of all the means of persuasion available to him—offices, pensions, and bribes. He introduced a new kind of professional management in recruiting and then directing the king's party in the lower house. Danby's efforts resulted in the foundation of what came to be known in 1679 as the Tory party (after the name for Irish Catholic outlaws). The Tory party is the beginning of the party system. But party loyalties were uncertain and fickle. The unpopularity of the king's policies and a well-founded suspicion of his intentions were too much for the lord treasurer. The efforts of the opposition led by Shaftesbury, which was given the name of Whigs (after truculent Scottish Presbyterians) in 1679 to distinguish them from Danby's Tories, gained an unexpected assist from the exposure of the "Popish Plot" in 1678.

The Popish Plot

This cruel hoax almost precipitated a revolution and kept the country in turmoil for the next three years. The "plot" was discovered by Titus Oates, a discredited Anglican clergyman, twice an apostate, who revealed a plan by Roman Catholics to murder the king after which James, with French support, would succeed to the throne. When the scheme was disclosed to the king and council, Charles immediately recognized the bogus nature of Oates's story. But Oates had unwittingly pointed to enough suspicious activities on the part of the English Jesuits and the duchess of York's secretary, who had been corresponding with French Catholics, that the alarm was raised. The death through misadventure of Sir Edmund Godfrey, the justice of the peace before whom Oates had sworn his story, provided further circumstantial evidence to confirm the validity of Oates's discovery.

Shaftesbury and his Whigs made the most of the opportunity. The king and his policies were discredited; thus the opposition-dominated Commons alone possessed popular confidence. Parliament stiffened the Test Act, removed Catholics from both houses, and attempted to disband the army and replace it with the loyal militia—all while it investigated unceasingly countless wild stories about a Catholic coup centering on the duke of York. Many innocent Catholics, including the queen herself, came under suspicion. More than a few peers, priests, and commoners who were so unlucky as to be incriminated were executed. The king was dangerously isolated and lost almost all power to protect himself. Not the least important consequence of the plot and its aftermath was the impact on the press. The censorship laws were allowed to lapse, and the court was powerless to curb the press. Newspapers, pamphlets, tracts, and books were published in wild profusion. The role of the press in influencing public opinion and in making the average Englishman aware of the torments his country was undergoing was one of the most important phenomena of these years.

The First Exclusion Parliament

The next two years were dominated by the struggle between the king and the opposition over a bill to exclude the duke of York from the succession. To appease his enemies Charles ordered his brother into exile at Brussels and remodeled his council by making places for the opposition, including Shaftesbury and the great moderating statesman George Savile, marquis of Halifax. The closest advisers included the new secretary of state, Robert Spencer, earl of Sunderland, who soon earned a reputation for industry and ability as well as deviousness and subservience. The election in February 1679 of a new Parliament was the first in which the two new parties of Whig and Tory contested for supremacy. The tone of conciliation employed by the king in his welcoming address to the new Parliament failed to appease his auditors. They took up the investigation of the plot again, ignored the king's pardon of Danby, and tried to pass an act of attainder to override the pardon granted by the king. Danby surrendered to the Lords and was incarcerated in the Tower for five years, narrowly escaping with his life. The main thrust of the Commons was to bar the Catholic duke of York from the succession. Charles responded that he was willing to give his assent to bills guaranteeing the Protestant religion and the laws of property; but he was indissolubly wed to the principle of hereditary succession. After passing a bill to further secure the right of habeas corpus, the Commons began work on an exclusion bill, and it was only halted by the king's prorogation and then dissolution of Parliament. A sudden and serious illness of the king resulted in the return of James and revealed the precarious state of the realm. If the king had died the Whigs would undoubtedly have precipitated a revolution rather than submit to James's rule. After

Charles recovered, James was persuaded to exile himself to Scotland. There he had the opportunity as high commissioner to give proof to the fears of his opponents about his rigid and uncompromising attitudes. The quid pro quo was the exile of the duke of Monmouth, the illegitimate son of Charles II who was the hero of the Whigs and the pawn of Shaftesbury. Monmouth was removed from the office of commander in chief and was sent to Holland.

The Second Exclusion Parliament

The king delayed summoning the new Parliament for an entire year while he regained some control over the government, allowing opposition passions to be expended in demonstrations, investigations, and condemnations. The ministry was again remodeled and more compliant officers were appointed, drawn from the Tory or king's party. The chiefs were Sunderland and two new treasury commissioners, James's brother-in-law by his first wife, Lawrence Hyde, and Sidney Godolphin. Rochester (as Hyde later became known) has never received full credit for his achievements at the Treasury. He and his fellow commissioners were able to commit the king to retrenchment in expenditures with such success that a surplus in income was achieved to apply toward the debt. Moreover, the new commission, also with Charles's acquiescence, was able for the first time to exercise some control over departmental expenditures, thus establishing a new pattern of government that was to be carefully exploited by their successors. Foreign affairs were also part of Charles's strategy to wrest the initiative back from Parliament. Charles's own principles and his financial need made France the preferred ally, and still another subsidy treaty was concluded in March 1681.

When the new Parliament assembled in October 1680, it joined the press wars by ordering its resolutions to be published daily as the *Votes*. A second exclusion bill that not only denied James the succession but also threatened him with the charge of high treason if he returned to England was only defeated in the Lords. Frustrated in this effort the Commons proceeded to address the king to remove Halifax for advising the dissolution of the previous Parliament, and then the Commons criticized or impeached ministers and judges who supported the king. The king responded to their precipitate action by yet another dissolution in January.

The Third Exclusion Parliament

One last time the king tried to come to terms with Parliament. The location was changed to Oxford, where the staunchly Tory and conservative church-dominated atmosphere would encourage a more tractable attitude than the Whig mobs of London and Westminster. At the same time the king made careful military preparations to protect his person and the capital. Five troops of the Royal Horse Guards were stationed along the Oxford road to escort the royal party. The garrison in London, the center of Whig support and organization, was doubled to prevent trouble in the king's absence. The parties were now experienced in election battles, and Shaftesbury employed all his energy and experience to secure control of the new lower House. He succeeded all too well. Meeting on March 21, 1681, the Commons devoted the first week to dredging up the old hostilities and platforms. Though Charles had indicated beforehand and in his opening speech a willingness to make major concessions to guarantee that the government would remain in Protestant hands during the reign of his brother, the Commons dismissed his proposals. Shaftesbury made a public offer to Charles to name Monmouth as his successor, which the king summarily refused. When the Commons rejected all compromise, Charles dissolved the Parliament on March 28. It would not meet again in his lifetime.

The Attempt to Establish Despotism in England

The Last Years of Charles II

Determined to rule without Parliament and to ensure his brother's succession, Charles was equally determined to bring all elements of government under his control. Diplomats who favored the French alliance were employed in the major English posts abroad. A scrutiny of the lists of justices of the peace was followed by a remodeling of local governments throughout the country to obtain Tory officers and, in the event a Parliament had to be called, a more sympathetic membership. The chief weapons of the crown, however, were directed against the Whig leaders. The Rye House Plot, revealed in June 1682, was hardly more credible than the Popish Plot, but the Court was able to exploit it with something like the same impact. Two radical Whigs, William Russell and Algernon Sidney, were executed as an example to the others. Shaftesbury was hounded into exile, his party broken. The process of calling in the borough charters was accelerated after London failed to win a stay, and with it the bastions of Whig power in local government were eliminated. When Charles died on February 6, 1685, his authoritarian policy had substantially strengthened his successor's hand.

The Accession of James II

James II (1685–1688) was fifty-two years old, an advanced age in the seventeenth century, when he became king. And his essential rigidity of thinking had only intensified with age. Intolerant of Charles's vices, though he had often shared them, he demonstrated a firmness and a sense of moral rectitude that in other individuals would have been admired. But wedded to these were a devotion to Roman Catholicism and a disdain for the hard-won and still vulnerable constitutional guarantees protecting the liberty of the subject and the

James II, when Duke of York, by Sir Peter Lely. By courtesy of The National Portrait Gallery, London.

inviolability of property. The new king immediately summoned a Parliament to meet in May. The Parliament that met was the most tractable since 1661, the consequence of the careful remodeling of the corporations under Charles II and Sunderland's assiduity in managing the elections. It confirmed James for life in the taxes he had already begun collecting. Responding to the king's assertions that he required additional income to satisfy the debts of his brother and the obligations of the services, they voted additional duties that gave him a combined income estimated at £1,900,000, almost double that awarded Charles in 1660.

In the midst of the Parliament's deliberations two invasions were mounted to unseat James, one by the duke of Monmouth in the southwest and another by the earl of Argyle in Scotland. Both invasions were poorly managed by their leaders, and the disciplined response of the king's troops put a quick end to both efforts. Monmouth was defeated at Sedgemoor on July 6, where the young John Churchill demonstrated his prowess for the first time with an English army. The manner in which the rebels were treated by the king and his minions was cruel and heartless. In England, Lord Chief Justice George Jeffreys dealt so harshly and punitively with those unlucky enough to be charged with complicity, whether innocent or not, that his court sessions have gone down in history as the "Bloody Assizes."

When Parliament reassembled in November the king used the failure of the militia in the recent crisis as a basis for requesting still more funds in order to support a standing army—a permanent, professional, active military force. The Parliament, stirred by a few old hands, demonstrated once again its unpredictability and resourcefulness by outspoken debates. Several members questioned the use to which the army might be put and warned that the king's introduction of Catholic officers made inadvisable this military strengthening. The Lords were even more independent and forthright than the Commons in their distrust of royal policies. The king, notoriously sensitive to criticism, prorogued the Parliament even before it concluded action on a bill to provide him with yet another £700,000, which it would undoubtedly have granted. Dissolved in 1687, the Parliament never met again during his reign.

James lost no time in placing Roman Catholics in positions of trust and importance in the revamped army, in the ministry, and in the church. From a few thousand men and officers in 1685 James increased the army to 13,000 in 1686 and to more than 53,000 in 1688. Accompanying the introduction of Roman Catholics into the army, a deliberate policy was introduced to isolate the army from society, to improve its discipline, and to make it totally subservient to the crown. The king came dangerously close to his goal of creating a professional military force. The law courts were an early target, and James removed four of the judges in the spring of 1686 when they refused to recognize his right to dispense with the test and penal acts. When the king placed Roman Catholics in benefices in the church, the attorney and solicitor generals quickly found themselves out of office when they refused to issue the necessary warrants. In July 1686 James created a panel of ecclesiastical commissioners to act in his name as supreme governor of the church in all its concerns. Though not a court—it was not granted the power to impose fines and penalties and its jurisdiction did not extend to laymen—the unconscious parallel to the twice-proscribed early Stuart Court of High Commission was indeed ominous. Exercising its visitatorial authority, the panel first suspended Bishop Compton of London for refusing to remove a preacher who had offended the king. It then intervened in the affairs of the universities, removing the vice-chancellor of Cambridge from his office as well as removing him from headship of a college for refusing to admit a Benedictine monk to the degree of Master of Arts. Oxford was even more abused when the king replaced the fellows of Magdalen College with Roman Catholics and then capped this audacity by placing one of the king's favorite priests in the presidency. James's threats to disturb the quiet possession of property were even more evident in the inquisitorial nature of his administration in Scotland. There his opponents were hunted out, tortured, tried, and sentenced to heavy fines, transportation (shipment to the colonies), or death.

Determined not only to restore the Catholics to an active if not predominant role in public life but also to guarantee this restoration after his own reign,

James decided in the summer of 1687 to summon another Parliament. Its charge would be to give legislative confirmation to a second Declaration of Indulgence, which he intended to issue in 1688. His first Declaration, issued in April 1687, had been grudgingly accepted in England and in an earlier version promulgated in Scotland. Now a committee directed by Sunderland sent out a questionnaire in October 1687 to the lord lieutenants with instructions to obtain replies from their deputies, the sheriffs, and the justices of their counties. There were three questions. Will you, if returned to Parliament, vote for the repeal of the penal laws and the test? Will you support candidates who are in favor of such a measure? Will you live neighborly and friendly with those of a contrary religion? An unexpectedly large number of lieutenants resigned rather than carry out the instructions. Many loyal Tories who had demonstrated extraordinary tolerance in their acceptance of the king's arbitrary actions were turned into active opponents by these measures.

The second Declaration of Indulgence, issued on April 27, 1688, was one of the two immediate causes of the Revolution of 1688. James ordered it to be read from every pulpit for the next two Sundays. Many faithful clergy refused, and the primate himself, William Sancroft, archbishop of Canterbury, together with six of his fellow ecclesiastics petitioned the king not to insist upon his order. The king was outraged by this show of resistance and was determined to set an example by prosecuting the offenders, not by a summons to the High Commission but rather by a trial for seditious libel in the Court of the King's Bench. The trial, which began on June 29, was one of the most famous and critical in English history. The judges abandoned their neutral role and risked the king's displeasure (two were subsequently removed) by supporting the defendants. The jury acquitted the defendants, who were triumphantly escorted out of the court and back to Lambeth Palace amid great public displays of attention and joy. Even before the trial started the die had already been cast for a rebellion when Queen Mary of Modena gave birth to a son on June 10. With the prospect of a Catholic succession even the most loyal Anglicans now realized that the threat to the liberties of the church could allow for no further delay. The means of their deliverance was at hand: the Prince of Orange.

William of Orange and Revolution

Since assuming the leadership of the Dutch Republic in 1672, William had been watching the conduct of his royal uncles with the closest interest and concern. His wife, Mary, would succeed James to the thrones of the three kingdoms (England, Scotland, and Ireland), and he was determined to gain the crown for himself. On every suitable ceremonial occasion he had sent emissaries to James mainly to conduct reconnaissance and to test the loyalty and strength of his English friends. Moreover, William had finally succeeded in constructing an imposing new coalition of European states against France, and he wanted to be sure of English support or neutrality. Unexpectedly, the birth of a son to James in 1688 meant that Mary was no longer the heir to the English throne. William sent a minister to congratulate his uncle on the birth of a male heir, but the minister's real mission was to secure an invitation for William to come to England. He fulfilled his instructions. On June 30, Edward Russell, cousin to William Russell, one of the Whig martyrs of 1682, made his way over to Holland with a document signed by himself and six other prominent leaders: Bishop Compton, Danby, three other peers, Devonshire, Shrewsbury, and Lumley, and Henry Sidney, brother of the other martyr, Sidney. William was invited to come to England with his troops to save the English constitution and the Protestant religion.

Meanwhile James, who was urged on by the aged Sancroft and other moderate advisers, began to take tardy steps to regain the support of his countrymen. Early in October he abolished the ecclesiastical commission. He then restored the old charters to London and to the other corporations that had been forced to give them up. Unlike his royal predecessor, James could not be brought to renounce his Declarations of Indulgence, so that his good faith was still suspect, and he refused to summon a Parliament at this time. Moreover, when he attempted to restore the natural leaders of local government to their posts, he found that the majority were unwilling to serve on his terms. This left the government in the hands of men who had been repudiated by their compatriots; the government was without the means to support the king in his troubles.

The imminence of William's descent was known to all, but the intended landing place was a well-guarded secret. James relied on his fleet under the Protestant Dartmouth to prevent a landing, but the fleet proved a broken reed. Dartmouth's own loyalty is doubtful, and the fleet had been subjected to a constant stream of propaganda to support Prince William rather than King James. Whether due to the accident of the winds or to deliberate inaction, Dartmouth's fleet allowed William to land unopposed at Torbay, in the west of England, on November 5. Announcing his mission to preserve the liberties and religion of England, William slowly moved toward London, gathering supporters along the way. The king summoned a new Parliament for January and sent commissioners to meet with the prince. But the desertions of John Churchill, who was his most trusted general and long-time adviser, his son-in-law, Prince George of Denmark, and then his Protestant daughter Anne, escorted by Bishop Compton, reduced the king to a state of total despair and helplessness. Having previously arranged for the passage of his son and wife to France, he embarked for France on the night of December 11. Caught by the tide, his ship was boarded by suspicious fishermen who forced the king to return to shore. James returned to London briefly, but his presence was now an embarrassment and an unwelcome bar to a speedy settlement. He was allowed to slip away again on December 23, never to return to England. The time for decision was now at hand.

SUGGESTIONS FOR FURTHER READING

A good general survey of the Stuart period is Barry Coward, *The Stuart Age: England, 1603–1714* (2nd ed., 1994). For the Stuart rulers see J. P. Kenyon, *The Stuarts* (1958). The fullest treatment of the Restoration era and the Revolution is to be found in David Ogg, *England in the Reign of Charles II* (2nd edition, 2 vols., 1956) and *England in the Reigns of James II and William III* (1955). Ronald Hutton, *The Restoration: A Political and Religious History of England and Wales, 1658–67* (1985) is authoritative. Robert M. Bliss reviews *Restoration England: Politics and Government, 1660–1688* (1985). K. D. H. Haley has written *Politics in the Reign of Charles II* (1985). Tim Harris examines *Politics under the Later Stuarts: Party Conflict in a Divided Society, 1660–1715* (1993). On foreign policy see J. R. Jones, *Britain and Europe in the Seventeenth Century* (1966).

Reliable accounts of "the Glorious Revolution" are J. R. Jones, *The Revolution of 1688 in England* (1972) and W. A. Speck, *Reluctant Revolutionaries: Englishmen and the Revolution of 1688* (1988). The definitive study of the ideas and goals of the Revolution is Lois G. Schwoerer, *The Declaration of Rights, 1689* (1981). She has edited *The Revolution of 1688–89: Changing Perspectives* (1992), a valuable collection of essays.

Charles Wilson reviews economic developments in *England's Apprenticeship, 1603–1763* (2nd ed., 1985), which can be supplemented by Ralph Davis, *English Overseas Trade, 1500–1700* (1973) and D. C. Coleman, *Industry in Tudor and Stuart England* (1975). Social history is reviewed in J. A. Sharpe, *Early Modern England: A Social History, 1550–1760* (2nd ed., 1997). *The Origins of English Individualism: The Family, Property, and Social Transition* (1978) by Alan Macfarlane is an influential book. General histories of London are Roy Porter, *London: A Social History* (1998), Francis Sheppard, *London* (1998) and Stephen Inwood, *A History of London* (1998). Studies of London in the Stuart period are Peter Earle, *The Making of the Middle Class: Business, Society, and Family Life in London, 1660–1730* (1989) and A. L. Beier and Roger Finlay, eds., *London, 1500–1700: The Making of the Metropolis* (1986). Peter Clark, ed., *The Transformation of English Provincial Towns, 1600–1800* (1984) and Peter Borsay, *The English Urban Renaissance: Culture and Society in the English Provincial Town, 1660–1770* (1989) are good introductions to smaller cities and towns.

For the Church of England see S. Doran and C. Durston, *Princes, Pastors, and People: The Church and Religion in England, 1529–1689* (1991). People outside the Church are covered by M. R. Watts, *The Dissenters from the Reformation to the French Revolution* (1978) and J. Bossy, *The English Catholic Community, 1570–1850* (1975). Religious dissensions are the subject of Gerald. R. Cragg, *Puritanism in the Period of the Great Persecution* (1957) and Douglas Lacey, *Dissent and Parliamentary Politics in England, 1661–1689* (1969). For one of the influential figures in Dissent see Richard L. Greaves, *John Bunyan and English Nonconformity* (1993).

Good introductions to science are A. R. Hall, *The Revolution in Science* (1983) and Richard S. Westfall, *Science and Religion in Seventeenth-Century England* (1958). A key figure may be studied in Westfall, *Never at Rest: A Biography of Isaac Newton* (1980). Among the many studies of Locke, one of the best is Maurice Cranston, *Locke* (1957). Richard Ashcraft considers

Revolutionary Politics and Locke's Two Treatises of Government (1986) and has edited the *Treatises* (1989). Ruth Grant shows the relevance of Locke's thought to the present in *John Locke's Liberalism* (1987). Standard works on the arts are John Summerson, *Architecture in Britain, 1530–1830* (1953), Ellis Waterhouse, *Painting Britain, 1530–1790* (1953), and Margaret Whinney, *Sculpture in Britain, 1530–1830* (1964).

Geraint H. Jenkins covers *The History of Wales, Vol. 4: The Foundation of Modern Wales, 1642–1780* (1988). Good general histories of Scotland are George S. Pryde, *Scotland from 1603 to the Present Day* (1962) and T. C. Smout, *A History of the Scottish People* (1969). A changing relationship is traced in *Scotland and England, 1286–1815* ed. Roger A. Mason (1986). Brian P. Levack examines *The Formation of the British State: England, Scotland, and the Union, 1603–1707* (1987). J. C. Beckett, *The Making of Modern Ireland* (1966) is an excellent introductory book. More detail is provided in T. W. Moody, ed., *A New History of Ireland, Vol. III : Early Modern Ireland, 1534–1691* (1976).

Standard biographies include Ronald Hutton, *Charles II: King of England, Scotland, and Ireland* (1991); J. R. Jones, *Charles II: Royal Politician* (1987); John Miller, *James II: A Study in Kingship* (1978); Stephen Baxter, *William III and the Defense of European Liberty* (1966); Andrew Browning, *Danby* (3 vols., 1944–1951); and K. D. H. Haley, *Shaftesbury* (1968).

CHAPTER NINE

Revolution and Succession
1689–1714

The Revolution of 1688, the "Glorious Revolution," is one of the great landmarks in English history, yet it was no more a revolution than previous accessions except for the manner of James's going. The Revolution was inspired and controlled by the aristocracy and landed gentry to preserve the constitution in its traditional state, so the Revolution settlement itself was conservative and limited in character. There is a European dimension to the Revolution that cannot be disregarded. It could not have occurred without William and his army; William could not afford to let England remain in the French camp. Furthermore, William III (1689–1702) was by any standard the most effective and most active chief executive of any Stuart sovereign. Finally, the legacy that he left in terms of England's new-found prestige and importance in Europe and the commitments he made for continued participation in the coalition against Louis XIV and the succession of the Electress Sophia of Hanover and her heirs all transformed the status and character of England and its dependencies.

THE REVOLUTION OF 1688

Goals of William III

But as important as these considerations are for an explanation of *how* the Revolution occurred, we must not lose sight of the fact that the reasons *why* it occurred were wholly domestic and internal. William's new subjects, preoccupied with domestic matters, were loath to heed the European situation or to accept England's critical role in it. Part of the disillusionment and ultimately the opposition of the Tories to William was the consequence of their realization of William's true motives and interests. The other part of their disillusionment came with the recognition that he was as forceful and domineering as were any of his predecessors. The control that this forbidding, cold foreigner soon obtained over the agencies of English government and the commitments he made of English men and English gold to European causes revived the traditional hostilities of the aristocracy and gentry to autocratic monarchs. This was the fate of William's ambition and reputation.

The Settlement of the Crown

The question of William's promotion to the kingship of England was never much in doubt, but the matter of securing the Revolution and his rule was far less certain. On the collapse of James's government the peers in and about London had met and had taken the government into their hands. Although the country was remarkably quiet, rioting in London and the burning of the chapels and homes of prominent Catholics required speedy action to preserve public order. The lords were soon joined by the surviving members of the Parliaments of Charles II. The assembled leaders requested the prince to assume the civil administration as he had already assumed control over the remnants of the military forces of the crown. A convention summoned by the prince met on January 22, 1689. This body divided essentially on the basis of attitudes toward the succession. Most Tories favored a regency to preserve a semblance of constitutionality and to honor their oaths to James as anointed sovereign. Only the most conservative element favored James's return under carefully controlled limitations. The Whigs were more united in their determination to assert the principles of parliamentary sovereignty by acknowledging a break in the hereditary succession. Most men recognized, albeit reluctantly, that English security was dependent on William's exercise of the executive authority. The question of the legal basis for this exercise was resolved by Mary's refusal to act as queen regnant and by William's equally positive assertion that he would not remain in England unless all executive authority was awarded to him for life. The activities of James II's supporters in the other two kingdoms cut short the discussion of constitutional safeguards in the convention, but before the crown was offered to William and Mary (with all authority vested in William) a Declaration of Rights was passed and was accepted by the new sovereigns; this was subsequently enacted into law to embody the essence of the Revolution.

The Declaration fundamentally changed the character of English kingship. The monarch was subordinated to the common law, the suspending and dispensing powers of the crown were severely restricted, prerogative courts were declared illegal, and the king was prohibited from levying taxes without parliamentary consent. A Whig document, it passed because the Tories supported it to embarrass William and hopefully to create a climate for a regency or rule by Mary alone. The result of their compliance was to enshrine in the constitution what for them was repugnant, a victorious Whig ideology. For the first year and even longer the fate of the Revolution was in doubt. William had only limited financial resources of his own, and they were exhausted by the expedition. Although he requested the same revenues that James II had, he was granted the customs for life but the excise for only four years. These and other revenues were not sufficient to supply the extraordinary requirements of a nation at war.

The Revolution in Scotland and Ireland

Preoccupied with the situations in England and in Ireland, the new king gave Scotland little attention, and consequently that kingdom worked out its own destiny with little interference. The Jacobites, as James's supporters were called, were made up of the Episcopalians in the Scottish Lowlands and the Roman Catholics in the Highlands and were thus more active and stronger in the northern kingdom than in England. William was only able to send part of the Scottish regiments in the Dutch service to Edinburgh to buttress his supporters. Before they arrived, a convention had met, and the crown was offered to William and his consort on April 11. Yet even as the convention sat, Edinburgh castle was in the hands of Jacobites, and forces were raised in behalf of James in Stirling. Fortunately the rebels obtained no reinforcements from abroad. By the end of the summer all the Jacobite troops had capitulated. Because the new government was little beholden to William it was also independent of his influence. The Scots were determined to remove the shackles that James had used to restrain them. The crown-controlled Committee of the Articles that dominated the Scottish Parliament was abolished, and the episcopal government of the church, a useful instrument for insuring royal control, was dismantled.

Ireland was the more immediate problem. Lord Lieutenant Tyrconnel, a Roman Catholic, was one of the most able and determined of James's supporters. He and his coreligionists planned to use this opportunity to secure full control of their own country for themselves. James II came to Ireland in March 1689 planning to use a loyal Ireland as a base for the conquest of England and Scotland. The Irish nationalists refused to submit to his plans, and so James soon found himself in the midst of a war to drive the English and Protestants out of Ireland, a war he pursued with ferocity and determination. With funds provided by the new Parliament, William sailed for Ireland in June 1690. The critical stage of the campaign was soon over. At the River Boyne, William routed

James's forces on the last day of the month. The mopping-up took another year, but William's attention was now directed to the continent.

The Nine Years' War and the Partition Treaties

The Nine Years' War, King William's War, the War of the League of Augsburg—it is known by all three names—had broken out in the fall of 1688 when Louis XIV laid siege to Phillipsburg and the Dutch took possession of towns on the lower Rhine belonging to the archbishop of Cologne. William had wasted no time in bringing his new kingdom into the war. Even before James II had left London for France, William had given orders to the English navy to attack French ships. The Nine Years' War is not one of the great European conflicts if measured in terms of notable battles or of major territorial transfers through the treaty that closed it. For England, the war served as a training session. The most seasoned officers in James's army were the Roman Catholics, and the remaining cadre of English officers and men were mainly raw, unseasoned troops. This fact, coupled with their dubious loyalty, caused William to employ foreign officers—Dutch, Germans, and Huguenots—in the commands. It was this apprenticeship that permitted the army to perform so well in the next war.

William personally commanded his armies in Europe from 1691 to the end of the war. He was not a great general, but he excelled in terms of organization, discipline, and care for his troops. The major sieges, with one exception, were won by the French. In part this was because the king was given inadequate financial support by the Parliament, except in 1690 and 1694. The French were always amazed at William's ability to regroup his forces after a defeat and to return to the field of battle more determined and stronger than ever. It was this war of attrition that eventually persuaded Louis XIV to agree to a peace. By the treaty of Ryswick that brought the war to an end in 1697, the French king was forced to recognize William as king of England, thus recognizing the Protestant succession, a major war aim of the English.

WILLIAM III, KING AND DIPLOMAT

War Finance—The Bank of England

The extraordinary cost of maintaining both a large army overseas and an expanded navy wrought a revolution in English public finance. The changes that took place in William's reign in this sphere are among the most important consequences of the Revolution of 1688. After a year's delay Parliament granted William the customs for only short terms. The king's recurring need for funds during the war required that Parliament be called into session each year. Because of the need for funds to maintain the army and to pay off debts, the

William III. Miniature by
Sir Godfrey Kneller.
Victoria & Albert Museum.

regular meeting of Parliament was guaranteed. Determined this time to exercise greater control over royal finances, Parliament now resorted to the expedient of appropriating funds for specific uses, and an accounting was required each year. The vast sums of money required resulted in new taxes, notably the land tax, a temporary expedient that became the basis for governmental income until it was transmuted by Pitt at the end of the eighteenth century. Because of this tax, landowners paid a greater proportion of taxes than at any other time in the eighteenth century. Other taxes were proposed, notably a general excise (a sales tax), but that was found to be intolerable politically, though the excise was extended on specific items.

The most important impact of the war was the new system developed to raise the enormous sums of money required. Formerly the king had to raise loans on the security of his name alone. Now Parliament, assured of its existence through the system of annual appropriations, itself undertook to guarantee the loans that were required to finance the war. With this kind of security the crown was able to secure funds much more readily and at much lower interest rates. The parliamentary guarantee of the king's credit was the basis for the new system of a national debt, a landmark in public finance. A body of trained civil servants was created to continue to carry the system throughout the violent alternation of party administrations that characterized the quarter century that followed the Revolution. The traditional sources of credit used by the crown proved inadequate to the huge demands placed upon them during the war. To compensate for this deficiency the Bank of England was created, a joint-stock, limited liability corporation authorized by act of Parliament in 1694. With seasoned officials at the Treasury—the veteran Lord Godolphin, the Secretary Henry Guy, and the brilliant young chancellor of the exchequer, Charles Montagu—working in collaboration with the predominantly Whig financiers who composed the Bank's board of directors, England was able to produce the funds needed to sustain it and its allies in the struggle with France. The capture of Namur in 1695 can be directly attributed to the success of the new banking establishment.

The Parties and the Cabinet

William's success in securing his three kingdoms, in restoring the strength and credit of the English army and navy, and in fighting Louis XIV to a standstill was not matched in his dealings with the parties and parliament. To begin with, the qualified support for his invasion and succession inclined many politicians to reinsure themselves with the exiled James in case of a Stuart restoration. William's refusal to give his confidence to any of his English ministers and his obvious partiality for his Dutch and other foreign aides created jealousy and resentment. William never really understood or accepted the party structure in England. His first ministries included representatives of all the major party groups as he endeavored to secure broad support for his program while keeping out of the clutches of one particular faction. Initially, he found the Tories most sympathetic to his views on government and the role of monarchy. In the early years of the reign the Whigs' desire to limit the power of the crown was ample reason to keep that party from dominating the ministry. But the setbacks in the land campaign in 1692 convinced the Tories that further expenditures on the army were wasted. William was forced to choose between fighting a war in Flanders with Whig support or pursuing the "blue water policy"—the reliance on the navy and not the army—favored by the Tories. He chose the former. By the end of 1693 the Whigs were in the ascendancy. Their promotion was advocated by Sunderland, who had emerged as the king's political broker or "manager," a practice necessitated by the rise of parties.

One of the most important constitutional innovations of the post-Revolution period was the Cabinet. The Privy Council had declined in authority as the Stuart kings expanded its membership to suit the vanity of the many courtiers who pressed to be included. Its work consequently fell into the hands of standing committees, of which the most important was the committee on foreign affairs. Managed by the senior secretary of state, it had developed into the principal advisory body of the crown. William III preferred the departmental style of government, by which he met separately with each minister. Circumstances dictated otherwise. When he went to Ireland in 1690 he left Mary as regent and instructed her to consult a committee of nine privy councillors who were given the designation of Cabinet Council. Continuing to meet during the king's absences, the Cabinet also met with the king during the winter of 1691–1692, though less frequently. William's attempt to replace it in 1694 with a smaller, less formal body failed. There were regular meetings in the winter of 1694–1695, and the members acted as lords justices for William after Mary's death when he was on the Continent. The continuous history of the Cabinet, an informal body unknown to the law, dates from this time.

The Succession in Spain and England

Throughout his reign William III was preoccupied with the problem of the succession to the throne in Spain. Louis XIV showed his concern for his own reasons. The Treaty of Ryswick was concluded in part so both monarchs could turn their attention to the disposition of the Spanish Empire upon the imminent death of the long-suffering Carlos II. Louis and the Austrian emperor, Leopold I, were each sons and husbands of Spanish princesses. The brides of the French kings in each case were senior but had renounced their claims to the Spanish throne both for themselves and their heirs. The other European powers did not want the crown of Spain to go either to the Bourbons or to the Habsburgs. Louis and William finally agreed that the throne would go to Leopold's grandson by his first wife, the son of the elector of Bavaria. The first partition treaty, concluded in 1699, provided for this settlement, but even as the treaty was being signed the young prince died. Louis and William, both anxious to avoid a major war over Spain, reopened their negotiations. A second partition treaty signed early in 1700 assigned the bulk of the Spanish inheritance to Archduke Charles, Leopold's second son by his third wife.

The death of another young prince, Princess Anne's only surviving child, the duke of Gloucester, meant that the Protestant succession in England was now in jeopardy. William had long favored vesting the succession in the Electress Sophia of Hanover, granddaughter of James I, and Sophia's heirs. But to do so required the assent of Parliament, and a majority of country members had been elected in 1698, many of whom were hostile to the king's continental interests and concerns. The Tory Parliament delivered a series of attacks on the aging king, sending home his Dutch guards and taking back the large grants of Irish land he had made to his favorites. The king seriously considered abdication. But though his health was failing his will remained strong and his ambition constant. These qualities were put to their greatest test at the end of 1700 when Carlos II died. He bequeathed his empire to the younger grandson of Louis XIV, Philip, duke of Anjou, and Louis accepted the inheritance in the name of Philip. A new English Parliament elected in the beginning of 1701 was slightly more Whiggish in composition, and it confirmed the succession of the crown to the Electress Sophia, though the Commons included a number of limitations upon the crown which reflected their dislike of William's foreign advisers.

The Legacy of William III

Though the Dutch were cowed into accepting Philip V's accession in Spain, England was not. The Tories found their public stock falling as a result of their vindictive measures, so to restore confidence and regain the king's favor they passed a resolution asking him to take steps to curb the exorbitant power of France. The king responded promptly, appointing John Churchill, earl of Marlborough, who was the principal adviser to the Princess Anne, as his agent to negotiate a new alliance with the Dutch and the emperor. Fortunately for William, Louis XIV now entered into measures guaranteed to provoke English hostility. He sent French troops into the Spanish Netherlands to shut off English commerce to the continent and sent other contingents into Milan and its dependencies, thus enraging the Austrian emperor, who claimed that territory for his family. Finally, Louis acknowledged the young son of James II as king of England when the old monarch died in exile in September 1701. Armed with a new grand alliance among England, the Dutch Republic, and the Austrian emperor, William returned to England in the fall of 1701, dissolved the Parliament, and began to transfer power once again to the Whigs, the party dedicated to support his continental policies. Though the election returns gave neither faction a real majority, he had the satisfaction of knowing that England would honor its commitments. The king died on March 8, 1702, after a fall from his horse. William died respected but unloved. His adopted country had been well schooled in the arts of war, diplomacy, and government but had not undertaken its tutelage willingly. Now, however, the benefits of William's rule were to be seen, and his successor was able to enjoy the fruits of his labors.

THE EARLY YEARS OF ANNE'S REIGN

The Accession of Queen Anne

The new queen (1702–1714) was hardly a prepossessing figure for the newly emerging power of England. Although Anne was only thirty-five years old, the toll of seventeen pregnancies, chronic ill health, and the gout had already made her old before her time and rendered her a semi-invalid. After the death of her sister, Mary, and her father, James II, she could be accepted as the rightful and legal heir to the throne. A true daughter of the church, her devotion to her people and her country enabled her to draw upon a reserve of affection and loyalty that united at least for a time most of the influential elements in society behind her government.

Anne was a woman who was wholehearted in her loyalties once they were fixed. She immediately turned over her affairs to her most trusted advisers and friends, a triumvirate remarkable in English history. Sarah, Countess of Marlborough, had been Anne's constant companion and closest friend for a score of years. She was given control of the queen's entourage and access to her person by the grant of the offices of Mistress of the Robes, Groom of the Stole, and Keeper of the Privy Purse. Her husband, the duke of Marlborough, was named captain-general of the English army in Flanders and ambassador to the Dutch Republic, with command of the armies of the maritime powers in the Low Countries. The final member of this close-knit circle was another lifelong friend, Sidney, Lord Godolphin. While Marlborough took over the principal direction of foreign affairs and the conduct of the war, Godolphin acted as prime minister at home, with sole responsibility for the Treasury and supervision of the executive. He was also the liaison between the ministry, the queen, and Parliament. If Marlborough as general and diplomat was the architect of England's greatness abroad, it was Godolphin as prime minister who made Marlborough's successes possible by the firm support he provided from home.

Queen Anne. An engraving, c. 1750. Kenneth Spencer Research Library.

The queen's predilection and the long associations with Marlborough and Godolphin meant that the ministry was initially composed almost entirely of Tories. No eighteenth-century ministry ever lost an election, and the new Parliament that was returned in the summer of 1702 followed the traditional pattern by containing a Tory majority. Although possessing the complete backing of the queen, Marlborough and Godolphin had to share power at first with the principal Tory leaders, Nottingham and Rochester, who returned to office respectively as secretary of state and lord lieutenant of Ireland. Both favored the now traditional Tory blue water policy, which ran counter to the Williamite policies adopted by Marlborough.

The War of the Spanish Succession—The First Phase

When England entered the war in 1702, campaigns were conducted by the French on three fronts: in Italy, on the Rhine, and in the Spanish Netherlands against the maritime powers. Spain was dynastically linked to France. The Grand Alliance—England, the Netherlands, and the Habsburg domain, Austria and Hungary—had only a few German princes in league with them initially. In 1703 Bavaria and Cologne joined France while Savoy and Portugal joined the Grand Alliance. As a condition to enter the alliance, Portugal insisted that the maritime powers open another front in Spain and endeavor to place the Habsburg candidate on the throne. Savoy brought some reinforcements to the Austrians in Italy, but the defection of Bavaria and Cologne laid the Rhineland and southern Germany open to French occupation and made an advance on Vienna a practical reality.

Marlborough had already shown superior tactical ability and generalship in the campaign of 1702. Contrary to the prevailing traditions of the time, which favored long and essentially static campaigns devoted mainly to sieges, he preferred to seek out the enemy's army in the field and destroy it, believing thereby that the fortresses would be cut off from resupply and would fall into his hands. The Dutch, whose political representatives at the field headquarters had to give their consent before their troops could be employed, regarded the army as a defensive weapon, as all that stood between them and a French invasion, so they were loath to risk it in battle. Determined not to return to the field in 1704 unless he was given greater authority, Marlborough persuaded the Dutch to let him take part of the troops for a daring march up the Rhine to save the Empire. At the Danube, Marlborough joined the imperial commander, Prince Eugene of Savoy, and deliberately provoked a battle with the Franco-Bavarian army. In one of the decisive battles of European history, they defeated the flower of the French army at the little village of Blenheim on the Danube. The victory saved the Austrian Empire from French control and provided Godolphin with the means to fight off the attacks of the parties at home.

The Church Settlement and Occasional Conformity

After the Revolution of 1688 it was expected that the Dissenters would be rewarded with a relaxation of the laws designed to suppress them as a consequence of their refusal to cooperate with James II against the Anglicans. William III, a Calvinist, was fully committed to religious toleration and was even prepared to go further and remodel the church so that it would be acceptable to Presbyterians if not most of the Dissenters. He was frustrated in his efforts because of the means he used to try to force the Tories to consent. They in turn were opposed to concessions, motivated not only by conscience but also by a desire to protect an Anglican monopoly of political offices. A compromise measure, the Toleration Act, was passed, though its terms were hardly very generous. It was the refusal of the crown to implement the more punitive measures still in force that really gave the Dissenters a measure of peace. Public office, both in the central government and at the local level, was restricted to communicants of the Church of England. Many Dissenters, however, would take communion in the established church once a year to qualify themselves for office and then return to their chapels. The high church party, synonymous with the Tories, was outraged at this behavior. After the dismissal of Rochester in 1703 and Nottingham and his colleagues from the ministry in 1704, the Tories seized upon the issue of occasional conformity to try to break

The Battle of Blenheim, 1704. An engraving, c. 1735. Kenneth Spencer Research Library.

the ministry. Two previous bills designed to eradicate this practice had been defeated in the Lords in 1702 and 1703. Now the Tories in the Commons moved to add the provision to a money bill in late 1704, intending to force its acceptance on both the Lords (who had earlier given up the right to alter money bills) and the queen. The motion to tack the provision onto a bill was defeated but only after a most desperate effort by both sides to garner the necessary votes. The man principally responsible for its defeat was the speaker and new secretary of state, Robert Harley.

Robert Harley versus the Whigs

Robert Harley was one of the most interesting, important, and yet enigmatic statesmen of the early eighteenth century. Born into a Dissenting family, he became the leader of the church party or Tories after starting his political career in Parliament as a country Whig. Elected speaker in 1701 and again in 1702, he proved to be one of the most successful managers of the Commons in English history. Godolphin and Marlborough came to rely on him heavily; by 1704 the three jointly managed affairs. Harley was persuaded to take high office as a secretary of state, though he retained the speakership until the dissolution of the Parliament in 1705. A man of the middle, he was suspicious of the extremists of either party. When Godolphin made an opening to the Whigs in late 1704 to save his majority, Harley was opposed and resisted all efforts to increase the Whig presence in the ministry. In December 1706 the earl of Sunderland, Marlborough's son-in-law and one of the Whig junto or ruling clique of that party, was made secretary of state. Harley was unwilling to accept Sunderland as a colleague and now began to undermine Godolphin. In February 1708 he advised the queen to remove Godolphin and to remodel the ministry. Marlborough refused to support this move and without his prestige Harley could not hope to achieve his aims, so he voluntarily resigned. Just when the Cabinet crisis reached its height, word reached London that the "Old Pretender," Prince James Edward, the son born to James II in 1688, was now on the sea with a French fleet, determined to invade Britain and regain the crown. His landing was thwarted, but the threat and excitement tended to reinforce the Whigs. When parliamentary elections were held later in the spring, the Whigs were returned with a solid majority.

THE LATER YEARS OF QUEEN ANNE'S REIGN

The War of the Spanish Succession—The Second Phase

After an abortive advance along the Moselle, Marlborough returned to the battlefield in Flanders in 1705 for another year of frustration. Only the successful landing of an allied fleet with Archduke Charles in Catalonia and the capture of Barcelona provided any relief from the dismal dispatches from the other theaters. The year 1706 proved to be the annus mirabilis of the war. Marlborough was able to engage the French in battle at Ramillies, south of Brussels, and the resulting victory put most of Flanders into his hands. The English and their allies won a number of important engagements early in the war, but soon the war situation began to deteriorate for the allies. In 1707 the Austrians concluded a truce with the French in Italy, which freed French troops for employment elsewhere. A severe defeat in Spain lost that country for the allies, though the war dragged on there for another four years. Marlborough cleared the rest of the Netherlands, but the Battle of Malplaquet in 1709 was so bloody that it sickened the civilians on both sides. The turn of events at home made Marlborough afraid to risk another major engagement. In spite of two further impressive successes against the French, Marlborough was dismissed from all his offices at the end of 1711, defeated not as a general but as a diplomat and politician.

During the first part of the war Marlborough had practically single-handedly held the Grand Alliance together. For several successive years he set out on exhausting trips around the capitals of Europe after the campaign to persuade the allied princes to contribute troops to the armies in the several theaters. In 1706 when the French first sued for peace, he was firm in his refusal to accept anything less than unconditional terms. When peace negotiations were undertaken in earnest in 1709, however, he insisted on a collaborator, the young Viscount Townshend, and Marlborough left the negotiating to him. It was the same in 1710 when the negotiations were again taken up after Louis XIV's rejection of the preliminaries the previous year. Marlborough's increasing caution and refusal to accept responsibility for anything but his own army was the consequence of political changes at home.

Blenheim Palace. Constructed for the first Duke of Marlborough. Private collection.

The Decline and Fall of the Godolphin Ministry

The duchess of Marlborough is often credited with almost complete control over the queen for the first half of her reign. Yet, in fact, she had lost whatever influence she possessed even before Anne's accession. The duchess, a convert to Whig principles, held views that were unpalatable to the queen. Disagreeing on politics as early as 1702, their relationship became more distant after 1703 when the duchess went into semiseclusion following the death of her only surviving son. Though placed in the queen's bedchamber by her cousin the duchess, the queen's dresser, Abigail Hill, later Mrs. Masham, worked to advance the interests and projects of another relation, Robert Harley. The duchess became increasingly outspoken and strident in forcing her unwanted advice on the queen. The queen turned increasingly to Masham and others, so that by 1710 all communication between the two former friends had ceased. At the end of 1710 the duchess was dismissed from all her offices. This estrangement was an important factor in the fall of Marlborough, Godolphin, and the Whigs.

The Godolphin ministry had fully earned the appreciation of the nation by its impressive accomplishments both at home and abroad. Besides maintaining English naval supremacy, a preeminence dramatized by the scuttling of the French fleet at Toulon in 1707, it had made possible the great victories of Marlborough in Flanders and Germany and had subsidized other allied victories in Italy and Spain. One must add to these accomplishments the taking of Gibraltar in 1704 and Port Mahon in 1708. At home the greatest achievement was the passage of the Act of Union in 1707. Precipitated by the Scottish threat to elect a sovereign other than the one to rule England after Anne's death, the English Parliament in 1705 had moved the queen to appoint commissioners to treat for a union. The Scots were encouraged to participate by the threat of the loss of their privileges in England as subjects of a common sovereign and by the promise of full participation in the lucrative colonial trade. The sixty-two commissioners (thirty-one from each nation) chosen by the queen did their work well. Completing their deliberations in July 1705, they recommended a parliamentary union in which 16 elected Scottish peers would join the House of Lords and 45 Scottish members would be added to the 513 members of the English Commons. After a stormy passage in the Scots Parliament, the recommendations were accepted without qualification, and the union came into being on May 1, 1707.

The increasing and irksome burden of taxation that fell heaviest on the landowners, the jealousy of those excluded from political power, and the growing frustration over the ministry's apparent inability to bring the war to an end, when combined with the estrangement of the queen, eventually brought down Godolphin and his colleagues. The instrument of the change was an unlikely object—an inflammatory, ultraconservative Tory parson. The high church clergy were among the most vociferous and influential opponents of the Godolphin ministry and were a key element in the strength of the Tories. In order to reduce the clergy to subservience, one of the most notorious members, Dr. Henry Sacheverell, a fellow of Magdalen College, Oxford, and a popular preacher in London, was impeached by the Commons before the High Court of Parliament in December 1709. This effort to muzzle the Tory churchman backfired on the Whigs. The martyr cleric became a symbol of Whig oppression and tyranny. All those dissatisfied with ministerial policies of every kind now used the parson to demonstrate their true feelings. Emboldened by the reaction and counseled by Harley, the queen removed her servants one by one, so that by the end of the year Harley and the Tories were in control of the executive. An election held in September returned an overwhelming Tory majority.

The End of Anne's Reign

Ignoring Britain's commitments to its allies, Harley opened secret negotiations with the French. By the winter of 1711–1712 the preliminaries were sufficiently far advanced that Harley, now raised to the peerage as earl of Oxford, felt confident enough to dismiss Marlborough and to make public the negotiations. The abandonment of Britain's allies on the battlefield aroused powerful protest at home and on the continent, but Oxford, now assisted by his principal colleague and rival for authority, Henry St. John (created Viscount Bolingbroke in 1713), proceeded to confirm his arrangements with Louis XIV in the Treaty of Utrecht. In addition to Gibraltar and Minorca, Nova Scotia was ceded to England, marking the beginning of a retreat for the French in North America. The fortifications at Dunkirk were to be razed. Important commercial concessions were granted in Spain and the Spanish Empire, and France recognized the Protestant succession in England. Nonetheless, the success of Oxford in turning out the Whigs and in restoring the Tories to power was ultimately his undoing. He found himself the prisoner of the newly dominant party, unable to play them off against the Whigs and thus retain control; meanwhile the sickly queen began to repent the abandonment of her old friends and advisers. With the queen's health failing, Oxford and Bolingbroke looked to the heir to the crown to shore up their positions. But George, Elector of Hanover, loyal to the imperial cause, could never forgive the ministers who betrayed England's allies in the late war. Oxford and Bolingbroke then sought, independently, to ingratiate themselves with the "Pretender," the son of the late James II. When he refused unequivocally to change his religion for the crown of England they realized his cause was hopeless. Thus when Queen Anne fell mortally ill at the end of July, the Tories were unprepared to manage the succession. The Whigs, on the other hand, were fully prepared to launch a coup if necessary to secure the Protestant succession and had secretly arranged a takeover of the army if this eventuality proved necessary. It was not. When Anne died peacefully on August 1, 1714, George I was proclaimed king without any challenge.

The Press and the Parties

The fall of the Godolphin ministry, the rapprochement with France, and the renewed attack on the Dissenters by the triumphant Tories, which was shown by the passage of the occasional conformity bill in 1711, all inspired political and press battles in England that exceeded even those of the exclusion controversy in their magnitude and ferocity. The party lines had hardened into a clear Whig-Tory split by the beginning of the reign. The successive replacements and then transformation of the ministry had changed its composition from Tory to Whig and back to Tory. The frequent parliamentary elections—1702, 1705, 1708, 1710, and 1713—were all fought on party lines. Though the parties lacked a formal national organization (that did not emerge until the mid-nineteenth century), the continuity of leadership and principles and the presence of some centralized management, both for elections and control of parliamentary sessions, are clear evidence of the existence of party in Anne's reign. These divisions are particularly well exemplified by the press.

With the lapse of the censorship laws in 1695 a steady increase in publications becomes evident. Newspapers and monthlies began to proliferate, and the first daily newspaper, the *Daily Courant,* made its appearance in 1702. In spite of a parliamentary prohibition, accounts of parliamentary debates appeared in annual histories at the turn of the century. The expanded activity of the press in Anne's reign, culminating in the great battles that dominated the last four years, is one of the most important phenomena of modern English history. By 1714 nearly all the features we have come to expect in modern newspapers—the editorial, the news, the advice to the lovelorn, the periodical essay—had all made their appearance. Newspapers began and ended in startling profusion. Press battles, such as those between Defoe's *Review,* Tutchin's *Observator,* and Leslie's *Rehearsal,* were the order of the day. By 1712 between 50,000 and 60,000 copies of newspapers were sold in London each week, in spite of a stamp tax imposed by Parliament to curb the Whig press. Nearly all the most celebrated writers of the day were drawn into the press wars. Joseph Addison, Jonathan Swift, Richard Steele, and Daniel Defoe were only the best known and the most active. A polemical tract could inspire literally dozens of answers. The most successful and influential tracts, such as Swift's *The Conduct of the Allies* (1711), were sold by the tens of thousands of copies and could swing the opinion of the whole country behind a change in policy. The attacks of Tory writers on Marlborough were sufficient to compromise his reputation for many decades.

The general election of 1710 was fought and won in the press as much as it was on the hustings. Even all the means of a powerful ministry were unable to save the French commerce bill in 1713 thanks to the efforts of the opposition. The electorate represented a surprisingly high proportion of the adult male population, although in many boroughs the right to return representatives was vested in a small number of individuals, often under the influence of a local patron. Nevertheless, recent studies of poll books have suggested the presence of a swing vote, beyond the control of borough-mongers and responsive to changing public opinion. The success of the Revolution of 1688 and the preservation of English liberties are no better illustrated than in the vigor of its press and the strength of its political parties.

GROWTH AND CHANGE

Mercantilism

England's rise to great power status at the end of the wars against Louis XIV was the consequence of English arms backed by English industry and finance. The exploitation of this new eminence was the province of the merchants. The impact of the wars on England and the other European countries has been hotly debated. The depredations of the French privateers on English merchant shipping were tremendous. Yet the English gained as well as lost, and thousands of French ships were taken as prizes during the same period and incorporated into the English fleet. Though the English merchant marine may have been only marginally larger at the end of the period, and little more than it had been a century ago, the contrast with the situation in France and the Dutch Republic was more important and ultimately decisive. Prior to 1688 Dutch ships carried much of the bulk cargo required by England. The Dutch navy also suffered at the hands of the French, and the great burden of war expense took its toll on this small nation: it never recovered from the drain of men, ships, and gold. France, though blessed with far greater resources, both human and material, likewise lost out in the competition with England. England emerged from the war unquestionably the strongest in terms of its fleet.

Some share of this economic success must be attributed to the mercantilist system that was developed in the Commonwealth period and reinforced during the Restoration. Given its classic statement in 1664 in Thomas Mun's *Discourse on England's Treasure by Forraign Trade,* mercantilism stressed the importance of a favorable balance of trade. If England exported more than it imported the consequence would be a steady flow of specie into the country and increased prosperity. The navigation laws, first passed in 1651 and reenacted 1660 to 1663, restricted the colonial trade and imports generally to English bottoms (ships), thus laying the foundation for the growth of the English merchant marine. As the colonies grew in size and the value of their exports increased, English merchants and the king's tax collectors were the beneficiaries. The colonies, restricted to England as a single trading partner, became a principal market for English goods just as they were an essential source of raw materials. The wars were fought to protect old markets as well as create new ones. When Philip V inherited Spain he excluded English and Dutch shipping from trading with the Spanish colonies—a trade regarded as vital to English prosperity. So, too, the Levant and Mediterranean trade was assured by the capture of Minorca and Gibraltar and the scuttling of the French fleet at Toulon in 1707.

The demand in unprecedented quantities for supplies for the services, clothing, sail cloth, armaments, and ships gave a stimulus to industry and larger commercial organizations. The lot of the lower classes, whether urban or rural, was not materially altered. But in general it seems that the trading and mercantile community and landowners benefited as well from the war. The unprecedented demand for money sired the Bank of England, encouraged the union of the old and new East India companies in 1709, created the South Sea Company, and thus established a pattern of large-scale increases in capital formation. The more effective mobilization of resources made England's advance to great power status possible. This was a legacy of William and Anne.

Foreign Immigration

One of the many elements that fired the economic expansion and development that characterized the reigns of William III and Anne was the influx of refugees from the continent. There were two major groups. The second of these was comprised of Germans, largely from the Palatine along the upper Rhine. Driven from their homes by the depredations of the French army during the two wars, they made their way down the Rhine to Amsterdam. From thence many went on to England. William Penn was active in recruiting the Germans for his new colony of Pennsylvania in North America. They were the progenitors of those who came to be called the Pennsylvania Dutch (actually "deutsch" or German). From the sacking of Heidelberg in 1692 down through the first decade of the eighteenth century this migration continued. The severe winter of 1708–1709 increased the flow. The Whigs, then in power in England, welcomed the refugees with an eye to settling them in Ireland to reinforce the Protestant population there. The German immigrants were artisans and merchants for the most part, rather than farmers, and the plantation concept failed. But the "poor Palatines," as they were called, went on to join their predecessors in the New World.

The more important refugee group of this time was the Huguenots. From the time of the revocation of the Edict of Nantes in France by Louis XIV in 1675, there was a steady exodus of Huguenots from that country. Fearful of losing the right to worship as Protestants in their own churches, they fled to the security of more hospitable, Protestant countries, notably the Netherlands and England. They were educated, professional people. Many joined the world of letters or the more prosaic field of journalism and became important middlemen in translating continental literature for the English and in performing a like service for English writings for the continent, where English political theorists were widely read. From their mercantile and banking experiences a network of Huguenots developed around the periphery of France, from Switzerland and Savoy in the south of Europe to England, the Netherlands, and Prussia in the north. They became essential in the rapidly expanding system of public credit and the transmittal of funds, critical to the financing of the French wars on both sides. A number of Huguenots came over with William III—generals like the earl of Galway and journalists like Guillaume de Lamberty and Abel Boyer. Huguenot bankers were instrumental in the establishment of the Bank of England. Others brought new trades and skills such as hatmaking, silversmithing, glassblowing, and silk weaving. Architecture, gardening, and furniture and cabinetmaking also were positively influenced by the newcomers. They were an invigorating and valuable new addition to England's resources, and their loss to France was a grave one.

The Growth of the Professions

The innovation, boldness, and expansiveness that marked the post-Revolution period is exemplified by yet another phenomenon—the rise of a new professional class. To be sure, it was not all new. There already existed lawyers, physicians, clergy, and military and naval officers. But in this period they took on a new kind of importance, increased substantially in number, and improved in expertise and training. Furthermore, they were joined by budding new professions: architects, landscape gardeners, musicians, and, above all, civil servants. The lawyers first came to prominence in the long struggle between crown and parliament that led to the civil wars. The Revolution brought stability and independence to the judiciary. The rise in commercial and political activity, and thus the new prosperity, also meant a rise in litigation. The senior members of the bar, the barristers who alone were permitted to plead before the courts, reaped great profit from their practices. The number of lawyers in the parliament steadily increased after the Revolution, and that meant greater access to places, capped by lucrative and prestigious posts both in the executive and judicial branches of government. The junior members, the attorneys, found increased demand for their services in the creation and management of great landed estates as well as the inevitable preparation and analysis of documents essential to the conduct of business. In all, the emoluments derived from the legal profession accounted for greater accumulations of wealth for this profession than did any other during the period.

The late seventeenth century also saw the emergence of the practice of medicine as a respectable and lucrative profession. The latter character is amply testified to by the sharp rise in the size of fees. In part the improvement in professional status was the consequence of a gradual consolidation of the separate callings of physicians, apothecaries, and surgeons. The first determined the cause of illness and prescribed treatment; the second provided the medicines; the third treated external afflictions. By the mid-eighteenth century the three heretofore distinct classes merged loosely into what were now called "doctors." The loss of control by the College of Physicians over its profession was one factor, as apothecaries and surgeons gained new respectability and the right to prescribe medicine and administer treatment to the sick. Professional training and education was another factor. The graduates of Oxford and Cambridge licensed by the College were augmented by doctors trained in the provinces through apprenticeship and licensed by the bishops. In the late seventeenth century they were augmented by foreign-trained physicians, notably of Leyden. After the turn of the century the Leyden contingent was composed increasingly of Englishmen. In the Georgian period it was the Scottish universities that took the lead, both in the number and quality of doctors produced. The third factor, allied to the second, was the grudging acceptance of the surgeon-barbers into the profession. The two great French wars were the impetus; the surgeons gained substantially in numbers, expertise, and prestige through the heavy demand for their services in the army and navy. After the wars they returned to civilian life and found a ready market for their talents. The surgeons, too, increased the rigor and standards of their training through the development of Surgeons' Hall in London as a training center. Moreover, all branches of the profession of medicine benefited from the proliferation of hospitals in the eighteenth century. These provided training sites and the opportunity to learn and test skills.

The origins of the civil service can be traced back to the clerics who provided the secretariat or scriptorium for the crown from before the Conquest, then to the expanded, more specialized bureaucrats assembled by the early Tudors to administer their new taxes and to manage the secularization of church lands. The next great development came with the assumption by the crown of the collection and management of taxes beginning with tenure of Danby as lord treasurer. It was completed by the great expansion of business generated by the French wars, wars that also greatly expanded the need for a large number of army and naval officers. By the death of Queen Anne one can see the presence of a proficient, indispensable body of civil servants in the treasury, at the court, in the offices of the secretaries of state, and in the army and navy and their support services. Their expertise and experience were so essential to the operation of the government that many civil servants were able to remain in office, secure in their tenure, in spite of the frequent alterations of ministers in the major posts and parties in control of parliament in the two decades after the Revolution. If Samuel Pepys was the Restoration prototype of the civil servant, the later officials who typified the new and enduring model included: the apolitical William Lowndes, employed at the treasury from 1679 and secretary from 1695 to 1724; Josiah Burchett, who commenced his career at the navy office as a clerk to Pepys in 1680 and eventually succeeded to the office of secretary in 1695, a post he held until his death in 1742; and Sir Christopher Wren, who began as a surveyor-general to Charles II's works in 1661, succeeded to the charge of all royal works in 1670, and remained in office until his removal in 1718 (at the age of 86). Nor should one forget that Sir Isaac Newton, in addition to his more celebrated accomplishments, was first warden and then master of the mint from 1696 until his death in 1727.

Suggestions for Further Reading

The New Columbia Encyclopedia (4th ed., 1975) is the single most useful reference work for students of history. It is a good place to check names, dates, places, and events. The Dictionary of National Biography (1917) provides articles on persons prominent in British history to 1900. The Concise Dictionary of National Biography (London, 1961) contains abridgements of every article in the complete DNB. Useful guides to important people are Lives of the Stuart Age, 1603–1714 (1976) and Lives of the Georgian Age, 1714–1837 (1978). A profusely illustrated overview is The Oxford Illustrated History of the British Monarchy, ed. John Cannon (1991). For constitutional development the standard work is D. L. Keir, The Constitutional History of Modern Britain (9th ed., 1969). See also Mark Thompson, The Constitutional History of England, 1642–1801 (1938). Betty Kemp, King and Commons, 1660–1832 (1957) is a lucid explanation of the shift in political power that began with the Restoration and ended with the Reform Bill of 1832.

For the later Stuarts, good surveys are J. R. Jones, Country and Court: England, 1658–1714 (1978) and Geoffrey Holmes, The Making of a Great Power: Late Stuart and Early Georgian England, 1660–1722 (1993). The fullest treatment is to be found in David Ogg, England in the Reigns of James II and William III (1955). The Stuart rulers are discussed and illustrated in J. P. Kenyon, The Stuarts (1958). For a broad perspective on the long-term consequences of the Revolution settlement see Paul Langford, Public Life and Propertied Englishmen, 1689–1798 (1991).

Good political histories are Henry Horwitz, Parliament, Policy and Politics in the Reign of William III (1977) and Geoffrey Holmes, British Politics in the Age of Anne (1987). Political parties are reviewed in Brian Hill, Early Parties and Politics in Britain, 1688–1832 (1996) and J. P. Kenyon, Revolution Principles: The Politics of Party, 1689–1720 (1977). Perhaps the most stimulating study of the Revolution era is J. R. Plumb, The Growth of Political Stability in England, 1675–1725 (1967). The influence of Plumb is seen in Britain after the Glorious Revolution, 1689–1714 (1969), ed. Geoffrey Holmes.

For court life see R. O. Buchholz, The Augustan Court: Queen Anne and the Decline of Court Culture (1992). An important perspective is provided by Gary S. DeKrey in A Fractured

Society: The Politics of London in the First Age of Party, 1688–1715 (1985). M. G. Dickson, *The Financial Revolution in England, A Study in the Development of Public Credit, 1688–1756* (1967) is a work of major importance. A broad and detailed appreciation of the period is available in George M. Trevelyan, *England under Queen Anne* (3 vols., 1932–1934).

On foreign policy see Jeremy Black, *'A System of Ambition': British Foreign Policy, 1660–1793* (1992); Paul Langford, *Modern British Foreign Policy: the Eighteenth Century, 1688–1815* (1976), and D. B. Horn, *Great Britain and Europe in the Eighteenth Century* (1967). Earl A. Reitan, *Politics, War, and Empire: The Rise of Britain to a World Power, 1688–1792* (1994) combines foreign policy, military factors, and imperial expansion. A good introduction to the many wars of the seventeenth and eighteenth centuries is M. S. Anderson, *War and Society in Europe of the Old Regime, 1618–1789* (1988). Britain's role in these wars is examined in Jeremy Black, *Britain as a Military Power, 1688–1815* (1998). John Brewer considers *The Sinews of Power: War, Money, and the English State, 1688–1783* (1989). The effects of war are examined by D. W. Jones in *War and the Economy in the Age of William III and Marlborough* (1988) and H. V. Bowen, *War and British Society, 1688–1815* (1997). A good account of the navy is G. J. Marcus, *A Naval History of England, Vol. I: The Formative Centuries* (1961). General surveys of the armed forces are Paul Kennedy, *The Rise and Fall of British Naval Mastery* (1976); James Stokesbury, *Navy and Empire* (1983); Corelli Barnett, *Britain and her Army, 1509–1970* (1970); and *The Oxford Illustrated History of the British Army*, ed. David Chandler and Ian Beckett (1994).

For the Church of England see Norman Sykes, *From Seldon to Secker, 1160–1768* (1959) and E. G. Rupp, *Religion in England, 1688–1791* (1986). People outside the Church are covered by M. R. Watts, *The Dissenters from the Reformation to the French Revolution* (1978) and J. Bossy, *The English Catholic Community, 1570–1850* (1975). G. V. Bennett, *The Tory Crisis in Church and State, 1688–1730* (1975) and Norman Sykes, *Church and State in England in the Eighteenth Century* (1934) are fundamental to an understanding of the relationship of Church and state. See also Geoffrey Holmes, *The Trial of Dr. Sacheverell* (1973).

Charles Wilson reviews economic developments in *England's Apprenticeship, 1603–1763* (2nd ed., 1985), which can be supplemented by Ralph Davis, *English Overseas Trade, 1500–1700* (1973) and D. C. Coleman, *Industry in Tudor and Stuart England* (1975). Histories of London are Roy Porter, *London: A Social History* (1998); Francis Sheppard, *London* (1998); and Stephen Inwood, *A History Of London* (1998). Peter Clark, ed., *The Transformation of English Provincial Towns, 1600–1800* (1984) and Peter Borsay, *The English Urban Renaissance: Culture and Society in the English Provincial Town, 1660–1770* (1989) are good introductions to smaller cities and towns.

Social history is reviewed in J. A. Sharpe, *Early Modern England: A Social History, 1550–1760* (2nd ed., 1997). For the leadership elite see J. V. Beckett, *The Aristocracy in England, 1660–1714* (1986) and Felicity Heal and Clive Holmes, *The Gentry in England and Wales, 1500–1700* (1994). Lawrence Stone, *The Family, Sex, and Marriage in England, 1500–1800* (1977) is interesting and important. See also Anthony Fletcher, *Gender, Sex, and Subordination in England, 1500–1800* (1995). The lives of the poor are examined by Paul Slack in *Poverty and Policy in Tudor and Stuart England* (1988). Standard works on the arts are John Summerson, *Architecture in Britain, 1530–1830* (1953), Ellis Waterhouse, *Painting Britain, 1530–1790* (1953), and Margaret Whinney, *Sculpture in Britain, 1530–1830* (1964).

Geraint H. Jenkins covers *The History of Wales, Vol. 4: The Foundation of Modern Wales, 1642–1780* (1988). Good general histories of Scotland are George S. Pryde, *Scotland from 1603 to the Present Day* (1962); William Ferguson, *Scotland: 1689 to the Present* (1968); and T. C. Smout, *A History of the Scottish People* (1969). The changing relationship is traced in *Scotland and England, 1286–1815*, ed. Roger A. Mason (1986). Brian P. Levack describes *The Formation* of the British State: England, Scotland, and the Union, 1603–1707 (1987). The Act of Union is covered in G. S. Pryde, *The Treaty of Union of Scotland and Ireland* (1950) and K. Brown, *Kingdom or Province? Scotland and the Regnal Union, 1603–1715* (1992). T. C. Smout explores *Scottish Trade on the Eve of the Union* (1963); and P. W. J. Riley examines the implementation of the union in *The English Ministers and Scotland, 1707–1727* (1964).

J. C. Beckett, *The Making of Modern Ireland* (1966) is an excellent starting place. More detail is provided in T. W. Moody, ed., *A New History of Ireland, Vol. IV: Eighteenth-Century Ireland, 1691–1800* (1986). See also Thomas Hachey, *The Irish Experience: A Concise History* (1996). *The Oxford Illustrated History of Ireland* (1991), ed. R. F. Foster is a lavish work. An important study is F. G. James, *Ireland in the Empire, 1688–1770* (1973).

Major biographies include Stephen Baxter, *William III* (1966); Hester Chapman, *Mary, Queen of England* (1953); Edward Gregg, *Queen Anne* (1980); J. P. Kenyon, *Robert Spencer, Earl of Sunderland* (1958); Angus McInnes, *Robert Harley, Puritan Politician* (1970); Winston S. Churchill, *Marlborough, His Life and Times* (1933–1938); Ivor Burton, *The Captain General* (1968); J. R. Jones, *Marlborough* (1993); Frances Harris, *A Passion for Government: The Life of Sarah, Duchess of Marlborough* (1991); Brian W. Hill, *Robert Harley: Speaker, Secretary of State and Premier Minister* (1988); and H. T. Dickinson, *Bolingbroke* (1970).

APPENDIX

KINGS AND QUEENS OF ENGLAND

Bretwaldas

ca. 560–591	Caelwin, king of the West Saxons
560–616	Ethelbert, king of Kent
ca. 600–616	Raedwald, king of East Anglia
616–632	Edwin, king of Northumbria
633–641	Oswald, king of Northumbria
654–670	Oswiu, king of Northumbria

King of Mercia

757–796	Offa

Kings of the West Saxons

802–839	Egbert
866–871	Ethelred
871–899	Alfred
899–924	Edward the Elder

Rulers of England

959–975	Edgar the Peaceful
978–1016	Ethelred the Unready
1016–1035	Canute

1042–1066	Edward the Confessor
1066	Harold Godwinson

Normans

1066–1087	William I
1087–1100	William II
1100–1135	Henry I
1135–1154	Stephen

Angevins-Plantagenets

1154–1189	Henry II
1189–1199	Richard I
1199–1216	John
1216–1272	Henry III
1272–1307	Edward I
1307–1327	Edward II
1327–1377	Edward III
1377–1399	Richard II

Lancastrians

1399–1413	Henry IV
1413–1422	Henry V
1422–1461	Henry VI

Yorkists

1461–1483	Edward IV
1483	Edward V
1483–1485	Richard III

Tudors

1485–1509	Henry VII
1509–1547	Henry VIII
1547–1553	Edward VI
1553–1558	Mary I
1558–1603	Elizabeth I

Stuarts

1603–1625	James I
1625–1649	Charles I
1649–1660	Commonwealth and Protectorate
1660–1685	Charles II
1685–1688	James II
1689–1702	William III and Mary II
1702–1714	Anne

Hanoverians

1714–1727	George I
1727–1760	George II
1760–1820	George III
1820–1830	George IV
1830–1837	William IV
1837–1901	Victoria
1901–1910	Edward VII
1910–1936	George V (House of Windsor)
1936	Edward VIII
1936–1952	George VI
1952–	Elizabeth II

PRIME MINISTERS OF ENGLAND

1721–1742	Sir Robert Walpole
1742–1744	John Carteret
1744–1754	Henry Pelham
1754–1756	Duke of Newcastle
1756–1757	William Pitt, the Elder
1757–1761	Pitt the Elder and the Duke of Newcastle
1761–1762	Duke of Newcastle and Lord Bute
1762–1763	Lord Bute
1763–1765	George Grenville
1765–1766	Lord Rockingham
1766–1768	William Pitt, Lord Chatham
1768–1770	Duke of Grafton
1770–1782	Lord North
1782	Lord Rockingham
1782–1783	Lord Shelburne

1783	Charles James Fox and Lord North	
1783–1801	William Pitt, the Younger	
1801–1804	Henry Addington	
1804–1806	William Pitt, the Younger	
1806–1807	Lord Grenville	
1807–1809	Duke of Portland	
1809–1812	Spencer Perceval	
1812–1827	Lord Liverpool	Tory
1827	George Canning	Tory
1827	Lord Goderich	Tory
1828–1830	Duke of Wellington	Tory
1830–1834	Earl Grey	Whig
1834	Lord Melbourne	Whig
1834–1835	Sir Robert Peel	Tory
1835–1841	Lord Melbourne	Whig
1841–1846	Sir Robert Peel	Tory
1846–1852	Lord John Russell	Whig
1852	Lord Derby	Tory
	and Benjamin Disraeli	
1852–1855	Lord Aberdeen	Coalition
1855–1858	Lord Palmerston	Liberal
1858–1859	Lord Derby	Conservative
	and Benjamin Disraeli	
1859–1865	Lord Palmerston	Liberal
1865–1866	Lord John Russell	Liberal
1866–1868	Lord Derby	Conservative
	and Benjamin Disraeli	
1868–1874	William E. Gladstone	Liberal
1874–1880	Benjamin Disraeli	Conservative
1880–1885	William Gladstone	Liberal
1885–1886	Lord Salisbury	Conservative
1886	William Gladstone	Liberal
1886–1892	Lord Salisbury	Conservative
1892–1894	William Gladstone	Liberal
1894–1895	Lord Rosebery	Liberal
1895–1902	Lord Salisbury	Conservative
1902–1905	Arthur Balfour	Conservative
1905–1908	Sir Henry Campbell-Bannerman	Liberal
1908–1916	Herbert H. Asquith	Liberal
1916–1922	David Lloyd George	Coalition

1922–1923	Andrew Bonar Law	Conservative
1923–1924	Stanley Baldwin	Conservative
1924	J. Ramsay MacDonald	Labour
1924–1929	Stanley Baldwin	Conservative
1929–1931	Ramsay MacDonald	Labour
1931–1935	Ramsay MacDonald	National Government
1935–1937	Stanley Baldwin	Conservative
1937–1940	Neville Chamberlain	Conservative
1940–1945	Winston Churchill	Conservative
1945–1951	Clement Attlee	Labour
1951–1955	Winston Churchill	Conservative
1955–1957	Sir Anthony Eden	Conservative
1957–1963	Sir Harold Macmillan	Conservative
1963–1964	Sir Alec Douglas-Home	Conservative
1964–1970	Harold Wilson	Labour
1970–1974	Edward Heath	Conservative
1974–1976	Harold Wilson	Labour
1976–1979	James Callaghan	Labour
1979–1990	Margaret Thatcher	Conservative
1990–1997	John Major	Conservative
1997–	Tony Blair	Labour

INDEX

Combined index for Volumes I and II.
Volume II begins on page 171.

The English Heritage, Third Edition
Developmental editor and copy editor: Andrew J. Davidson
Copy editor and production editor: Lucy Herz
Photo editor and proofreader: Claudia Siler
Cartographer: James Bier
Printer: Versa Press, Inc.
Cover designer: DePinto Graphic Design